ISSUES IN POLITICAL THEORY

Political Theory has undergone a remarkable development in recent years. From a state in which it was once declared dead, it has come to occupy a central place in the study of Politics. Both political ideas and the wide-ranging arguments to which they give rise are now treated in a rigorous, analytical fashion, and political theorists have contributed to disciplines as diverse as economics, sociology and law. These developments have made the subject more challenging and exciting, but they have also added to the difficulties of students and others coming to the subject for the first time. Much of the burgeoning literature in specialist books and journals is readily intelligible only to those who are already well-versed in the subject.

Issues in Political Theory is a series conceived in response to this situation. It consists of a number of detailed and comprehensive studies of issues central to Political Theory which take account of the latest developments in scholarly debate. While making original contributions to the subject, books in the series are written especially for those who are new to Political Theory. Each volume aims to introduce its readers to the intricacies of a fundamental political issue and to help them find their way through the detailed, and often complicated, argument that that issue has attracted.

PETER JONES
ALBERT WEALE

D0474866

ISSUES IN POLITICAL THEORY

Series Editors: PETER JONES and ALBERT WEALE

Published

David Beetham: **The Legitimation of Power**
Tom Campbell: **Justice**
John Horton: **Political Obligation**
Peter Jones: **Rights**
Albert Weale: **Democracy**

Forthcoming

Bhikhu Parekh: **The Politics of Multiculturalism**
Hillel Steiner: **Utilitarianism**

Democracy

Albert Weale

First published 1999 by
MACMILLAN PRESS LTD
Houndmills, Basingstoke, Hampshire RG21 6XS
and London
Companies and representatives throughout the world

ISBN 0–333–56754–4 hardcover
ISBN 0–333–56755–2 paperback

A catalogue record for this book is available from the British
Library.

This book is printed on paper suitable for recycling and made
from
fully managed and sustained forest sources.

10	9	8	7	6	5	4	3	2	1
08	07	06	05	04	03	02	01	00	99

Typeset by EXPO Holdings, Malaysia

Printed in Hong Kong

Published in the United States of America 1999 by
ST. MARTIN'S PRESS, INC.,
Scholarly and Reference Division,
175 Fifth Avenue, New York, N.Y. 10010

ISBN 0–312–22092–8 PBK
ISBN 0–312–22091–X HC

Contents

Acknowledgements

I have acquired many debts in writing this book. Peter Jones, co-editor of this series and a long-standing friend, has helped me over many years. He has been unstinting with advice, constructive in criticism and supportive throughout. My publisher, Steven Kennedy, has been patient above and beyond the call of duty. There must have been many occasions on which he will have thought that, in the race between Achilles and the tortoise, Achilles would never catch up. I thank him for his understanding.

I do not follow the current fashion in thinking that teaching and research are incompatible activities. Indeed, not only do I find I learn much myself from trying to put my thoughts into order, but I am constantly intrigued by the insights that students bring to the logic of democratic theory. In recent years at the University of Essex I have taught much of this material to my graduate students in my course 'Political Principles and Public Policy' as well as lecturing on democratic theory to first-year students in the 'Introduction to Politics' course. I have always enjoyed the experience, and I hope the same can be said for those who have taken the courses.

I have also given various papers related to this work at different universities, including Cambridge, City University Hong Kong, East Anglia, Essex and the London School of Economics. I am grateful to the participants on all occasions for the constructive discussions I have had.

I have learnt many things from conversations and discussions with colleagues at Essex, especially Michael Freeman, Tony King and Hugh Ward. In addition, a number of people have kindly read, sometimes in great detail, all or part of the draft manuscript. They include: David Beetham, Ian Budge, David Held, Ron Johnston, Geraint Parry and John Street, as well as an anonymous publisher's reviewer. Their comments were always pertinent and acute, and

I hope they see some signs of their influence in this version. I am particularly grateful to those where I have ventured, and sometimes even persisted, in disagreeing with their views.

One person who read the draft manuscript was the late Martin Hollis, who offered comments that were typically astute. Although I had been familiar with his work for many years, I came to know him personally when I worked at the University of East Anglia. He combined philosophical rigour with a wide understanding of the social sciences and a deep commitment to the values of a critical, academically independent educational system. He will be deeply missed by many.

Throughout the period of writing Jan Harris has been a constant companion, but the writing itself has all too often intruded upon time that we should have had together. That is why I only give two cheers for democracy.

ALBERT WEALE

1 Introduction: Democracy and Political Theory

In the last twenty years, there has occurred a 'global resurgence of democracy' (Diamond and Plattner, 1996). The collapse of communism in central and eastern Europe, the democratization of Latin America and the transformation of some African one-party systems into multi-party systems have had profound effects upon patterns of government throughout the world. Democratization in places as diverse as Zambia, Argentina, Poland and South Korea has occurred with a speed and vigour that has surprised informed and knowledgeable observers. Formerly closed, authoritarian political systems have become open to new influences and political ideas. These events and trends have prompted many observers in recent years to claim that 'we are all democrats now', having reached 'the end of history' (Fukuyama, 1989) or, to put the point less poetically but more accurately, the end of political controversy about systems of government. Democracy – it would seem – has ceased to be a matter of contention and has become a matter of convention.

Yet, however superficially appealing this judgement may seem, it needs to be qualified in various ways. Firstly, it is clear that the legacy of authoritarian rule is far from extinct. In the lead up to the hand over of Hong Kong from the UK to China, the Chinese government installed its own appointed legislative body to replace the democratically elected legislative council. Within China itself, political dissent has been suppressed, most notably in the violent putting down of the democracy demonstrations in Tiananmen Square and the subsequent persecution and imprisonment of political dissidents. Moreover, the 1990s appear to have witnessed a slowing down in the rate of democratization compared to the 1980s

1

(Diamond and Plattner, 1996, p. x) and authoritarian rule has been defended by arguments, sometimes advanced in good faith, to the effect that democratic practices are culturally specific and that in some cultures, for example, those influenced by Confucianism, authoritarian systems of government are not only politically defensible but morally justifiable (Freeman, 1996).

The second qualification arises from the observed consequences of the collapse of communist and authoritarian systems. Far from leading to liberal democracy these collapses have often unleashed nationalist and ethnic forces that are difficult to contain within the scope of democratic norms and practices. The civil war in Bosnia following the breakup of the former Yugoslavia, the war in Chechnya or the suppression of electoral results in Serbia all testify to the complexity and difficulty of the transitions.

Thirdly, even in well established political systems that like to think of themselves as being democratic, there are persistent and pertinent questions about the quality of performance of the political system. Italy perhaps is the most conspicuous example of this questioning, with the seismic shocks to the political order in recent years reflecting the disillusionment on the part of citizens with the performance of the established democratic system. Thus, the demand within Italy for more issues of public policy to be decided by referendum can be seen as an attempt to overcome the blockages to decision-making characteristic of the post-war political system.

Doubts about democratic performance are not unique to Italy among liberal democracies, however. Political systems that were once taken to be paradigmatic of a form of democracy to be emulated, like the UK's Westminster system, have fallen into disrepute for their inability to cope with long-standing problems of post-imperial economic adjustment and it is clear that the Labour government elected in 1997 is pursuing vigorously a programme of constitutional reform. In New Zealand, at one time the prime example of the Westminster system at work (Lijphart, 1984, pp. 16–20), fundamental constitutional change has taken place. In presidential systems, like that of the US, signs of political disillusionment are abundant, manifested not least in low electoral turn-outs and the tendency of candidates for office running on an anti-Washington ticket.

One striking instance where democratic values have yet to flourish is in the European Union. Many observers have noted the existence of a 'democratic deficit' in the decision-making procedures of the Union. Indeed, it has been said that if the European Union itself applied to become a member state, it would be rejected because its political system was insufficiently democratic. Moreover, it is clear that this is not simply an oversight or accident of history, but that executive government by a political elite was integral to the Monnet method of European integration in the post-war years (Featherstone, 1994) and reflects the interests of key political actors who currently have power within the present system.

It might be said that these examples merely show how political practice can lag behind political theory, and that in time political and institutional changes will mean that political institutions will come to reflect democratic norms. However, it is not so easy to draw this conclusion. Democratic principles are neither self-evident nor universally accepted. In fact, if we look at influential strands of contemporary political theory, it is clear that some theorists at least express considerable scepticism about democracy as a system of government.

One clear example is to be found in Robert Nozick's (1974) libertarian theory of the state. Although he has subsequently recanted his earlier views (Nozick, 1989, pp. 286–96), Nozick's 'invisible hand' theory of political legitimacy left no clear room for democratic institutions. According to this theory, the state emerges from a series of bilateral contracts that individuals make with protective associations in a Lockean state of nature. However, there is no reason to assume that the contractual relations that prevail between individuals and the protective associations that guard them should be democratic. Indeed, according to the logic of contractual arrangements, it would presumably be up to the contracting parties to negotiate how protective associations would make their decisions. And on this account, even monopoly suppliers of protective services might be more fully constrained in their actions by the contestability of their market position, with the possibility of other suppliers entering the market, than by the institution of democratic procedures.

Sceptical doubts about democracy are not confined to the libertarian portion of the political spectrum, however. In many of his essays, Dworkin (1977, 1985 and 1996) gives primacy of the place to the independent judiciary as interpreters of the political morality of a community, rather than to its elected legislators. Although there are some issues left over from constitutional interpretation on which Dworkin thinks that legislators are free to act, many of the most fundamental questions that a political community can face – equality in employment and education, freedom of association and protest, or the imposition of censorship – are off limits to legislative action, once the judges have interpreted the political constitution by reference to the principle of political equality (see Chapter 9).

In short, despite many celebrations of democracy and democratization, there is also ambivalence about the legitimate scope and range of the authority of democratic institutions among both political observers and political theorists. At this point it is clear that we are confronted by fundamental questions of normative theory. Once we abandon the view that the development of democratic practice is an inevitable consequence of the progress of history and recognize that articulate political theories are often sceptical of democracy as an ideal, we see that certain questions of political principle cannot be avoided, if democracy is to be properly understood. Why is democracy valuable, and can it be justified as being better than alternative non-democratic forms of government? What assumptions about the moral standing of persons lie behind democratic practice, and how far are these assumptions justified? How is democratic performance to be evaluated, and what would count as an improvement in performance? Why should certain features of democratic practice – for example, rule by the majority – be thought superior to other ways of making political decisions? How do democratic values relate to the values of constitutional government in general, especially personal freedom, human rights and the rule of law?

The most important feature of these questions is that they concern the principles of political morality. Although responding to them in full may require us to understand how in practice democratic institutions function, it should be clear that we cannot answer such questions merely by empirical description and analysis. We also need to engage in normative argument. To be sure, our reasoning cannot ignore empirical evidence, since we need to understand how the elements of democratic practice hang together and what the consequences are of adopting one set of institutions rather than another. Equally, however, we cannot rest content with empirical evidence alone, since the evaluation of institutions and practices requires us to have some independent standard in terms of which we can judge the adequacy of practice. To say this, however, is to raise the question of how we might determine the content and form of such standards, and this in turn raises questions about the appropriate methods for approaching questions of political morality.

Political Principles and Political Theory

I have argued so far that we cannot take for granted the theoretical basis of democratic government. Once we enquire more precisely into its scope, nature and moral appeal, we find the potential for controversy and political disagreement. It is at this point that we need to consider the methods of political theory, and the extent to which we can (and cannot) expect these methods to be of use.

Normative political theory is concerned with the analysis and understanding of political principles. The need for a systematic study of political principles arises, because, as soon as we seek to consider what should be done in particular cases, we find ourselves involved in the assertion or refutation of political principles of one sort or another. Consider, for example, the question of whether there should be a death penalty for certain crimes, or the issue of the age at which people should be entitled to vote. In answering these questions members of a political community will usually give different and competing answers, but in doing so disputants will also typically appeal to certain principles, for example the sanctity of life or the principle of deterrence in the case of the death penalty or principles of personal responsibility in the case of determining the age of voting. The presupposition of such arguments therefore is that principles are crucial to arriving at a reasonable answer to such questions, even if there is disagreement about what the relevant principles should be.

Moreover, the political principles invoked in arguments about particular issues are often thought to have a certain general pattern or structure to them. That is to say, they are used not only to assert solutions to particular issues of policy but also to define a stance, or political position, towards a wide range of questions. For example, when people defend the principle of majority rule, they normally think about it as applying across a whole range of political decisions, and not simply to one set of political issues. To be sure, they may think that there are limits to the scope of majority rule that may properly be imposed within a justifiable political morality – for example, they may hold that a majority is not entitled to deprive a minority of its political rights – but here again the limits are defined in terms of classes of issues, and not simply to a one-off decision.

At any one time there will be a number of such general principles informing judgements of political morality. In the case of democratic theory, for example, such principles might include the following: no one should be unreasonably denied the opportunity to express their interests; no one should be regarded as especially competent to make political decisions; each person is to be regarded as the best judge of his or her own interests; majority decision-making should decide most issues of political decision-making; a minority should not be deprived of the opportunity to become a majority; and so on.

It is an important feature of a political morality that the scope and content of the principles that form its corpus are indefinite and prone to conflict with one another. If we consider the principles of democratic theory, for example, it is clear that intuitively attractive principles may clash. It is easy to see that allowing a minority to become a majority may impose restrictions upon what a majority can do, but this will conflict with the principle that the general method of taking decisions should be majoritarian. The chief intellectual task in relation to such a morality is therefore to achieve as precise a statement of the principles as we can and to establish the relation of the principles one to another, so as to minimize the occasions of inconsistency and conflict, or identify their precise nature when they occur.

What is the test of how far we have been adequately to define the principles or standards of a political morality? One test has been implicitly referred to in the argument so far, namely that there should be a reasonable coherence among the principles that make up a political morality. I say 'reasonable coherence' rather than 'complete consistency' deliberately. Any political morality will be the accretion of different elements and there may well be conflicting portions of the morality, as the conflict between majority rule and minority rights goes to show.

However, even if we have a reasonably coherent body of political principles, it does not follow that we have done all that we theoretically need to. For there may be competing bodies of principles, internally coherent in themselves but nevertheless inconsistent with one another. It is unlikely, for example, given the amount of intellectual effort that has gone into the development of their respective traditions that either libertarians or social democrats are going to be able to fault one another by finding some serious inconsistency in their respective body of principles. The theoretical argument needs to be conducted in a different way.

It is at this point that the method of 'reflective equilibrium' enters. So far as I am aware, this method was first formally adopted by Sidgwick (1901) and is now widespread in normative theory (compare Feinberg, 1973, p. 3; Rawls, 1972, pp. 20–1; and Scanlon, 1982). The crux of this method is that the body of political principles to which we subscribe should be consistent with our most deeply held convictions about what is right or wrong. For example, it is a widespread and deeply held conviction that slavery is wrong as an institution. But we only begin to think about the issue in a theoretical way (which is not to say that this is the only, or even most important, way in which we should think about it), when we consider the grounds upon which we regard slavery as being wrong. Once we have identified these grounds we then consider other cases to which they might apply and see whether we come to the same judgement, or whether we think that some other principle applies in that case. For example, some people think that poverty in a market economy is akin to slavery, since it makes people work at unreasonably low rates of pay, whereas others think that the analogy is not that close or that other principles apply (for example, that of freedom of contract). Similarly, some people might think that being deprived of the vote was rather like being a slave, whereas others might hold to the view that, though true for those born in a society, it was not true for those who voluntarily choose to live and work in a foreign country which did not give them the right to vote.

The method of reflective equilibrium therefore works by seeking to build out from agreement on particular institutions to more general principles and thereafter to other institutions that may fall within the compass of the principle. As Joel Feinberg (1973, p. 3) says, correct general principles 'do not reveal themselves spontaneously,

nor are they deduced from self-evident principles'. We have to continue to move between judgements, principles and institutional
applications iteratively, in order to establish any conclusions, and
to come to the point of reflective equilibrium where we feel we
have a reasonably comprehensive and coherent point of view. At
some point on this journey we may well lose certain people, whose
views about the judgements we make, the principles we hold or the
institutions we endorse differ from ours. But they, after all, are
always free to define their own reflective equilibrium. There is
no such thing as logical coercion. Only the appeal to certain
sorts of arguments, which we hope that others will find convincing,
plausible or justifiable.

The Circumstances of Politics

I have so far distinguished normative arguments about the political
morality of institutional arrangements from empirical arguments
about how institutional arrangements work, what their consequences are and what the conditions are under which they emerge.
However, a distinction does not imply an absence of relation, and
in this section I shall set out what I take to be a plausible account
of this relation.

One argument that can be appealed to in this context is the doctrine that ought implies can. That is to say, if we hold to a principle
implying that a certain set of institutions ought to be maintained
or brought into being, then we are also committed to saying that
such institutions can be feasibly maintained or introduced. For
example, if I say that the members of a society ought to be able to
decide all important issues directly through such devices as a referendum, then I am implicitly saying, according to the principle that
ought implies can, that it is feasible or practicable for a society to
run its affairs in this way.

Such a principle, if accepted, would suggest that there is often
quite a close relationship between empirical claims and normative
analysis. If we require of any principle that the institutions it
endorses should be practicable, then we are saying that the only
institutional arrangements we should countenance theoretically
are those that have at least a prima facie claim to be considered
feasible from our understanding of how societies work. Thus, we

should need to ensure that our principles of democratic theory were consistent with what political science currently thinks to be feasible as a set of workable institutions.

To impose this requirement of consistency between feasibility and moral desirability is often taken to be a purely formal matter, but it should be clear that it is more than such, and indeed that it has some substantive implications for political theory. One effect, for example, is to rule out of consideration from the start certain sorts of utopian political theorizing. For some, this is a disadvantage, since utopian theorizing, it is argued, has its own purposes and merits, alerting us to possibilities that our lack of imagination, rather than any state of the world, rules out of bounds. Despite this insight, I shall stick to the principle that ought implies can, recognizing its limitations. In part this is simply to make the argument manageable, but in part my decision rests upon the belief that there are no general reasons stemming from the findings of empirical political science to rule out a wide range of institutional democratic forms. There is quite simply a wide range of institutional choice that confronts the citizen of most societies and the selection from among the alternatives rests ultimately upon arguments of political principle.

However, the openness of this choice does not mean that anything goes, and we should recognize that the set of the ethically desirable is bounded by the set of the feasible. What can we say of relevance about these constraints of feasibility? Modern political theory normally aspires to be relatively modest about the empirical assumptions it makes. Modern analytic political theorists are unlikely to go around letting blast with Bentham (1780, p. 11) that nature has placed mankind under two sovereign masters: pain and pleasure. The reason for this modesty largely stems, I suspect, from acknowledging that the social sciences have shown how difficult it is to sustain such bold generalizations about how the world works and an awareness that there is great variety in human interaction and social structures. Hence, there is a desire not to make conclusions depend upon particular empirical claims that may well turn out to be false or limited in scope.

Despite this understandable modesty, one is unlikely to get very far in thinking about the institutional consequences of political principles unless one makes certain assumptions about how political institutions work. In the rest of this section, therefore, I shall

try to define the conditions of what I shall term, by obvious analogy
with Rawls's (1972, pp. 126–30) concept of the circumstances of
justice, the circumstances of political organization. These conditions are intended to embody middle-range empirical generalizations about how social and political institutions work. As empirical
generalizations they are obviously prone to revision in the light of
further experience, although as I shall hope to show the reasons
for adopting them are not always entirely empirical.

I shall take a society to be characterized by a mixture of conflict
and cooperation (compare Scharpf, 1989). A society is cooperative
in so far as broad agreement on the structure of basic social institutions is necessary in order to provide the conditions under which
individuals can escape the state of nature as described by Hobbes
(1651), that is the hypothetical condition in which life is solitary,
poor, nasty, brutish and short. By avoiding the state of nature, individuals are free to enjoy the products of their labour and activity.
The sort of institutions that are necessary to create this productive
surplus over and above what would be achieved in the state of
nature involve, among other things: a legal system, including a
functioning system of property rights; institutions for coordinating
behaviour to mutual advantage; means of educating new generations; and institutions to protect people from the vicissitudes of life
(ill health, disability and so) to which flesh is heir.

The conflictual element in a society arises because there is no
one form that these institutions have to take in order to perform
the function of enabling individuals to avoid the state of nature,
and different institutional arrangements will typically bestow different types of relative advantage on different types of people. For
example, a system of private property will benefit people with
entrepreneurial skills, whereas collective property will benefit
people with political skills. Moreover, conflict will also arise over
the functioning of the institutions that a society has and not simply
over the choice of institutions. The allocation of rights and the distribution of benefits is seldom rigidly fixed in any institutional
arrangement, and controversy can arise over the basis upon which
alternative allocations or distributions can be made.

Within this situation of partial cooperation and partial conflict,
individuals have only constrained generosity. Although there will
be saints and heroes who are prepared to act selflessly for what is
taken to be the common good, most individuals will want to protect

what they regard as their legitimate interests from others. This protective motive is not one of predation, as it would be in the Hobbesian state of nature, but it is sufficiently strong to create the basis for organized and opposed interest groups, based on class, ethnic, linguistic, religious or regional identities. Limited generosity therefore involves an unwillingness to carry disproportionate burdens or disadvantages relative to one's reference group, but it does not involve a desire to disrupt a satisfactory balance of interests among potentially antagonistic groups if it can be established.

Social cooperation and conflict exists in the context of bounded rationality (Simon, 1983, pp. 17–23). Bounded rationality arises because human beings have limited processing capacity for the information they need to conduct their lives in a satisfactory way and no one agent is able to understand all the issues that relate to a particular society. To say that human rationality is bounded is to say that there are pervasive and ineliminable information asymmetries in a society, so that some individuals will always know more about some particular facet of social life than any other individuals could. This in turn leads to pervasive problems of trust and commitment.

Bounded rationality is likely to lead to differences of political perspective in various situations. Among these situations the following are most prominent: an extensive division of labour (so that individuals in one occupational grouping are simply unable to know what is involved in some other occupation); differences of language (limited information processing meaning that few individuals will be functional in non-native languages); differences of religion (where again limited information processing will preclude mutual understanding); or ethnic differences (in which different formative experiences may be effectively unbridgeable for those with a different background). Other possible sources of mutual incomprehension include gender and age.

As a result of these circumstances, political interaction and decision-making are needed not only to resolve the conflicts of interests that arise inevitably in institutions, but also to reconcile differences of view about what is in the common interest, such differences arising from diverse positions that individuals occupy in society. Moreover, political choices have to be made in definite and limited periods of time. We should not conceptualize politics as an open-ended conversation stretching indefinitely into the future, but as a practical activity directed towards solving the inevitable problems that emerge continuously as individuals and groups negotiate with one another over the terms of their cooperation and the resolution of their conflicts. If we accept this characterization of the circumstances of politics, there will be clear implications for the evaluation of political institutions.

Firstly, we should think of the political problem as one in which there is limited mutual understanding and constrained generosity, but not as one in which there is an overriding imperative towards selfish behaviour irrespective of the behaviour of others. One can understand the logic of the war of all against all in a Hobbesian state of nature (though even in this case there are reasons for thinking that it rarely exists in pure form; see Taylor, 1976), since in being subject to the predation of others, all individuals have to be ultra-cautious about their interactions. However, within an established and on-going political community, it is more reasonable to think that the willingness of individuals to cooperate with one another will depend upon their past experience of cooperation, and in that sense will rest upon a principle of reciprocity rather than selfishness.

Secondly, we need to decide what theory of human motivation we should adopt when considering the evaluation and design of political institutions. In a famous argument, David Hume (1742, pp. 117–26) cited the maxim that in the design of political institutions everyone should be supposed a knave. The argument is that in politics knavery should be assumed, not on the grounds that everyone is a knave, but on the grounds that the consequences of knaves holding political power are potentially so serious that any prudent person would want to guard against the possibility. We shall find ourselves at various times returning to this problem, particularly in chapter 9, when we consider the limits that might justifiably be placed upon the scope of democratic decision-making. However, I shall simply assert here, in the context of the circumstances of politics, that it would be unreasonable to make the supposition of knavery a general rule.

Thirdly, there is the phenomenon of what has come to be known as 'path-dependence' (North, 1990, pp. 94–102; Putnam, 1993, pp. 179–81). In essence what this means is that the changes it is feasible to envisage in a set of institutions will depend upon the history of those institutions. Thus, Latin America has a poorer economic record than North America, despite their similarity in natural resources, because it inherited a political system based upon hierarchy rather than decentralized parliamentarianism, and once boxed in to these institutions, it was difficult to escape their consequences. Similarly, we can ascribe the higher level of crime in the US, compared to Canada, to the fact that in the latter the Royal Mounted Police in the nineteenth century were able to establish law and order before new settlers arrived in the western territories, whereas no equivalent institution existed in the US. Path-dependence thus suggests that the changes it is sensible to introduce into a political system will depend upon what has happened before, and that fundamental constitutional changes are rare, seismic events.

Taking these features – constrained generosity, bounded rationality and path-dependence – together, it might be thought that we are severely limited in the extent to which we can subscribe to general principles of institutional evaluation. All evaluative judgements, it would seem, have to take note of the circumstances of particular cases to such a degree that it ceases to be plausible to invoke general principles. However, this would surely be too strong a conclusion to draw. Political principles are not a blueprint, but a standard. They do not tell us what to do in the design of political institutions, since knowing what to do in any particular case always involves a great deal of local and contextual knowledge, but they do provide a criterion for assessing whether what we are doing is aiming in the right direction. The circumstances of politics thus set constraints on what it is feasible to expect from the construction of any set of political institutions. However, a great variety of political institutions could be constructed in accordance with the characteristics so far identified. Even if we limit ourselves to recognizably democratic political institutions, they are still a diverse set. The circumstances of politics should lead us to be cautious in our evaluations, but not morally agnostic.

The Definition of Democracy

So far I have referred to the global resurgence of democracy and assumed a notion of democratic government without offering a formal definition of what we are discussing. The definition I shall use is intended to capture the thought that democracy is best defined by contrast with non-democratic forms of government and also attempts to identify elements that are common to the variety of forms that democratic government can take. Accordingly, the definition should be regarded as stating the minimal conditions for a system of government to count as democratic. The definition I offer may be stated as follows: in a democracy important public decisions on questions of law and policy depend, directly or indirectly, upon public opinion formally expressed by citizens of the community, the vast bulk of whom have equal political rights.

In this definition government policy depends in some formal and regular way on the state of public opinion. It is precisely the dependence of government upon opinion that was the object of classical critiques of Athenian democracy by Plato in *The Republic*, on the grounds that knowledge (*episteme*), not opinion (*doxa*), should steer the ship of state. In offering this definition, I therefore seek to defend the role of opinion as a source of political authority, but I do not intend to assert that in a democracy public policy always needs to track public opinion across the full range of decisions that governments make. I merely mean to assert that if we came across a system of government in which there was no dependence at all in important public choices on public opinion, then we would withhold the name democracy from that system.

The link with public opinion may be direct or indirect. A direct link with public opinion exists when choices on law and policy are made by citizens themselves, for example by voting in a binding referendum. However, the choices may be far less directly dependent than in that sort of example. Provided that political representatives can effectively be turned out of office by reasonably regular elections, the political system is a democracy according to the definition I am working with. However, such indirect links must involve a recognized rule of the political system. Someone once said of government in late eighteenth-century Britain that it was 'despotism tempered by riot'. But according to the definition I am offering, even when effective in changing government policy, rioting crowds are not democratic citizens exercising their rights. So in saying that the link is formal, there is no implication that it is ineffective. Rather, on the claimed definition, a democracy achieves its effectiveness through the formal features of the relevant institutions.

Note too that the definition requires an equality of political rights among the vast bulk of the citizens in a democratic community. This qualification identifies two dimensions of democratic institutions as being important. The first is the sharing of the same rights among the citizens of a political community. How stringently one should insist on this criterion is a matter for judgement in particular cases, and it is difficult to come up with a general formula (neither is it necessary) to cover all cases. However, even in the absence of a definite criterion, we can still make distinctions. Thus, I take it that many states in the US were not democracies until African-Americans obtained the effective right to vote and organize politically on a par with other citizens, but that Britain was still a democracy when university graduates had two votes compared to everyone else's one. The second dimension is the requirement that the vast bulk of citizens be given political rights and this picks out a requirement of inclusiveness. On this test, political systems were not democratic which deprived women of the vote, even if there was a high level of participation among men in political decision-making, as was true of Switzerland at the federal level until 1971.

It will be helpful in seeing the force of the definition to identify cases with which democracy in this sense is contrasted. The definition excludes two possible systems of government from being called democratic (there are many others of course that could never aspire to the title). The first is benign authoritarianism, or what Finer (1970) termed 'quasi-democracies', a type of political regime that is supposed to prevail in some east Asian societies influenced by Confucianism. Under benign authoritarianism, it is asserted, governments take decisions in the interests of the citizens, but they substitute their own judgement about what those interests are for the views of citizens themselves. By contrast, on the definition I offer, democracy is a system of government in which the policies and decisions of government on an important range of issues depend, to a greater or lesser extent, on public opinion as expressed in elections or other forms of aggregating opinion.

The definition also denies the title of democracy to what has been termed 'vanguard democracy' (Macpherson, 1966). Vanguard democracy is simply the former Communist Party's version of benign authoritarianism, on the understanding that the scientific insight by the party leadership into the march of history replaces the wisdom of the rulers. One might extend the courtesy title of democracy to this system of government, if it was clear that it was aiming firmly at the inauguration of a democratic regime. However, as Trotsky notoriously pointed out about Lenin's version of vanguard democracy, it too ends up as a sort of 'substitutionism' (see Knei-Paz, 1978, pp. 192–9).

In defining democracy I have been referring to systems of government. The main reason for approaching the topic in this way is that, whatever else we might want to do with a theory of democracy, we certainly need it to evaluate governments. Does this imply, however, that there are no other social institutions that we might wish to classify as democratic or non-democratic? What about the democratic workplace, the democratic school, the democratic university, the democratic church or the democratic family? If we say that the principle of democracy applies to systems of government, should we not also say that it applies to these other institutions, and, if so, should we not also expand our definition to include these other institutions?

There is a perfectly clear sense in which we can distinguish such institutions as being democratic or non-democratic. For example, we can say of a firm either that its organization is based on principles of worker democracy, in which those in the firm choose who is to run it and what decisions are made, or it may be based on the non-democratic principle of hierarchy. The same can be said for the other institutions I have mentioned. However, it does not follow from this definitional point that we should seek to construct a normative theory of democracy on the assumption that all these institutions are covered by the same arguments. There are a number of reasons why this is so.

Firstly, the state – the collection of institutions that governments occupy – may be defined, following the famous definition of Weber (1947, pp. 154–7) as that association with the legitimate monopoly of coercive force in a given territorial area. To be sure, we must be careful in the way that the notion of legitimacy is defined here (Beetham, 1991). None the less, no other association typically rivals a stable state in its ability to raise revenue, impose laws and fight wars. It would seem to be an obvious question to ask how the distinctive power that is generated by the state should be used and directed.

Secondly, governmental politics deals with the articulation and aggregation of what are relatively permanent interests. With their retentive memories, human beings may be able to recall for some time their being jostled out of turn for a place in the bus queue or the kindness of strangers who shared their firelighters at the camp-site (compare Leftwich, 1983, pp. 11–12). But these memories are not part of the fabric of basic and long-term interests – like the conditions of employment, the provisions made for economic secur-ity in the event of loss of earnings or the character of an educa-tional system – that are the elements of political contestation within systems of government.

Both these features – the monopoly of legitimate coercive force and the relevance to permanent and basic interests – distinguish the activity of government from other spheres of human activity and, taken together, they mark government out as a significantly distinct institutional realm. Provided we continue to remain open about the possibilities of seeing analogies between politics and other forms of activity, it is simply intellectually confusing not to distinguish issues that arise in the practice of government from issues that arise from other practices.

By extension, one should remain open-minded about the degree to which we can carry over arguments about the justification and form of democracy from one sphere of human activity to another. Participatory democracy in, say, the university need carry no implica-tions about the form of democracy in the nation-state in the absence of any special argument to show how the former could be a model of the latter. Conversely, democracy in the nation-state need not imply, again in the absence of special argument, democracy in the work-place or the church. To be sure, there may be a frame of mind we could call, to use Davie's (1961) term, a 'democratic intellect' that is constant across different areas of activity. But, unless we wish to say that members of churches whose government is non-democratic cannot be good political democrats, we have to acknowledge that arguments about the principles of government do not have straight-forward application to other spheres of activity and vice versa.

The definition offered is intended to be minimal, in the sense that it designates a class of political systems without distinguishing between the members of that class. Hyland (1995, pp. 49–50), however, reminds us that definitions can involve 'scalar' as well as 'sortal' concepts. Sortal concepts designate a class – for example, it is sortal concepts that distinguish lions from tigers – whereas scalar concepts identify a characteristic – for example, warmth, that objects can have to a greater or lesser degree. Why should we regard democracy as a sortal rather than a scalar concept? Why not say that political systems can have certain characteristics, for example their degree of inclusiveness or their extent of citizen participation, and such systems are more or less democratic depending upon where they are located on the appropriate scale? In this approach we would not be looking for the minimum conditions that a political system would need to satisfy in order to count as democratic, but the ideal scheme of democratic political organization against which actually existing examples could be assessed.

The answer to this question is complex, but I suggest that it falls along the following lines. From the point of view of making practical decisions of political morality, there is some value in distinguishing democratic from non-democratic political systems in the sense that the democratic systems meet some minimal conditions that are stipulated. For example, such distinctions may be important in answering the question of whether international aid should be made conditional upon the accomplishment of democratic reforms in some countries. In such contexts, it would be impracticable, and perhaps counter-productive, to set the standard so high that imperfect human societies could not reach it. Even if our underlying notion of democracy is scalar rather than sortal, we may still need to impose some cut-off points on the scale.

In addition, to define democracy in scalar terms carries the implication that having more of a certain characteristic, for example citizen participation in the making of decisions, makes the political system more democratic *as such*. But we should at least be open to the possibility that representative government is at least as democratic a form of government as direct democracy, even if there are good substantive reasons for wishing to increase participation. There are a variety of conceptions of democracy that have been advanced as justifiable all of which are compatible with the definition I have offered. The definition is intended to be a criterion, distinguishing democratic from non-democratic regimes, it is not intended to be a full characterization of the full range of democratic polities. In the next chapter, I consider how we might understand this range of possibilities and how we might begin to understand the way in which we could evaluate their respective merits with some intellectual plausibility.

2 Varieties of Democracy

We have seen that democracy is a form of government in which public policy depends in a systematic, if sometimes indirect, way upon public opinion. However, subject to this criterion, there are various forms that democratic governments can take. Indeed, looking at the literature on democracy, it is clear that it reflects this diversity with classifications, categories and typologies in abundance. We read of pluralist democracy, radical democracy, liberal democracy, socialist democracy, one-party democracy, deliberative democracy, polyarchy, elitist democracy, equilibrium democracy and so on. (For examples of such typologies, see Held, 1996; and Macpherson, 1977.)

The reasons for this proliferation of categories is not hard to find. First, democracy, whatever it is, is a complex phenomenon, and it is bound to take a variety of forms. To understand and account for this complexity requires us to have some typology in mind that will reduce the complexity and clarify our thinking. Second, given the favourable connotations the term 'democracy' often seems to possess, it is not surprising that many people from different ideological persuasions have wished to identify their preferred arrangement of political life with the ideals of democracy. Whatever the merits of liberalism, socialism, capitalism, republicanism and so on, each ideology will receive considerable intellectual and moral support from being associated with a plausible account of democracy. In consequence, ideas like 'liberal democracy', 'social democracy' and so on are bound to flourish.

Amid so many competing typologies it is hazardous to offer another. Yet, simply in order to organize the subsequent discussion, it is necessary to offer some particular account of the varieties of democracy, and this is what I shall seek to do in this chapter.

I do not claim that this is the 'best' or 'most desirable' typology. Typologies are essentially instruments of enquiry and which instrument one chooses depends upon the job at hand. I do want to claim, however, that for the purposes of normative political theory a relevant typology ought to be based upon institutional, rather than behavioural, features of political life. Let me explain the distinction and why it is important in this context.

An institution can be defined, in the words of Oran Young (1989, p. 5), as 'identifiable practices consisting of recognised roles linked by clusters of rules or conventions governing relations among the occupants of these roles'. Institutions in this sense may be highly informal. The practice of leaving your coat on your seat in the train when you want to keep your place is an institution in this broad sense, as is the practice of shaking hands when meeting people. But institutions may be formalized into organizational structures such as firms, political parties or systems of government. If we offer an institutional account of democracy, therefore, we essentially make our typology turn on the way that we characterize and categorize the rule-governed and convention-governed system of roles and practices that constitute a mode of politics. Examples of institutional accounts in this sense include the following: the scope that the rules of decision-making assign to popular participation; the division of authority between the government of the day and the courts that guard the constitution; the ways in which membership of the polity is assigned or denied to individuals; and the processes by which statements of popular preference are amalgamated into a collective choice.

A behavioural typology of democracy, by contrast, would focus upon how people act within institutional constraints and possibilities. It would ask whether citizens at large avail themselves of the institutional possibilities open to them to influence public policy, or whether decision-making in practice is largely concentrated in the hands of a few people. It would examine the ways in which powerful political actors use the rules of the game to maintain or enhance their own strategic advantage, say by moving amendments and procedural motions during the passing of legislation. It would assess the extent to which social agents have the ability to ignore, bend or alter the rules to their own advantage given the political resources they are able to mobilize. In short, a behavioural account shifts attention from the institutional structures of government to the actions of individuals and groups within those structures.

There is a strong intellectual current in the history of political science which argues that in studying politics we should look at behavioural and not institutional questions. In part, this emphasis arises from an attempt to liberate political science from legal studies, and to study not what the legal and constitutional rules say should happen but what in practice does happen. A good example of the attempt to get behind the appearance of modern politics in order to understand how things work in practice is provided by Bagehot's (1867, p. 61) distinction between the 'dignified' and the 'efficient' elements of the English constitution. According to Bagehot, although the formal rules of the nineteenth-century constitution stipulated that parliament was sovereign, if one looked at how in practice decisions were made it became clear that it was the cabinet which governed. Many British political scientists have embraced a similar 'realism' (compare Gamble, 1990, p. 410).

There is a temptation in discussions of political science for the choice between institutional and behavioural approaches to be polarized, so that one approach comes to dominate the other. This can even apply to authors who show great sensitivity to institutional questions. Thus, in the heyday of the behavioural revolution in political science, Robert Dahl argued that

'in so far as there is any general protection in human society against the deprivation by one group of the freedom desired by another, it is probably not to be found in constitutional forms. It is to be discovered, if at all, in extra-constitutional factors' (Dahl, 1956, p. 134).

Among these extra-constitutional factors Dahl included such things as the distribution of preference intensities in society, a factor that is not related in any straightforward way to a society's institutional arrangements. Yet, without seeking to underestimate the importance of behavioural accounts for political science generally, there are powerful arguments for taking an institutional focus within normative political theory when constructing a typology of democratic forms.

The principal reason for taking such an approach is that political choice can be exercised over institutional arrangements in a way that it cannot easily be exercised over behavioural regularities. Countries can adopt systems of proportional representation where previously they had use first-past-the-post electoral systems. They can open up their decision-making to the greater use of referendums or other forms of citizen participation. They can entrench a bill of rights. They can extend the franchise to resident aliens. They can adopt a constitution that gives a supreme court restraining powers in the action of a legislature. And so on. By contrast, it is more difficult to change behavioural regularities and the results, when tried, are likely to be unpredictable. Patterns of economic occupation, the division of labour by gender, ethnic and linguistic composition or the balance of religious sentiment are clearly important in shaping political behaviour, but they are influential precisely because they are the unintended consequences of multiple interactions among members of society that take place over time. Moreover, causes of political behaviour are only partially related to political decisions. In designing political institutions we may hope that certain patterns of behaviour will result, but we have to reckon with a number of other influences, some of which may be deeply rooted in social structure.

To accept this argument, however, does not imply that an understanding of political behaviour is irrelevant to normative theory. However, rather than directing normative principles at political behaviour, behavioural considerations enter as evidence pertaining to the choice of institutions. Consider, as an example of how this works, Arend Lijphart's account of consociational democracy (Lijphart, 1968; 1977). Lijphart argued that there was a class of segmented societies, in which the behaviour of their members was bounded by close social ties based upon language or religion. Patterns of work organization, marriage, recreational life and so on were structured by the existence of segmented groups so that, for example, Catholics did not marry, form trades unions with or spend much of their free time with Protestants. Lijphart argued that in such circumstances a political system built upon the principle of simple majority rule would not work, because the members of each group would fear that the other group would take too much advantage of the opportunities for power that were offered. In this context one needed institutions built upon a super-majority principle with opportunity for each group to veto the political proposals of the other.

In this sort of argument behavioural and historical evidence is clearly relevant to evaluating the merits of alternative political institutions, but it is taken as a given and attention is directed at the choice of a pattern of institutions rather than at questions about how one might go around changing the underlying social structure that gives rise to the problem. This is not to deny that the structures will change, as indeed they have in the Netherlands, the paradigm of the consociational state, where religious differences have weakened and the tradition 'pillars' have ceased to play the dominant role in shaping behaviour. But it is to say that, insofar as any political prescriptions do emerge from normative argument, they are more likely to make sense when applied to institutions than when applied to structured patterns of political behaviour.

It might be thought that, if social structures so shape behaviour, they leave no room for political choice whatsoever. To speak about institutional choice related to behavioural evidence in the way I shall in this chapter is to reject that form of sociological determinism which asserts that political institutions are simply a manifestation of underlying social forces in relation to which institutional design is purely epiphenomenal. However, rejection of sociological determinism in this form is not rejection of the claim that there may be social conditions that facilitate or enable on the one hand or prevent or inhibit on the other the adoption of certain institutional arrangements. Lijphart's own argument essentially turns on considerations of how social conditions may prevent the emergence of one stable pattern of institutions. More generally, the statistical association between economic development and democratic stability is strong and well documented, and it is not difficult to think of reasons why this association should hold, as well as reasons why it is sometimes overridden (for discussion, see Rueschemeyer, Stephens and Stephens, 1992). To reject a strong form of sociological determinism is merely to say that there are degrees of freedom within sociologically defined boundaries and that choice within these degrees of freedom is politically important. It may also be to say, as I shall argue later in chapter 10, that there can be an obligation upon policy-makers to bring about the social conditions – like generalized prosperity or higher levels of popular education – that make democracy easier to maintain.

If we are to examine institutional alternatives in the way I have suggested, then we shall need some classification of the possibilities in order to make our task manageable. In the next section, I suggest one such classification, and provide some account of the traditions of political thought with which each alternative is associated.

A Typology of Democratic Forms

If the general concept of democracy is given by the criterion of a systematic and non-trivial relationship between public policy and public opinion formally expressed by the bulk of citizens with equal political rights, what variety of institutional conceptions are compatible with this view? A conception of democracy is a specific way of describing a set of institutions which relate public opinion to public policy.

The typology I offer is built upon two stages of classification. The first stage is simply defined by the familiar distinction between direct and indirect democracies. In a direct democracy the people choose the content of public policy. In an indirect democracy the people choose representatives who in turn determine the content of public policy. The second stage of classification further divides each of these two categories into sub-categories. Two forms of direct democracy are identified: unmediated popular government and party-mediated popular government. For the forms of indirect democracy the classification is a little more complex. It builds on work in comparative politics, including Lijphart's (1984) distinction between consensual and majoritarian forms of representative government, and in particular Bingham Powell's (1989) scheme for classifying modern democracies. One category can be called 'representational government' and the other 'accountable' or 'responsible' government. ('Representational government' is an ugly neologism, but I cannot think of an alternative. 'Representative government' refers to all forms of indirect government. I intend the term 'representational' to highlight one important and salient feature of this form of government, namely that decision-making processes reflect inputs from a broad range of social groups.) I shall also distinguish a third form of representative government, namely liberal constitutionalism. We therefore have five possible versions of democracy: unmediated popular government; party-mediated popular government; representational government; accountable government; and liberal constitutionalism. To the description of each I now turn.

1   *Unmediated popular government.* The first form of democracy that we can envisage is that of unmediated popular government as conceptualized by Rousseau (1762). Central to this conception is the

idea that legitimate government will only exist if citizens determine for themselves the rules and laws that they will be obliged to
follow. Citizens assemble together and decide on the content of
laws and public policy without the mediation of political representatives. In their decision, each seeks the common good or general
will of all. According to this view, persons are naturally free, and
their moral autonomy requires that obligations are self-willed.
Under certain conditions (notably a rough equality of economic
circumstance and willingness on the part of citizens to think about
the general interest), these separate autonomous wills combine
into a general will. Under the same conditions the obligation of
citizens to obey the government is complete in the sense that they
can properly and legitimately be forced into compliance, in a way
that would not be possible before the expression of the general
will.

One important element in Rousseau's conception is the prohibition upon factionalism. The distinction between the general will
and the will of all is precisely that the latter is simply the sum of
wills when people vote thinking of their own interests whereas the
general will arises when people think of the public interest.
Rousseau's own example of a decision on whether or not to have
the death penalty provides a good instance of this distinction
(Rousseau, 1762, pp. 189–91). Likely criminals, consulting their
own self-interest, would vote against it, and likely victims, consulting their own self-interest, would vote in favour. Citizens, seeking
to identify the general will, will say to themselves that they could
fall into either category, and will balance the competing interests
involved. This balancing may seem to be both psychologically possible (think of the way that causing death through drunken driving
has attracted less penalty than other ways of causing death, presumably because those responsible for making a decision, including
juries, think that they too might easily have been guilty) and a
reason for Rousseau's views on the importance of economic equality (since the ability to put oneself in the shoes of another is likely
to be easier when all share similar circumstances).

As autonomy is the central underlying value constraining the
construction of political institutions in the Rousseauian conception,
it follows that participation is an essential element in the
justification of legitimate government. When Rousseau wrote that,
though the people of England regarded itself as being free, it was

in fact free only during the election of its members of parliament (Rousseau, 1762, p. 240), he was expressing this sentiment. Without participation by citizens in the formulation of the general will, there can be no legitimate way of making public decisions. In this sense the connection between public opinion, suitably defined, and the making of rules and laws is direct and constitutive. Public opinion defines the content of the laws and rules by which citizens are to be governed.

Rousseau is clear that there is a moralization of individual human beings in the process of social life. The social contract transmutes natural freedom into moral obligation by the participation of citizens in forming the general will. Moreover, the scope of the general will is in principle unbounded. It has to be. Since persons are morally autonomous, there can be no *a priori* limitations upon what they might will (for example, there can be no requirement that their choices be consistent with the demands of a traditional religion). Hence the only source of obligation is the general will as defined by a majority of those voting. Those who are in the minority simply realize that they have mistaken the general will.

Although this last element of Rousseau's thought has often been held to have totalitarian implications, it is in fact no more than a logical inference from the strong assumption of moral autonomy. If strong moral autonomy exists in the way that Rousseau supposes, then moral rules and principles can be nothing other than conventions adopted by societies for the regulation of their conduct. This conventional character of morality will mean that a majority is likely to be right, since conventional behaviour is simply what most people will do under given circumstances. To see this, consider a case that we recognize to be purely conventional. If I turn up at a party wearing a suit and others are in jeans and a tee-shirt, I have simply mistaken the operative convention, and in this sense the general will.

The conception of democracy that emerges in the Rousseauian tradition is both an ideal and an idealization. It is an ideal in the sense that its proponents have thought that it incorporated the value of moral autonomy, and it is an idealization in the sense that it does not describe any particular functioning democracy, but is meant instead to identify some important characterizing features of any democracy. Rousseau's own models were ancient Sparta and republican Rome, though given the reference to Geneva as a free state at the beginning of *The Social Contract* Rousseau also seemed to think that there were contemporary examples that approximated the ideal. In the twentieth century it has been argued that certain forms of African democracy have Rousseauian elements – in particular, Julius Nyerere's conception of *ujamaa* in Tanzania, with its emphasis upon consensus and the outlawing of factions, supposedly building upon what were taken to be traditional African forms of government (see Nursey-Bray, 1983, pp. 101–3). Neither is it difficult to see Rousseauian elements also in a number of radical social movements in liberal democracies.Maier (1992, p. 145) has drawn attention to the echoes of Rousseau in the 1962 Port Huron statement, which was a rallying cry for American radicals, and there are certain styles of green politics that stress consensus and absence of factional struggles as central to their way of working – at least as an ideal.

2 *Party-mediated popular government.* Instead of direct democracy in its Rousseauian version, it is possible to imagine a form of direct democracy that took to their limits participatory devices, like the referendum or the citizen initiative, that currently exist only in restricted form in representative democracies. Ian Budge (1996) has recently proposed a conception of democracy along these lines, arguing that information and communications technologies now make possible extensive citizen involvement in the making of public policies.

How would such a form of democracy differ from its Rousseauian variant? One important difference is that, contrary to Rousseau's strictures on sectionalism, a direct democracy of the sort that Budge envisages would still have political parties, who would perform their traditional functions of organizing the agenda, defining alternatives, seeking for compromise packages and offering candidates for executive office. The chief difference from their role in existing representative democracies is that instead of providing the representatives who decide legislation, voting on laws, rules and policies would be done by the people at large registering their preferences electronically. This characterization of a direct democracy looks more like the example of ancient Athens, where there were clear factions organized in the

governing meeting, than it looks like the idealized version of
Rome or Sparta that Rousseau envisages. (It does not look much
like the idealization of the Athenian *polis* to be found in the works
of Hegel (1956 edn., pp. 258–62) or Arendt (1958, pp. 192–9), but
then neither did the actual Athenian *polis*.)

One of the principal differences between unmediated popular
government and party-mediated popular government is that there
is no need in the latter account to imagine that voters go through
the mental exercise of seeking to find the general will. Just as party
representatives at present vote for measures for a variety of
reasons, not all of them by any means related to an attempt to
define a public good, so citizens in a party-mediated direct democracy might in some cases vote from high motives and in others
from considerations of self-interest or partisan advantage. No
doubt, if there is a refining and elevating effect from having to
present one's arguments in the forum of public opinion, as a
number of deliberative theorists suggest (a view well discussed by
Elster, 1997), this process would operate too in a party-based direct
democracy. However, we should not have to make it a defining
requirement of such a system. In such a system public policy could
be regarded as much as a balancing of interests as the expression
of a view about the public good.

Budge argues that such a system is feasible given new information and communications technologies. He cites the growth of
citizen participation in the United States through such means as
referendums, citizen's initiatives and the recall of representatives,
to show that some of the obvious practical objections to such a
scheme can be overcome. He is also insistent that direct democracy
of this sort is quite compatible with the familiar range of constitutional devices – the separation of powers, the provision of checks
and balances, the existence of bills of rights, the power of courts to
engage in judicial review of measures that are passed and so on –
that are intended to control the abuse of legislative power. It is
simply that the controls are exercised on the people at large rather
than upon their representatives. Here again there is a significant
contrast with Rousseau. There is no assumption that 'the general
will is always right' (the logical consequence of Rousseau's commitment to a strong form of moral autonomy). Instead, the assumption is that though public choices should properly only be made by

the people who experience the consequences of the choice, it may be necessary to constrain the operation of electoral decision-making through constitutional means.

Again by contrast with Rousseau, there is no commitment in such a model to equalizing the economic circumstances of citizens. Such an equalizing of material circumstances was necessary for Rousseau so that each person could have the imaginative identification with others necessary to form a general will. Within the party-based model of direct democracy factions would still presumably reflect associations of citizens with similar interests and perspectives to each other and distinct interests or perspectives from competitor groupings. Such groupings would presumably include factions based upon economic differences, though no doubt these would not be the only source of difference and political competition.

Almost by definition, it is difficult to find examples of this conception of democracy in action, since its operation depends upon the advancement of new information and communication technologies that, though in existence, are not yet widespread. However, there is no reason to believe that such a system of government is not possible, and one imagines that it would look like an enlarged version of current local politics in places where citizen participation is at high levels.

3 Representational government. In order to introduce the conception of representational government, I need first to distinguish two main forms that political representation can take. I shall do this by introducing Bingham Powell's (1989) typology of representative democracies. This typology depends upon classifying political systems according to two principal dimensions: the extent to which the electoral system encourages elected party majorities in the legislature as against encouraging a broad reflection of party votes; and the extent to which legislative committee rules encourage opposition participation in the making of laws and public policy as against the extent to which they encourage executive dominance of the legislature. Table 2.1 shows how contemporary democracies may be classified on these two dimensions.

The most striking feature of Bingham Powell's classification is that it distinguishes clearly between two polar forms of representative

Table 2.1   *Powell's Classification*

	Legislative committee rules encourage		
Election rules encourage	*Government domination*	*Mixed*	*Opposition participation*
Party majorities	Australia France (Fifth Rep.) New Zealand UK	Canada	USA
Mixed	Ireland	—	West Germany Greece Japan Spain
Reflection of party votes	—	Finland	Austria Belgium Denmark Italy Netherlands Norway Sweden Switzerland

Source: Powell (1989, p. 113).

government. It clusters together Westminster systems and the strong system of government inaugurated in the constitution of the Fifth French Republic on the one hand as distinct from the smaller European democracies on the other. Taken together the electoral formula and the committee rules of the legislature characterize the salient distinctive features of two broad types of political system. Most countries fall into the diagonally opposite parts of the table, and off-diagonal elements are countries where mixed systems of government were often self-consciously adopted. It is also a merit of Bingham Powell's classification, in my opinion, that the US is placed in a category of its own.

If we were looking for instances of the principles of representational government, we should find them in the practices of the smaller north European democracies, among the countries that occupy the bottom right corner of Bingham Powell's classification. If we ask what political theory might justify such a form of democracy, then the obvious place to look is John Stuart Mill's *On Representative Government* (J. S. Mill, 1861a), but without the fancy franchise that Mill thought necessary to give the more able and intelligent a greater say in political power than others.

A central principle of representational government is that major decisions should be taken by political representatives meeting in a legislative chamber, who reflect in their characteristics and opinions a wide variety of views and experience. The idea in this conception is that, for various reasons largely to do with size, we should not expect the people to rule directly, but nevertheless policy choices should still reflect opinions that are representative of a broad swathe of opinion in society.

Undoubtedly, the most central institutional principle for Mill, about which he is quite explicit, is achieving proportionality between electoral opinions and the balance of representatives (Mill, 1861a, chapter 7). Mill is clear that the chief reason for wanting proportionality is that it is the only way of ensuring that a majority of the electorate actually decide policy through their representatives. Moreover, Mill supported Thomas Hare's proposed electoral reforms, in which there was an (impractical) attempt to allow the free association of voters in the selection of candidates, because of the diversity of views that could be expressed in society. Moreover, given Mill's general views about independence of spirit – as well as his own practice when an MP – executive dominance of parliament is hardly a logical implication of his theory. He thus provides the theoretical foundations for the representational systems identified by Bingham Powell.

There are two respects in which Mill's normative theory goes beyond the practice of some of the smaller European democracies. The first is his stress upon popular participation in politics at local level, not as a rival to representative government but as a complement to it. It is central to this conception that public spiritedness can only be built through the experience of citizens participating in the processes of government, so that in consequence there is an emphasis upon local democracy and other forms of citizen's participation, for example in the jury system, that would promote increased civic awareness among citizens. Such a conception does not go as far as

Rousseau in thinking that citizens can so internalize a sense of the common good that there will, in effect, be unanimity, but it does stress the extent to which citizens must learn to put their own prejudices and partial sentiments to one side when participating in the making of public decisions.

Because Rousseau thought that the people should be the sovereign, he saw no possibility that the people would pass laws against their own interests. Mill sees much greater scope for the tyranny of the majority and for the need to protect individuals from any harmful effects of collective decision-making (Mill, 1859). It is therefore consistent with Mill's theory of democracy that there should be some separation of powers and protection of individual interests through a bill of rights. None the less, these individualistic elements of his political theory should not detract from the distinctive democratic conception that he also advances.

4 Accountable government. Taking the polar opposite group in Bingham Powell's classification, we find political systems built not on the idea of representativeness but on that of accountability. As with the system of representational government, the principles of accountable government assume that political representatives, rather than the people themselves, make most important political decisions. However, accountable government differs from the conception of representational government in thinking of the legislative chamber not as a mirror or microcosm of the population, but instead as a device for choosing a team to make decisions for a limited term of office at the end of which they render an account of their tenure through the medium of competitive elections.

One form in which this conception of democracy has been instantiated is in Westminster systems. The most distinctive feature of Westminster systems has been the lack of proportionality between electoral opinion and the choice of representatives. In part this is obviously to be accounted for in terms of an implicit theory of elections, in which their purpose is to choose a government rather than mirror opinion. If this is the purpose of elections, then some features of the Westminster system can be seen to have a coherent logic and rationale. For example, it is a feature of first-past-the-post electoral systems that they magnify the share of the vote that locally strong political parties receive in the share of the seats in the legislature they are allocated. If the point of elections is to choose a government, rather than reflect popular opinion, this will be a desirable feature, since it will serve to make those governments that are elected more stable. Although Lijphart (1984) calls such systems 'majoritarian', this is misleading, precisely for the reason that governments within the Westminster system typically do not represent a majority of the electorate's first preference. A clearer designation would therefore be 'pluritarian' (Nagel, 1998), since in such systems the government is usually drawn from parties that represent the single largest block of voters. The extent to which the accountability of government is at issue is magnified by the rules of committee in the legislature, which give pre-eminence to the governing party.

Within pure forms of accountable government the role of citizens is limited, though important. Their primary task is to choose between teams that present themselves for office. There is no assumption that political participation is a good in itself, and the system of decision-making does not assume that citizens will be active in public affairs, although it does assume that citizens can be reasonably disinterested in their political choices.

In Lijphart's (1984) classification of political systems, one distinguishing feature of Westminster systems is the absence of checks and balances on the operation of legislative majorities. It has certainly been a feature of Westminster systems that they have made less use of formal institutional and judicial constraints on legislative majorities than other political systems. For example, the UK has not had a written constitution or a bill of rights, and second chambers are relatively weak or non-existent in Westminster systems. However, it may well be that the formal institutional measures are rather misleading in this respect, in the sense that there is nothing intrinsic to the idea of accountable government to prevent the use of checks and balances. Dicey certainly argued that individual rights were better protected in the Westminster system that in political systems in which there were formal bills of rights on the grounds that where the law was silent there was a presumption of non-interference (Dicey, 1885, p. 195). Whatever may be one's views of the merits of Dicey's argument in this particular case (see Chapter 9), it does at least suggest that a notion of minority protection is not inconsistent with the principles of accountable government.

5   Liberal constitutionalism. The use of the term liberal constitutionalism in the sense I intend it here is supposed to reflect the use of
the notion of Whig constitutionalism in Riker's (1982) *Liberalism
against Populism*. It refers to a form of government in which the
emphasis is upon the capacity of electorates to turn politicians out
of office, rather than upon their capacity to achieve an expression
of their views in public policy. It is also sometimes known as 'protective democracy' and is the sort of view than one might associate
with Schumpeter's (1954) writing on democracy.

A distinctive feature of this view is that popular participation is
low and decision-making power is exercised by a political (and in
Schumpeter's view at least social) elite. In this form of democracy
the people do not rule, they merely choose who is to rule them.
Indeed, the stress on the lack of popular participation can be taken
a stage further, with the thought that the task of electorates on the
constitutional view of democratic government is negative rather
than positive. If we ask where the democratic element is in this
theory, the answer is that it lies in the capacity of the people 'to
throw the rascals out'. In other words, the purpose of making government depend upon popular elections is not to guide the government in the choice of policies, but instead to provide an incentive
for rulers not to become tyrannical.

One reason why it is assumed that it is not the task of government to pursue the will of the people is that it can be held that the
popular will is not coherent or stable. On classical versions of
liberal constitutionalism, for example *The Federalist Papers* (1787),
the popular will is not stable or coherent because the people in
general are assumed to be turbulent, with fickle preferences. In
modern versions, like that of Riker, other reasons are invoked for
being sceptical of the idea of a popular will – as we shall see in
Chapter 7. So, unlike those versions of the Westminster system in
which it is assumed that is a mandate that the government should
implement, Whig constitutionalism may (and in Riker's version
does) assume that there is no underlying popular will, and that the
task of government is to govern in the sense of maintaining a
certain pattern of inherited rights and duties in being.

If constitutionalism sees a small role for popular organization
and politics (even smaller than in the Westminster system of
accountable government), it sees a correspondingly greater role

for judicial and other counter-majoritarian devices. Typical institutional proposals that emerge from the constitutionalist perspective include: an elaborate system of checks and balances to
prevent majorities using political power to their own advantage;
independent judicial systems with the powers to strike down legislation that is unconstitutional; constitutional restrictions on the
powers of legislatures to raise taxation, via such devices as the
requirement to maintain a balanced budget; control of the money
supply that is independent of the legislature; reductions in the
role of parties in the conduct of government; and insulation of
decision-makers from the pressures of social groups and interest
organizations.

Summary of typology. The various elements of the typology are summarized in Table 2.2, where I have sought to bring together the
points made in the discussion so far. The ideal-types are shown
according to answers that they characteristically give to various
questions about the way that democracy should be organized. In
the next section, I consider some general features of this typology
before going on to the question of whether it is possible to construct arguments that would enable us to choose among these
various possibilities.

Choosing Forms of Government

In setting out the above typology of forms of government, I have
been describing ideal-types, in Weber's (1947, p. 92) sense, namely
simplified descriptions of the distinctive characteristics of each
form. There is no supposition that any of these ideal-types either
does exist or can exist in anything resembling these ideal forms.
We have seen that Bingham Powell's typology clearly distinguishes
actually existing systems, with a core of Westminster systems on
one side and the parliamentary systems of the smaller European
democracies on the other. Yet, we should also recognize that there
are variations in practice within these two broad classes. Among
political systems that have inherited the Westminster pattern,
some are federal (Australia and Canada) and others are unitary.
Similarly, the degree of popular participation through institutionalized devices like the referendum varies among the representational

Table 2.2 *Features of Democratic Models*

	Rousseauian	Party-mediated	Representational	Accountable	Liberal constitutional
Direct decision	yes	yes	no	no	no
Broad opinion	yes	yes	yes	no	no
Shared legislative competence	inapplicable	inapplicable	some	no	yes
Counter-majoritarian	no	some	some	some	strong

democracies, for example between Switzerland, where it is high, and the Netherlands, where it is low.

One obvious way in which actual examples of political systems depart from the ideal-types is that different institutional rules and practices may operate at different levels of government. Typically, for example, sub-national governments offer more opportunities for participatory devices than national governments. Thus, the use of devices like the referendum and citizens' initiative is well developed in many states of the USA, but not used at all at the national level. Similarly, in international systems of governance different institutional principles may operate in structuring patterns of decision-making than those operating at the national level. Thus, the EU may be compared to a system of liberal constitutionalism, with elaborate checks and balances and a leading role given to the judicial institution of the European Court of Justice, even when the political systems of member states are based on models of accountable or representational government.

It is also worth noting that all these forms of government make processes of deliberation central to the way in which decision-making is conceived. It has become common in recent discussions to identify a category of 'deliberative democracy' (see Bohman and Rehg, 1997) and to contrast it with competitive party models. In fact, where the model of deliberative democracy is not simply a variant on the Rousseauian conception, it rests on a contrast with an implausible, if widely held, view of democratic decision-making in which choices are made as a result of competing pressures. The institutional theories of all the variants of democracy that I have been discussing stress the importance of deliberation, including liberal constitutionalism (Sunstein, 1991, p. 4). Indeed, if deliberation is really an issue, it is an irony that it was Rousseau who imagined that in a true democracy the first person to speak merely says what all have felt when arriving at the general will (Rousseau, 1762, p. 247). Not much deliberation there.

Despite these complications, the models of democracy are intended to be alternatives, resting on distinct assumptions and principles about such matters as the value of political participation, the role of representation, the definition of the popular will and so on. In other words, insofar as we are confronted with a choice about institutional arrangements, each of the models will appeal according to distinct and incompatible evaluative criteria and standards.

Does it make sense to think in this way, however? On one influential account of political theory it is impossible to choose rationally among these varying conceptions of democracy. Democracy, it is often said, is an essentially contested concept. In the original formulation of this view (Gallie, 1955–6), essentially contested concepts were marked out by their having two features: there were multiple criteria for their application to particular cases and those contesting an application normally stressed the relevance of one criterion relative to others. Subsequently, this thesis has expanded to the claim that there are irreducibly ideological assumptions involved in the application of terms like 'democracy' (or 'justice' or 'freedom' and so on), so that any contestation of the term inevitably involves calling upon these wider ideological disputes. Since such disputes are thought to be insoluble, it follows that there is no theoretically plausible way to choose one version of democracy over others on intersubjectively reasonable grounds. Conservatives like Whig constitutionalism. Radicals like Rousseau. And liberals are somewhere in between. End of story.

In the remainder of this work a rather different tack will be taken. The thesis of essential contestability will be taken as a hypothesis to be tested rather than as an organizing assumption to be adopted. One reason for this is that differing conceptions of democracy are supported by arguments of varying kinds on the part of their rival supporters. These arguments are complex and often rather indeterminate, but they are not like contests in which the aim is just to amass supporters and see which side can cheer the loudest. Instead, they purport, at least, to be reasoned claims.

Consider, as an example, one of the most notorious of the claims that has been made for the Whig constitutional view, namely Schumpeter's (1954, p. 262) assertion that people drop down to a lower level of mental performance when they enter politics. This is an empirical claim and if it were true it surely would be some sort of argument that a Rousseauian, with a commitment to the view that individuals can reason through to the general will, would have to take seriously. This is not to say that taken on its own it is going to be decisive for either party. But the claim is perfectly intelligible to each side of the argument, and in principle it is possible to envisage the sort of evidence that might decide the matter one way or the other, or at least allow us to suspend judgement until further evidence comes in.

Not all the points at issue are empirical claims, of course, and much of the disagreement about the relative merits of the conceptions turns upon judgements about the value and place of principles like autonomy in a political morality. But here again it would merely be a prejudice to suppose that we could not discuss these questions intelligently before at least trying to see whether there are arguments at hand that will enable us to advance our understanding of the issues. Indeed, it was the early evidence on lack of voter information that originally led to a reappraisal of certain models of democracy (Berelson, Lazarsfeld and McPhee, 1954, chapter 14).

So in what follows I shall try to isolate the various arguments that can go into favouring one conception of democracy rather than another. I shall do this by considering the various dimensions in which the conceptions differ from one another. In particular, I shall suggest that each of these models implicitly makes claims about such matters as the value of participation, the nature of representation, the most appropriate way of aggregating preferences, the criteria for inclusion and the duties of citizenship. If we examine each of these issues in turn, we can come to some conclusion about which view it is reasonable to adopt, or at least what is the range of permissible variation. However, before getting on to these differences I shall look in the next two chapters at the underlying justification of democracy treated as a system comprising all the above forms.

The Justification of Democracy

To justify a practice like democracy is to show either how the practice conforms to a principle or how the consequences of the practice lead to a state of affairs that can be judged good in principled terms. In this chapter I want to consider what kind of justification may be offered for a belief in democracy as a form of government superior to others. For the purposes of this chapter, then, I shall treating the competing conceptions of democracy that I identified in the previous chapter as members of the same class, contrasting the notion of democratic government, whatever specific form it takes, with that of non-democratic government. At this stage, therefore, I shall be laying greater stress on what elements these varying conceptions have in common than on the features that distinguish them.

Someone might think that there was little point in seeking to justify the practice of democracy, since there is now such widespread agreement on its value that the whole task is rather redundant – rather akin to a detailed demonstration that apple pie was tasty. But this would be too quick a move for various reasons. Firstly, insofar as the justification of democracy in general points to specific conceptions in detail a useful purpose is served. It is unlikely that the particular justification for democracy one adopts has no implications for assessing the relative merits of the differing conceptions that I identified in the previous chapter. Secondly, for the reasons I gave in chapter 1, I do not think that the theoretical foundations of democracy elicit as much widespread agreement as the point supposes, and indeed in this chapter and subsequent ones I shall seek to highlight the non-democratic implications of various widely believed theories. Thirdly, fashions change in politics as in every other sphere of life. Opinion-formers may be enamoured of democracy now, but perhaps disappointed expectations about the benefits that may be thought to flow in the wake of democracy will lead to disillusionment. Intellectual conviction is the surest security against such changes in fashion. It is not fool-proof; but it is the best we have.

A large number of principles have been advanced in the justification of democracy. For example, Pennock (1979, pp. 130–60) invokes the principles of human worth, autonomy, freedom, distributive justice, equality and the rejection of tyranny in his discussion of the justification of democratic theory. Such a list opens up the thought that the practice of democracy might be justified not by reference to one principle but by the fact that it was at the confluence of a number of distinct principles. Moreover, if we can invoke a wide range of principles in the justification for democracy, this might in itself suggest an interesting point of interpretation. The collective justification might be more powerful than the justification in terms of one particular principle, by analogy with the methodological principle of 'triangulation' in empirical research: the fact that a finding is established by different methods of enquiry makes its more plausible precisely in virtue of that fact.

Despite the appeal of this approach, one must be careful in simply seeking to amalgamate different arguments purporting to justify democracy. When examined in detail the premises of the arguments within which these principles appear may not always be compatible with one another, so that we may find ourselves invoking contradictory conceptions of society, citizenship or other features of political life simply by amalgamating different principles. This is not to say that we should adopt a monistic, rather than a pluralistic, justification of democracy. It is merely to say that such pluralistic justifications should contain elements that are compatible with one another.

In this chapter I shall offer a line of argument for justifying democracy that follows a broadly instrumentalist pattern. In this account, the practices of democracy are justified because of the interests that they serve, in particular because of their role in serving certain common or public interests. This instrumentalist justification needs to be supplemented, however, with the assumption of fallibilism, the belief that no one occupies a privileged position with respect to their political knowledge or judgement and that contestation and criticism of what at any one time is judged to be in the public interest is therefore necessary. Even with this supplementary assumption, appeal also has to be made to at least one intrinsic value of democracy, namely the sense in which it incorporates the idea of political equality, understood as the protection of the dignity of citizens. In sum, therefore, democratic institutions are justified as those practices that promote and protect the common interests of the members of a political community, when those persons regard themselves as political equals under conditions of human fallibility.

To establish the first part of this argument I shall begin with the shortcomings of a purely protective justification of democracy of a traditional sort. Even if we grant that democracy is not always needed for protection from tyranny, as the traditional argument assumes, we shall still need democracy for other purposes. At this instrumentalist stage of the argument, the primary mode of analysis that I shall employ in arriving is what I shall call 'derivation'. Derivation requires us to imagine a possible world in which democracy did not exist or was at a minimum, and then to consider what would be missing in such a world. It is not a state of nature theory of the sort that Nozick (1974) used to derive his account of the legitimate functions of the state, since it does not purport to offer a hypothetical explanation of how an outcome arises. It is rather akin to Feinberg's (1970) notion of 'a world without rights' in providing us with an intellectual device for highlighting what would be missing from a political morality if certain concepts were not available. Feinberg argued that in a world without rights persons would not be able to insist upon their claims but would be mere supplicants, so that a world without rights would be missing an important moral dimension. I shall argue that in a world without democracy it would be impossible to articulate and act in favour of certain sorts of interests. Of course, this notion of justification via derivation suffers from the weakness that it is always open to someone to say that a world without X, whatever X was, was perfectly all right as it was. But then this is no more damaging to justification as derivation than someone saying of state of nature theory 'Why should I begin from there?'. To see the need for this mode of analysis, we first need to look at the traditional argument for democracy in terms of protection from tyranny.

The Protective Case for Democracy

If we ask what the varying conceptions of democracy that I identified in Chapter 2 have in common, it is that they all share the concept that the law, rules and policies that define the public life of a society – including the rules that define what is to count as part of that public life – should be the product of decision-making by a body that is, in some systematic way, dependent upon the views of those who are citizens of that society. Even in constitutional democracy, where a central fear is that ordinary citizens will engage in too much back-seat driving, there is still an insistence that the device of elections is the principal means by which citizens can 'throw the rascals out', if that is what they judge their professional politicians to be. In this sense decision-making over matters of public policy is dependent upon the views of citizens within constitutional conceptions of democracy. In the other conceptions that I discussed, there is a more positive view of citizen opinion, culminating in the Rousseauian conception of a society which moralizes its members through the collective self-determination of its general will. Thus, we may say that what the varying conceptions have in common is the idea that the resolution of political questions is made by a body that is at some point at least dependent upon the views of citizens.

In treating a variety of conceptions of democracy as a class, it is helpful in clarifying our thoughts to ask what the members of that class are being contrasted with, since finding the contrary of a concept is often a good way of defining its meaning. Here we come across an interesting question of method: should we contrast democracy with its historically most prevalent alternatives or with its theoretically most plausible alternative? If we choose the former contrast, we shall be looking at what can be plausibly taken as feasible contrasts with democracy; if we choose the latter contrast, we shall be putting up the most stringent test that the justification of democracy will have to face.

To see this point, consider first the option of contrasting democracy with the historically most prevalent alternative forms of government in the modern world. These alternatives have been, in the classification due to Finer (1970), façade-democracies, quasi-democracies and military dictatorships. In terms of political morality, none of these is likely to be a serious alternative to democracy, as Finer's account of façade-democracy serves to illustrate:

> 'until recently most of the Third World was as though stuck in the first, pre-Reform Bill stage of British parliamentarianism – compounded, however, by a marked scarcity or total absence of indigenous liberal institutions; a disregard for civil liberties; a high degree of formal centralization; assiduous and ruthless police; and the pretensions of large standing armies.' (Finer, 1970, p. 444)

This could hardly be described as an appetizing prospect by comparison with functioning democratic regimes, whatever the faults of the latter. Thus, if this is the sort of political system that is being contrasted with democracy, then the latter would win hands-down. Totalitarian systems and military dictatorships, the other two specimens in Finer's classification, would hardly do better in the competition.

The tradition of the protective theory of democracy has sought to ground this conclusion in a more general theory of political behaviour (compare Held, 1996, pp. 70–100; and Lakoff, 1996, pp. 99–117). Theorists in this tradition start from the Hobbesian assumption that government is necessary in order to avoid civil war and social breakdown and to these ends governments are needed with enough power to enforce order (Hobbes, 1651). But at this point democratic theorists note a problem which Hobbes paid less attention to: if governments have enough power to stop civil war and social breakdown, they almost certainly have enough power to exploit their own populations. A government needs power to protect you from the theft and violence of a lawless neighbour, but what if government itself becomes a source of theft and violence?

Locke's famous comment on this dilemma is worth quoting. Assuming that the deficiencies of the state of nature are sufficient to induce its occupants to set up a system of political authority, he rejects the claim that people would contract into a form of government with absolute power:

> 'This is to think that men are so foolish that they take care to avoid what Mischiefs may be done them by *Pole-Cats*, or *Foxes*, but are content, nay think it Safety, to be devoured by *Lions*.' (Locke, 1690, p. 372)

Madison put the problem of political design to which this leads very well in the *Federalist Papers* No. 51:

'In framing a government which is to be administered by men over men, the great difficulty lies in this: you must first enable the government to control the governed; and in the next place oblige it to control itself.' (*Federalist*, 1787, p. 322)

The protective theorist argues that the institutions of democracy are the solution to this design problem.

The most systematic presentation of the argument was provided in the *Essay on Government* by James Mill (Mill, 1820). Mill seeks to derive the necessity of democracy from judging the effects of what he takes to be universal propositions of human nature. In schematic form, his argument can be stated as follows:

1. In order to build up prosperity in a community, people need to be assured of the fruits of their own labour.
2. Government is necessary to enforce rules of property and protection of the person.
3. The whole of the community cannot be expected to defend itself, because people acting together in an assembly simply cannot conduct business effectively.
4. A self-appointed minority cannot be expected to protect the people from tyrannous government.
5. But the people can elect a set of representatives whose function is to check the abuse of power, and if those representatives are subject to sufficiently frequent re-election, then their interests would be brought into accord with the interests of the community as a whole.

Essentially what Mill argued was that, human motivation being what it is, in the absence of any restraint, those who governed would simply abuse their powers to appropriate to themselves as much of the cooperative surplus of society as they could. Finer's characterization of non-democratic systems is just what we should expect, given the conditions that Mill supposes.

Note that this argument for democracy is founded on a pessimistic view of human nature. The theory of democracy in this protective version does not assume that people are naturally good,

and that they should participate in government as part of their own
self-development. Rather it assumes that people are rather nasty
and need a representative body to restrain their tendency to abuse
power. It is for this reason that some critics have said that the protective theory 'is neither inspiring nor inspired' and that in this
conception responsible 'government, even to the extent of responsibility to a democratic electorate, was needed for the protection of
individuals and the promotion of the Gross National Product, and
for nothing more' (Macpherson, 1977, p. 43).

Whether this evaluation of the argument is valid is a moot point.
Read more charitably, the argument can be seen as one about securing the necessary conditions of any self-development, so that although
democracy does have a protective rationale, economic interests are
not the only ones protected. However, in the present context, there is
another, and arguably more serious, problem with the argument,
namely the extent to which its general and abstract form enables it
genuinely to provide a foundation for what would otherwise be merely
a partial empirical generalization contrasting tendencies in democratic and non-democratic regimes. The historian Macaulay, commenting upon Mill's *Essay*, pointed out the problem in a barbed way:

> 'We have here an elaborate treatise on Government, from which,
> but for two or three passing allusions, it would not appear that
> the author was aware that any governments actually existed
> among men. Certain propensities of human nature are assumed;
> and from these premises the whole science of politics is syntheti-
> cally deduced!' (Macaulay, 1829, p. 273)

Macaulay goes on to point out that even Mill himself acknowledged
that the people of Denmark were governed well under an absolute
monarch, and alleges that Mill's method not only leads him to
adopt a theory that is contrary to the facts, but also to adopt a
theory *because* it is contrary to the facts. Claiming that Mill's theoretically derived account of non-democratic government simply
failed to take into account those non-democratic forms of government that were not tyrannous, Macaulay argued that Mill had not
demonstrated a general reason why democracy is the only response
to the problem of tyranny.

Macaulay's criticism, while it strikes home in some respects, is
not entirely fair. To be sure, Mill does admit exceptions to his

generalization, like the state of Denmark, but he also cites what might be termed 'crucial cases', one of which was the English practice of slavery in the West Indies. Appealing to the prejudices of his readers, Mill assumes that they will agree that English gentlemen are likely to be as civilized as one can imagine slave-owners to be, and then goes on to point out that in the English West Indies slaves were mercilessly exploited and oppressed (Mill, 1820, pp. 15–16). In other words, even in favourable circumstances, so Mill's argument runs, we cannot *guarantee* freedom from oppression when some people are given absolute power over others.

It is possible to buttress Mill's argumentative strategy here by appealing to Hume's supposition of knavery in institutional design. Hume (1742, pp. 117–18) quoted with approval the maxim that in 'contriving any system of government ... every man ought to be supposed a *knave*, and to have no other end, in all his doings, than private interest'. The same principle has been endorsed by modern writers, for example Brennan and Buchanan (1985, p. 59). By this principle even the exceptions to Mill's generalizations ought to be regarded as suspect, since we can never know whether or not someone occupying a position of political authority will abuse it. It is better to be safe than sorry, and hence it is better not to give too much weight to the apparent counter-examples when trying to assess in any particular case whether unaccountable power will be misused.

As a practical guide to the design of political arrangements, this is probably a satisfactory assumption. However, it still suffers from the defect that it only shows democracy to be superior to historically observed alternatives rather than showing that democracy has merits against the theoretically most compelling alternative. Suppose we could contrive non-democratic checks on government to circumvent the problem of tyranny. How would democracy perform against that sort of alternative? In other words, how does democracy fare against the best form of non-democratic government that we can envisage?

Democracy *versus* Adjudication

Since all the varying conceptions of democracy have in common the idea that decisions should be made by legislators who depend upon the views of citizens (including the case where citizens are the legislators) about collective choices, one obvious way of finding a theoretically plausible alternative to democracy is to consider a form of government that reduced or dispensed with the function of legislation. One form this could take would be a judicialized form of government resting upon a body of rules for governing social relations that, rather than being decided by a legislative body, evolved incrementally over time on the model of the English common law. Sidgwick described such a possibility with his usual clarity:

> 'a great part of the rules enforced by Government in our own society have not had their origin in express legislation; they have been gradually brought to the degree of precision and elaborateness which they have now attained, by a series of judicial decisions which ostensibly declared and applied rules and principles handed down from time immemorial. And it might be held that this judicial quasi-legislation is, even in a highly civilised society, the best machinery for introducing such improvements as may be required in the definition of the fundamental rights and duties that constitute the "individualistic minimum".' (Sidgwick, 1891, p. 324)

As the reference to the individualistic minimum suggests at the end of this passage, the conception of government that most naturally fits with such an institutional structure is that contained in the idea of the minimal or night-watchman state (not an alternative that Sidgwick was advocating incidentally). In this conception, the function of government is to define a framework of rights and obligations that enables individuals to interact with one another to their mutual advantage, but without prescribing some common course of action upon those individuals that they would not themselves choose when exercising their rights.

If this close association between the idea of a judicialized, non-democratic, form of government and the idea of the individualistic minimum is correct, then we should expect to find in libertarian writers a theory of government in which the opportunities for democratic choice and deliberation were attenuated or reduced and in which control of social relations was conceived primarily in terms of adjudication among individuals by reference to a customary or otherwise implicit body of rules, akin to the English common law. And indeed, if we turn to libertarian writers like Nozick or Hayek, or even Oakeshott in his libertarian moods, this is exactly what we do find.

Consider, for example, Oakeshott's discussion of the 'civil condition' (Oakeshott, 1975, pp. 108–84). According to Oakeshott, the distinguishing feature of the civil condition is the way in which its members, *cives*, are related to one another. In particular, the member of the civil condition are not related to one another as partners in an enterprise, but in terms of their subscription to a common practice. At the centre of this common practice is a system of rules, the chief characteristic of which is not to tell *cives* what to do but to prescribe the obligations of *cives* in respect of one another in the pursuit of their self-chosen purposes. As Oakeshott clearly puts it, '... it belongs to the character of *cives* (as it does not belong to the character of agents joined in an enterprise association) to be related as suitors to a judicial court' (Oakeshott, 1975, p. 131).

Legislation does take place within a civil association, but the most striking thing about Oakeshott's discussion of this function is how little he has to say about its deliberative basis. He does speak about what the deliberative basis of law in civil association is *not*. Thus, it is not the expression of preference, the exhibition of a will, it cannot be deduced from reason, it is not the pursuit of common purposes or interests, it is not 'managerial', and there is no ready and indisputable criterion for determining the desirability of a legislative proposal (Oakeshott, 1975, pp. 139–40). But the list does not end in anything positive, and though he later specifies three conditions on legislative deliberation (Oakeshott, 1975, p. 178), it is clear that these are merely formal conditions that many rules could satisfy. Most importantly, there is no account of how those undertaking the legislation are supposed to be chosen and to whom they are accountable. Indeed, the 'glimpses', to borrow his metaphor, of civil association that Oakeshott sees in the work of political theorists make it clear that democratic responsibility is not an essential element of the civil condition (Oakeshott, 1975, p. 181). Sidgwick's non-democratic judicial form of government is clearly then represented in Oakeshott's account of civil association.

It may be that we can nevertheless assert that Oakeshott's view of government is compatible with democracy, holding with Mapel (1990, p. 405) that an Oakeshottian perspective enables us to see democracy with a certain detachment and irony. Yet, it is equally true that democratic forms of government are not *implied* by Oakeshott's conception of politics. As noted in chapter 1, similar points could be made with respect to Nozick's account of political authority (Nozick, 1974). Although Nozick's basis of the political morality is distinct from that of Oakeshott, being founded in a notion of pre-existing rights rather than in customary law, the function of government is focussed upon its adjudicative role. Protective agencies grow up to perform the function of adjudication, and the dominant protective agency that ultimately becomes the state is just the best body to provide adjudication for its subscribers.

What distinguishes this judicialized form of government, in which the explicit legislative function is reduced, from all the varieties of democracy that I identified in the previous chapter? The first distinguishing characteristic is that the principles of adjudication that the judges are supposed to be using are derived either from a pre-existing notion of rights or from customary, traditional codes, the basis of both of which are beyond the scope of discussion and deliberation of a legislative assembly. For someone like Oakeshott this is, of course, an advantage, since it means that the development of political principles does not rest upon a constructivist rationalism which seeks particular ends, but merely states the general conditions in which individuals can pursue their own ends.

The second distinguishing characteristic is also one that Oakeshott and others, including Hayek (1973, chapter 2), have found attractive, namely that it rests upon a conception of society as being made up of a collection of individuals with their own, typically divergent, purposes, rather than a conception of society in which individuals are conceived to share purposes in common. On this conception of the social order, the principles that judges apply impose limits on the freedom of action of individuals, rather than prescribing a substantive purpose. Thus, the law will forbid theft, force and fraud, but within the limits implied by these proscriptions individuals are allowed the freedom to pursue their own individual purposes. In the pure form of this doctrine, the only substantive performance that the law will prescribe is the fulfilment of contractually incurred obligations, a substantive performance that could notionally be rendered as simply forbidding one individual defrauding another.

The third distinguishing feature of this conception of government is that those with responsibility for formulating principles for the regulation of public affairs are not to be made accountable to or dependent upon an elected assembly or the opinions of citizens at large. This absence of democratic dependence makes a great deal of sense within the overall conception, not least because judges are conceived of as developing a customary or otherwise pre-legislative code of principles, rather than implementing the decisions of a legislative assembly or popular referendum. Since the source of their authority is to be found in custom, not the resolution of a legislature, it would be completely otiose to make judges accountable to an elected body. Indeed, since the chief measure that a legislature has for controlling governments is to dismiss them once they have lost the confidence of legislators, the prospect of dismissal is thought to be the best way to control democratic governments, whereas the traditional means for securing judicial independence is to provide that judges cannot be removed from office by politicians.

In characterizing what a plausible theoretical alternative to a democratic system of government might be, I have of course only provided a sketch, rather than given the full picture, but it is, I think, suggestive even at that level. For if the *most plausible* alternative to a democratic form of government we can find has the characteristics identified, then it is already possible to see how it is *implausible* as a conception of government.

The first problem with this conception of government is one that Sidgwick himself recognized in his own discussion. In any system of government in which there is no legislative body, and consequently in which there are no explicitly formulated legislative rules, there is a large penumbra of uncertainty surrounding individual legal obligations. Courts proceed by making decisions on individual cases that are brought before them, and although their decisions are binding as precedents within a common law system, they do not seek to anticipate the future judgments of courts on related matters by making rules that clearly demarcate the class of cases that are covered. Thus, for example, in matters of product liability, a court may well decide that widget manufacturers are liable for defects in their widgets, but it will not be clear if consumers are able to claim reparations for purchases of goods that are like widgets in some respects but unlike them in others. This uncertainty may make it difficult, perhaps impossible, for individuals to coordinate their activities with one another for mutual advantage.

This problem of uncertainty is related to the second problem with our hypothetical form of judicialized government, which is its inability to anticipate, rather than merely react to, problems. Consider the problems associated with environmental protection. Experience in industrializing countries with the growth of pollution in the nineteenth and twentieth centuries shows that the control of pollution through the legal remedies of actions under the tort of nuisance must always wait until the damage has been done before a rule is formulated. If we now think about emerging technologies with environmental implications, most notably biotechnology and genetic manipulation, it is clear that an anticipatory capacity is needed to deal with the problems that might arise, since, as one expert in the field has said, it is as though the piano had just been invented and all the sonatas had still to be written (Woolhouse, cited in Roberts and Weale, 1991, p. 163).

In the third place, a judicialized conception of government has no way of dealing with the cumulatively undesirable consequences of individual interactions. Social problems such as environmental pollution, traffic congestion and urban sprawl arise as the cumulative effect of a series of individual actions each one of which is entirely legitimate taken on its own. In the absence of any governmental capacity to take stock of the whole series of actions, and not simply particular instances, individuals in a society will find themselves worse off than they otherwise need be. In effect, each individual is locked in an n-person prisoners' dilemma with every other individual, where the only rational action is not to cooperate with others in producing some social good, because it is rational to free ride on the efforts of others. In Fred Hirsch's (1977, p. 49) evocative image, when all stand on tiptoe, no one sees any better. They simply get tired legs.

It is helpful at this point to introduce a distinction between interactive choice on the one hand and social or collective choice on the other (Hargreaves Heap *et al.*, 1992). Interactive choice is typified by the pattern of behaviour in a market. The outcomes of a market are a result of the interactions of buyers and sellers with one another, and no individual or set of individuals has a particular overall outcome in mind. Although the individual transactions in a market may be planned, the sum of transactions is not. In a social or collective choice, by contrast, the aggregate outcomes are planned, though the individual outcomes may not be. Thus, a local authority imposing planning controls on land use will limit the number of houses to be built in a given area over a given period of time, though it will not typically say which builders shall build the houses or which occupiers shall buy them. In other words, it constrains the aggregate results of the individual transactions with some overall goal in mind. It is just this collective perspective that a legislative capacity in political decision-making provides.

Yet this, in turn, raises another function for which a legislative capacity is needed. When individuals interact with one another, they do so under the terms and conditions that are already established. Thus, traders bring to a market the produce they own and and its value is largely determined by circumstances beyond their individual control, including the material and human capital they control as well as the demand for their products or services prevailing at the time. Even when individuals successfully bargain to mutual advantage within these background circumstances, there is no way in which the structure and form of these background circumstances can be adequately addressed within the process of interactive bargaining itself. The only way in which that can be done is through legislative action that changes those terms and conditions. This is particularly important in labour markets where, for obvious reasons, employers usually have no incentive to pay regard, for example, to the family circumstances of their workers so that wage-rates will not normally compensate workers for the number of dependants that they have.

The argument so far has been that there are matters of common concern that need to be resolved if successful cooperation is to take place, but which cannot be resolved by individuals in the conduct of their own business. These common matters include the institutional preconditions for economic and social life, including the system of property rights and civil liability prevailing in the community, as well as the provision that it to be made for dealing with the cumulative consequences of individual interactions, of which environmental protection is the most conspicuous. Although we can imagine a form of polity which dispensed with a legislative function in respect of the resolutions of disputes between individuals, it would by its nature be incapable of satisfactorily resolving the collective problems to which any system of interactive choice gives rise.

Democracy and Political Equality

The argument so far has been that in order to promote or protect certain common interests, it is necessary for the members of society to establish a legislative capacity that can remedy the defects that arise from interactive modes of choice. Whatever the merits of this argument, it may be thought to leave out something of importance, namely why the legislative capacity should be democratic. To be sure, we can always reintroduce the protective argument, but this would throw us back onto empirical generalizations and this would make it a weaker case for democracy than an argument that succeeded against the most plausible alternative. After all, if we are considering the most plausible alternative, one possibility we should consider is that of a self-perpetuating meritocratic elite, with a strong internalized sense of the public interest acting on behalf of citizens at large. Some have argued, for example, that this was just the view that inspired the creation of the Commission of the European Community (Hayward, J., 1996, p. 252).

By contrast with this meritocratic notion, democracy seems founded on the idea that each citizen is to be given equal status within the system of collective political authority. The political equality of democracy means not simply that everyone is equal before the law, that is to say that as a subject of political authority everyone should be treated equally; it also means that everyone should have a place in the exercise of political authority, even if this only involves electing those who are to constitute the government. To deny the validity of an idealized meritocracy is thus to assert that political equality is a central component of democracy. But what is the ground of this claim exactly?

One version of the principle of political equality may be expressed in the maxim that each citizen is as well qualified as any other to contribute to the formation of a political community's decision-making and policy-making (compare Sidgwick, 1891, p. 587). This maxim rules out the idea that there is a special political faculty of governing that some people possess but which is not possessed by others, and it also rules out the claim of a 'ruling class', for example, an heredity caste, to enjoy privileged access to the political machinery of the community. Sidgwick points out that the institutional embodiment of the principle in Athenian democracy was selection by lot among the whole citizen body for certain offices (see Manin, 1997, chapter 1, for details). We can note an analogous institutional embodiment in modern democracies in the progressive removal of the disqualifications from serving in public office on such grounds as property ownership, sex, race and class.

This principle of political equality is close to, but not identical with, the principle that Thompson (1970, pp. 13–19) has identified as one of the presuppositions of democracy, namely the non-paternalist principle that each citizen is to be treated as the best judge of his or her own interests. (Thompson calls this a principle of 'autonomy', but I shall avoid this term to avoid confusion with the discussion in the next chapter.) How does this non-paternalist principle compare with the equal qualification principle that I have defined as part of the notion of political equality?

From one point of view the equal qualification principle appears to be weaker than the non-paternalist principle, since the former rests only upon a putative capacity of citizens, namely their ability to make a contribution to collective decision-making, whereas the latter claims that persons usually are in practice the best judges of their own welfare. Thus, the equal qualification principle does not say that the democratic capacity of persons is always realized, it only makes the assumption that it could be realized under appropriate circumstances. By contrast, the principle of non-paternalism asserts that persons are typically, not just potentially, the best judges of their own welfare.

This difference of emphasis most probably reflects the contexts within which the two principles are commonly used. Contrary to Thompson, it seems to me that the most obvious context for the non-paternalist principle is not that of collective political decision-making, but in the arrangement by citizens of their private or domestic affairs. To say that persons are the best judges of their own interests is not to say that they are perfect judges. It is to say that no one else is better placed to make decisions on their behalf. Such a principle would appear to be an empirical generalization that is likely to hold under certain circumstances, most importantly when the knowledge required for making a prudent decision is not easily available to anyone but the person or persons on whom the consequences of the decision might fall. The equal qualification principle, by contrast, does not assume that citizens are always in possession of the knowledge that would best place them in a position to make a decision, merely that there is in principle nothing

stopping them appreciating and understanding the relevant knowledge. In this sense, the equal capacity principle makes fewer
demands upon the abilities we ascribe to citizens than the non-
paternalist principle.

From another point of view, however, the equal capacity principle may be said to make somewhat stronger assumptions than the
non-paternalist principle. Whereas the non-paternalist principle
may be read as saying that in the sphere of their own interests
persons are likely to be better than others at making prudent decisions, the equal qualifications principle says that one person's contribution to collective decision-making is as likely to be as good as
that of someone else. At first blush, taken in this sense, it would
seem that political equality understood as an equal capacity is an
implausible assumption. Since in other spheres of life we regard
expertise as unequally distributed, why should we regard the capacity for political judgement as equally distributed? It is a point as old
as Plato to point out that in steering the ship we trust the captain,
who is trained, not the other passengers, who are not. Of course, it
is possible to hold that ethical and political disagreement is about
ends rather than means, in which there are no specialists
(Bambrough, 1956, p. 109). The analogy is not with who should
steer the ship, but with the direction in which the ship should head.
However, in politics and policy-making, ends and means are not
always easily distinguished, and if this is so, there surely will be
some place for expertise and merit.

The principal argument against giving too strong a place to meritocratic expertise relies upon an analogy in political affairs with
the argument underlying the principle of non-paternalism more
generally. For the non-paternalist persons are the best judges of
their own interest (by and large) because only they are in a position
to appreciate the consequences of the decisions they make. Even
good-natured persons only have a limited incentive to acquire
information about the circumstances of others. But this self-same
reason also means that in cases of collective decision-making,
where the consequences are public in the sense that they fall upon
all and sundry in a general way, no one person has the incentive
fully to investigate what the decision will mean for others. Hence
all should be able to contribute to the decision, to ensure that the
collective deliberations take account of all relevant points of view.
It may be better to render the principle of political equality here,

as Dahl does, in negative rather than positive form. In this formulation political equality would mean that no one is so definitely
better qualified as to be presumed capable of acting on behalf of
others (Dahl, 1989, p. 98; compare Lakoff, 1996, p. 20).

In some sense, this derivation of the principle of political equality relies upon a sort of fallibilism. Any one of us can make mis-
takes, and so, one might suppose, even meritocrats cannot be
granted unaccountable political power because they may err in its
use. But fallibilism on its own will not yield the democratic alternative. Civil servants or technocrats might regard themselves as fallible, but think that the only people qualified to criticise their
reasoning and detect their fallacies were other civil servants or
technocrats, as Lucas (1966, p. 9) once pointed out. In order to get
from fallibilism to a democratic conclusion, we need Popper's
assumption that we should, if we are rational, consider the argument rather than the person who is making the argument. It
requires the view that we must recognize everybody with whom we
communicate as a potential source of argument and reasonable
information (Popper, 1945, p. 225).

So far we have considered the ideal of political equality in the
form in which it precludes an appeal to the rights of a privileged
group to control the machinery of political decision-making within a
community. This approach is most at home in context where we
might be thinking of the political rights of the whole body of citizens
against the claims of a 'ruling class'. However, we also have to consider the value of political equality as it applies to the relations of
citizens to one another. In this context, in addition to the fallibilist
case for political equality, there is also, I suggest, a purely deonto-
logical element tied to the idea of respect for persons, even though
that notion is notoriously vague (compare Larmore, 1987, p. 61).

To make this idea clear, we need immediately to dispense with
one notion of respect, the sense of the term in which it means
acting in the interests of another. For example, proponents of
various forms of restrictive legislation in the fields of censorship
and sexual behaviour often argue that they are seeking to show
respect for persons. On this account respect for persons would be
compatible with compelling people to act for their own good,
despite any protestations on their part to the contrary. This may be
a case of loving the sinner while hating the sin, but it is not the
notion of respect for persons that I am seeking to define here.

Larmore (1987, pp. 64–5) comes closer to the notion I am seeking when he says that the notion of equal respect means that whatever we do when we affect others we must deal with them from within their own perspective. This means explaining our actions and acknowledging an obligation of justification towards others. There are, I think, two ideas contained in this formulation. The first is a form of non-paternalism, in which there is an unwillingness to see elites impose solutions on others. The second is a commitment to the principle that we have an obligation to explain, discuss and negotiate about proposals with others before we put them into practice.

Even this latter formulation does not, however, capture the minimum sense of political equality founded on a principle of respect, as I understand it. The essence of this stronger position is to note that the common enterprise of political life is one in which all members of the community have a place. Hence, the requirement of political equality is not simply one in which there is a mutual obligation on persons to justify their policy positions to one another, it also involves the acknowledgement that each member of the community has a place in the determination of the common interest.

If political authority is thought of as something that is exercised by citizens collectively to promote and pursue their common interests, then a failure to include all citizens as equals in the possession of that authority is an assault upon the dignity of the excluded. Dignity in this context is not the same as self-respect. To possess a sense of self-respect is to be in a certain psychological state, and it is perfectly possible that those excluded from the exercise of political authority could still maintain their self-respect provided that they had internalized sufficiently an ethic of 'my station and its duties'. But to be excluded from one's share of political authority is of itself to be treated in ways that do not accord with the principle that each person should be treated as having equal dignity.

Beitz comes close to this notion when he identifies an argument for political equality arising from the higher-order interest in recognition. Political procedures, on this view, define the terms on which citizens recognize one another as participants in the public processes of deliberation and choice. To be excluded from the public forum is to be 'socially dead' (Beitz, 1989, p. 109). However, it is unnecessarily restricting to formulate the point about dignity in terms of a 'higher-order interest'. For Beitz this formulation is important because his general account of political equality is contractarian, and in such a contractarian framework it is important to be able to identify, notionally, the interests on which citizens would not compromise in agreeing to a social contract. But if the notion of recognition and the importance of upholding dignity that underlies it could be a reason for agreement within a process of contractual negotiation, there is no reason why it cannot be treated as a first-order moral claim within political argument (Weale, 1998). If citizens lose their dignity by being treated as less than equal to other citizens under a set of political arrangements, we add nothing of moral force to say that they would not have consented to such an arrangement in a hypothetical social contract.

Common Interests and Common Ideals

On the account of democracy I have been seeking to develop, democratic political institutions are to be seen as the means by which citizens advance their common interests, conceiving themselves as equals in conditions of fallibility. This immediately raises a question of political agency. What account of political agency is presupposed in such a conception, and how far would it allow us to speak of the advancement of common ideals as well as common interests?

Of course one of the things that we must say is that *from the viewpoint of individual citizens* much that is a matter of the common interest is an issue of political ideals. Thus, it may simply be a matter of common interest that there be a system of property rights or that there be the means of environmental protection, but each individual will be living up to an ideal of citizenship when he or she acts in order to promote and protect these common interests (compare Chapter 10). Hence, from one point of view, we cannot make too sharp a distinction between ideals and interests.

Since the ideal of citizenship that is implicit in this approach does not presuppose that citizens hold a distinct set of personal ideals, the view set out here is compatible with a form of liberalism in which the liberal ideal is that of society maintaining neutrality between competing conceptions of the good held by various citizens, as for example in Ackerman (1980). Insofar as common interests need to be protected in order for individuals to pursue their own interests, the ideals of citizenship to which individuals need to be held by the democratic polity are in principle no more than in a society in which any form of public goods was protected. However, it could properly be said that the principle of democratic coopera- tion that I have used to justify democratic government does imply some collective ideals, that is to say ideal arrangements predicated of the polity rather than just of the individuals who compose it. For example, even a concern for the collective consequences of individ- ual interaction on the physical and social environment may be said to presuppose certain shared ideals among citizens.

Much at this point depends upon the level of abstraction that we are prepared to countenance in the description of social ideals. Thus, even a political theory like that of Rawls, which is insistent that political arrangements must respect competing and incom- patible conceptions of the good, will nevertheless appeal to the common political purpose of 'achieving peace and concord in a society characterized by religious and philosophical differences' (Rawls, 1993, p. 63). This is clearly a reasonable goal in the abstract, although equally clearly it presupposes that individual conceptions of the good can be fashioned so that they share an interest in peace rather than the pursuit of metaphysical truth. Moreover, as Mulhall and Swift (1992) have pointed out, Rawls's theory is not devoid of a conception of the common good, since the end of justice is what is seen as holding the members of a society together. So within a theory that is sometimes taken to be a para- digm of liberalism, there is scope for the notion of collective ideals.

Even in this case, however, it may be said that the collective ideal is one that plays a crucial part in facilitating the pursuit of individ- ual purposes, and that it was the latter idea, rather than the collec- tive ideal itself, which was at the heart of the theory. The situation may be different when we have to consider what may be regarded as irreducibly collective ideals, like the protection of a national or local architectural heritage, the development of distinctive per- forming arts, or the protection of a language and literature. The interest that individuals have in these matters will clearly vary, and the attempt to uphold collective ideals in respect of these matters may not involve a direct relation to their own interests for certain individuals.

However, rather than suggest an anti-democratic conclusion, this would seem to support the practice of democracy. That different citizens weigh the importance of collective outcomes differently provides a reason for ensuring that these disparate evaluations are included in the balance of political decision-making. In other words, to the extent that political decision-making calls upon a concern for ideals as well as interests, it presupposes the possibility of collective deliberation about the balance to be struck between competing common interests and the ideals they involve.

4 Autonomy, Virtue and Consent

In the previous chapter I sought to justify democracy as a form of government in terms of certain common interests that could not otherwise be attended to. The argument moved from protective considerations, through a thought-experiment about the most plausible alternative to democracy to considerations of political equality under conditions of human fallibility. Someone might argue at this point that, despite the role of the principle of political equality in this account, the pattern of justification used makes the defence of democracy external to the attitudes and perceptions of citizens. On this account democracy is primarily a means by which citizens attend to certain common interests rather than a practice through which individuals develop themselves and their potentialities. Does this not miss certain intrinsic merits that democratic government might be thought to have? Instead of a largely instrumental argument for democracy, should we not seek to ground the practice of democracy is something more internal to the conception of an individual's good? As Hannah Arendt (1958, p. 198) once put it, there is an interpretation of the political, in which the distinctive human capacities of speaking and writing not only have 'the most intimate relationship to the public world common to us all, but is the one activity which constitutes it'.

One starting-place here is the claim that democratic government is a form of self-government and hence involves autonomy. 'Autonomy' literally means prescribing a law to oneself (from the Greek *autos*, 'oneself' and *nomos*, 'law'), so that a democratic community would be one the members of which prescribed the laws of their collective life to one another. As Lakoff (1996) has pointed out, however, there are at least three forms of autonomy that have been associated with the idea of democracy. The first is that of communal autonomy, or the notion that a political unit should be independent of outside control. The second form is that of plural autonomy, or the idea that different social groups should share in political power. The third form is that of individual autonomy, resting on the idea that individuals should control their own lives.

Although the idea of communal autonomy was important in ancient Athens and arguably in subsequent civic republican conceptions of democracy (Skinner, 1992), its connection with democratic government is only partial. Those who enjoy self-government within a democracy will think it part of their good to preserve their communal autonomy, but it does not follow that all who wish to preserve communal autonomy will think democratic self-government a good. For example, native peoples may desire some form of tribal autonomy, protecting customary forms of authority from external control, even though those customary forms of authority might be non-democratic. The most consistent attempt to take the idea of communal autonomy seriously is to be found in the work of Castoriadis (1987), who places the source of autonomy in the collective consciousness of the 'social imaginary'. But even Castoriadis (1993, pp. 81–123) has to admit that the identification of the contents of the social imaginary with democracy is an historical contingency for those who are heirs of the Greeks.

Lakoff's second notion of autonomy comes closer to a distinctively democratic notion with the idea, which he traces back to republican Rome, that groups should share in the the political process. Autonomy in this sense is not an attribute of individuals, but rather a characterization of a certain form of political life. Held (1995, p. 156) sets out a not dissimilar notion when he claims that the principle of autonomy entrenched in democratic public law is not an individualistic principle of self-determination, but a 'structural principle of self-determination' where the 'self' is part of the collectivity or the 'majority' enabled and constrained by the rules and procedures of democratic life.

Taking autonomy in this sense raises the question of what could justify this form of political life. Clearly, one set of answers would be given by the protective and instrumentalist justifications that I discussed in the previous chapter. However, if we wish to go beyond such justifications, it looks as though we shall have to employ a notion of individual autonomy, seeing democratic practice as aspect of the free expression of human personality that the value of autonomy is supposed to capture. So in the next section, I seek to review those arguments that justify democracy by appeal to the principle of autonomy in this individual sense, before going on to look at other intrinsic goods with which democracy might be connected.

Democracy and Autonomy

A number of writers have advanced the principle of autonomy in its individualistic sense as being essential to the justification of democratic government. Lakoff (1996, p. 163), for example, writes that the capacity for autonomy is the ability to make a number of important and related judgements and to act on them, requiring the right to liberty, so that modern 'democracy is the form of social organization and government in which that right is protected and expressed as a matter of basic principle'. David Beetham argues that, if the core meaning of democracy is the popular control of collective decision-making by equal citizens, then the key value in terms of which it can be promoted and justified is that of autonomy or self-determination (Beetham, 1993, p. 61). On this view, autonomous action as a form of self-government would therefore seem to find its most natural expression in the practice of democracy.

In these versions of the argument, the principle of autonomy enters as a *ground* or *presupposition* for democratic decision-making. The thought is that being autonomous creatures means that human beings are self-determining and that collective self-government is the most appropriate way of reflecting this aspect of their moral personality. However, taken in this way, the principle of autonomy is ambiguous. One interpretation of the principle of autonomy is a strong one in the Kantian tradition, well expressed by Wolff (1970, p. 14): 'moral autonomy is a combination of freedom and responsibility; it is submission to laws which one has made for oneself'. Autonomy in this sense is thus the idea that persons are by their nature self-governing creatures, that is beings whose moral personality finds its fulfilment in their prescribing principles of action to themselves. But the idea of autonomy can also be given a weaker non-Kantian sense. In this weaker sense, it simply amounts to the proposition, discussed in the previous chapter, that each person is the best judge of his or her own welfare. This is the sense in which Thompson (1970) for example takes the principle of autonomy. He asserts that the principle of autonomy is one of the presuppositions of democratic citizenship, but makes it clear that what he means by autonomy is the non-paternalist proposition that people are the best judges of their own interests. This would not imply necessarily that persons prescribed their own principles to themselves, since it would be compatible with persons prudently, but unreflectively, acting in accordance with the norms of the community in which they lived. If I lead a conventional life out of unreflective habit, I may act prudently, but I do not act autonomously.

Clearly the link between autonomy and democracy in the second weaker sense is no problem, as we have seen in the previous chapter. Taking autonomy in the stronger sense, however, raises difficulties, since this move requires an explanation of how one moves from the ascription to *individuals* of the capacity for autonomy to the conclusion that democracy is an appropriate form of *collective* decision-making. In particular, it is not clear why the collective authority implied in democratic decision-making should be thought to flow from a principle that stresses individual autonomy. The natural correlate of individual autonomy would appear to be not democracy but anarchy. The notion of anarchy here does not mean chaos, but simply a political system in which no one is forced to act against his or her will. Robert Paul Wolff (1970) has pressed the argument that autonomy in the strong sense is compatible only with anarchy and not with democracy. As soon as we move from a system in which all collective decisions are determined by unanimity with all persons voting directly, we are saying that individuals have to accept the authority of an agency which is other than themselves, and this violates the principle of autonomy. The gap that appears to open up here between the logic of autonomy leading to anarchy and the logic of collective authority leading to democracy is not accidental, I conjecture, but a consequence of the fact that whereas the practice of democracy needs a notion of purposes common to a group of people in relation to a set of common interests, the principle of autonomy is fashioned for a world in which people only haphazardly or contingently share common purposes.

It has been argued in reply to the Wolff position that the justification of democracy in terms of the principle of autonomy does not carry these individualistic and anarchistic consequences, since there are inevitably collective choices to be made in the way in which individuals arrange their common affairs. Beetham (1993, p. 62) for example explicitly refers to Wolff's argument but insists that Wolff's criterion of autonomy 'simply refuses to recognize the necessary compromises and give-and-take that are an inescapable feature of social living, and that make collective necessarily different from individual decision-making'. This argument is fleshed out by Graham who suggests that collective decision-making need not violate the principle of individual autonomy, since there is a distinction between the conditions under which we can truly say that a collective has decided – namely that certain agreed procedures have been followed – and the conditions under which an individual ought to sacrifice his or her view about what is right (Graham, 1986, pp. 112–13). Thus, on both of these views, the value of autonomy remains central to the justification of democratic procedures, but this is not taken to mean that individuals can claim the right to act in accordance with their consciences against what the collectivity has decided. Considerations of practicality, if nothing else, mean that the effective scope of individual judgement is limited, but this is not the same as limiting the scope of individual autonomy, contrary to the arguments of Wolff.

This is obviously an attractive line of argument, but the trouble is that it either demonstrates too little or too much. On the one hand it demonstrates too little in that it is inevitably tied to the prevailing technological possibilities of what is a matter for individual choice and what is a matter for collective choice. There are what Raz (1986, pp. 198–203) has called intrinsically collective goods (like the benefits of living in a tolerant society, for example), but a number of other collective goods are such only by virtue of technological limitation. Consider the case of pure water supplies to households. At present this is secured through purification plants that serve whole communities. But it is clear that technical possibilities mean that individual households could install their own purification equipment, thus rendering their decisions about the quality of water they consume independent of a more general social decision. The 'inescapable compromises' of social living need not always be so inescapable after all.

Someone could always argue that the individualistic technology was more expensive than the collective alternative. (This is surely true in the case of water, just as it is in similar cases like crime prevention and urban transport.) But, as an argument of principle, this is too weak to sustain much burden. To say that autonomy is a value in any sense is to say that it should be upheld when it conflicts with other values, like economy in the provision of public benefits. This is a necessary condition for our saying that a principle had some value at all. So if we are to take individual autonomy as a value, we should be prepared to sacrifice other goods for it. Hence, a community that respected autonomy would impart a bias to its own collective decision-making, insisting that as much as it reasonably could should be exempted from the scope of collective responsibility and placed in the hands of individuals. It could do this partly by fostering investment in individualistic technologies or by promoting alternative non-political decision-making procedures, for example the law courts or alternative dispute resolution procedures. There is no reason, however, why a *democratic* decision-making procedure should want to impart this bias to its deliberations. Full democratic decision-making requires that citizens weigh up the arguments for and against certain alternatives, not that they give special weight to one particular value in their estimation of those alternatives.

If for these reasons the arguments against the non-democratic character of autonomy carry too little weight, it can be argued that the purported reconciliation of collective decision-making and autonomy demonstrates too much. There are occasions when there will be a straight conflict between what the demos decides and what individuals' consciences tell them should be done. This is most obviously the case in the circumstances where the doctrine of conscientious objection was first developed, namely those of war. In these circumstances it may be impossible for people to distinguish in the way Graham's account requires between the authority of the collective and the autonomy of their own conscience, since even passive acceptance of the majority's preference is taken to involve complicity in a wicked act. (This, after all, is the force of popular sayings like 'The only thing necessary for evil to triumph is for good persons to do nothing.') Autonomy here seems to have the connotation of holding out against the collective, and the problem of conscientious objection is one that any doctrine of political authority has to wrestle with. A clear gap opens up between the concern for democracy and the concern for autonomy.

Democracy and Deliberative Autonomy

So far I have argued that there is a disjunction between the principle of autonomy taken in its strong form as a ground of democracy
and the presuppositions of democratic practice itself. We cannot
move easily from the notion of the self-government of individuals of
themselves to the notion of democracy as a form of popular self-
government. But someone might say at this point that I have begged
the central question in connection with autonomy, since the notion
of common interests that I have so far invoked is not one that can be
made sense of unless we also invoke the notion of autonomy, but we
only need do this in its weaker, non-Kantian, version that insists that
people are the best judges of their own interests.

Again the crucial argument here has been made by Beetham,
who argues as follows:

> 'if the idea of interest-maximization is to deliver a defence of
> democracy, rather than of paternalist forms of rule, then it must
> contain the implicit assumption that people are the best judges of
> their own interests; that is it must embody a concept like that of
> autonomy, on which it is in effect parasitic.' (Beetham, 1993, p. 61)

Clearly, the crucial point of this argument is whether there is the
close connection posited between the principle that people are the
best judges of their own interests and the claim that therefore
the concept of interests is *parasitic* upon the concept of autonomy.
We might think for example that people were the best judges of
their own interests, but deny the alleged dependence of their judgement of their interests on the idea of autonomy. Indeed, the proposition that the notion of interests is thereby parasitic upon the notion
of autonomy moves, I shall argue, in unjustifiable ways from the
weaker notion of autonomy as non-paternalism to the stronger
Kantian notion, in which form it cannot do the task expected of it.

Let us first of all consider the sense in which the idea of autonomy necessarily enters our account of interests. The basic insight
here is that interests are never fixed in a rigid way. Consider, as an
example, the case of health interests. Most people would agree that
health interests are basic in the sense that to say that a policy or
practice had adverse effects on people's health would normally be
to provide a reason for not adopting that policy or practice, and

conversely to say that a policy or practice promoted health would normally be a good reason for adopting it. However, even if we accept that the protection and promotion of health is generally in the interests of persons, we cannot infer from this that policy-makers or practitioners can move straight from this assumption to a view about what should be done in particular cases. We still need to invoke something like the anti-paternalist principle that people are the best judges of their own interests for one simple reason. There often arise cases in medical practice where the response to a diagnosis involves balancing risks in the treatment of a disease, say between surgery, carrying its own risks, and watchful waiting. How the risks of these alternative consequences are balanced seems to be properly a matter for the individual patient than it does for anyone else, including medical practitioners.

Similar trade-offs can occur at the collective level. Thus, a community may be faced with the choice of environmental protection or economic well-being. A particular manufacturing plant in a locality may be an important source of jobs, but also be a source of health risks for the population of the community, as was clearly the case with traditional coal mining communities exposed not only to the occupational risks associated with working in the mines but also with environmental risks like land subsidence or avalanches of waste material. Provided that the risks are bounded within that community, it seems arguable at the very least (many people would take it to be axiomatic) that the members of the community should determine the balance of risks for themselves.

In the sense conveyed by these examples, a non-paternalist principle of autonomy is a necessary condition for acting in the interests of the people involved. Does this mean, however, that the concept of interests is *parasitic* upon that of autonomy? In the logical sense of the question the answer is clearly no. These are cases of competing interests, the appeal of which we understand before we introduce the notion of autonomy. True, we cannot define the correct policy without consulting individuals and finding out how they balance these competing goods, and in this sense our judgement of interests is dependent upon their choices. But this is not to say that the concept of interest is parasitic upon that of autonomy. Rather our interpretation of what should be the definition of a person's interest depends upon our that person balances conflicting goods.

However, someone may argue that this is to interpret the notion of autonomy in too restricted a way. The weak notion of autonomy is defined precisely as the principle that each person is the best judge of his or her own interests in balancing these conflicting goods, but there are other circumstances of choice in which the problem is not how to make a balanced choice between conflicting goods antecedently defined, but how to define what is the good for persons at all. This takes us back to a stronger Kantian conception of autonomy in which the notion is that autonomous persons define their own principles of action, and thereby define their own good. They live, that is to say, according to a law prescribed by themselves.

At the level of collective decision-making this line of argument has been most effectively worked out in recent years in a series of writings by Jürgen Habermas. Summarizing a complex body of writing, we may say that the root idea here is that modernity frees the citizens of contemporary societies from the traditionally pre-scribed social roles that would have defined in the human good in former times. The Weberian disenchantment of the world means that persons can no longer rely upon pre-formed notions of the good either of individuals or of the communities in which they live, leading Habermas to pose the question for example:

> 'In which direction would the structures of the life-world have to
> vary if the undistorted reproduction of a concrete form of life
> were to be less and less guaranteed by traditional, customary,
> time-tested, and consensual stocks of knowledge and had to be
> secured instead by a risky search for consensus, that is, by the
> cooperative achievements of those engaged in communicative
> action themselves?' (Habermas, 1985, p. 344)

In forming our view of collective choices we therefore have to appeal to the results of a social dialogue, constrained only by the requirements that the participants to the dialogue can enter it freely and that the process of collective will formation is uncoerced and undistorted. Whatever emerges from this dialogue will then count as constitutive of human interests in the full sense.

Clearly, this account would make the concept of human interests depend upon the notion of autonomy. It is certainly true that Habermas seems at times to appeal to a notion of interests that exists prior to the notion of discursive exchange (for example, the interest of coming to an understanding with a person with whom one communicates), but these pre-discursive interests are rather formal in character, corresponding to the constraints on negotiation that we find in Rawls's (1972, pp. 118–92) account of the original position. When we think about the social choices that face a community, say in whether there should be nuclear power or not or whether public transport should replace the private car, it is clear that Habermas's approach would not license a simple appeal to an antecedently identified human good, but would instead make the choices logically depend upon what came out of the social dialogue. (Of course there is not much doubt about where Habermas's own sympathies lie, or what choices he thinks would emerge from the dialogue – see Habermas (1979, p. 199), where he talks about the pursuit of happiness as being one day constituted not in the possession of material objects but in bringing about social relations in which mutuality predominates.)

If the notion of interests were to stand to the notion of autonomy in this way, then the concept of interests would be parasitic, in a strict sense, on that of autonomy. Moreover, Habermas's ideal speech situation looks rather like a certain sort of participatory democracy, so that the gap between the moral concept of autonomy and the political principle of democracy is correspondingly narrowed. Thus, in Habermas's ideal speech situation there is no domination arising from inequalities of power, and participation in the speech situation is open to all on terms of equality.

If we were to make this further connection, then it is easy to see how the practice of democracy could be linked to the idea of autonomy in a way that would also make the account of human interests depend upon the notion of autonomy. Human interests would be the result of deliberation by autonomous agents in the ideal speech situation, and the ideal speech situation in turn could be seen as the limiting case of democratic dialogue. Actual democratic dialogue would then variously approximate the conditions of the ideal speech situation, depending upon the conditions that were satisfied in particular cases. Brian Barry (1989a, pp. 347–8) has shown how this might work in an analogous case with his idea of the circumstances of impartiality. In brief, what he shows is that certain democracies (in his view roughly those of the Scandinavian type) can be said to approximate conditions of equal power and absence of domination that one would expect to see in idealized situations of political negotiation. Although the actual democratic practices are merely evidence of what would happen in such situations of negotiation, it is clear that in the limit the successive approximations will become criterial (see Weale, 1998).

Here we have, therefore, the articulation of a theory of democracy in which autonomy in the requisite sense is foundational, and in which we cannot have an account of democratic practice without also being able to specify what would be the conditions in which autonomous agents would be able to negotiate with one another and come to a collective decision about their common affairs. How far can this account of democracy be maintained?

One obvious problem is that the Habermasian account seems to replicate a difficulty inherent in the Kantian tradition of moral reasoning, namely that it merely provides a formal account of conditions that need to be satisfied for legitimate decisions, but without indicating what the substantive content of those decisions is. A familiar charge against Kant's test of moral principles based on the idea of universalizability is that it offers merely an 'empty formalism', in the sense that an indefinitely large number of principles could satisfy the test. Similarly, one might argue of the test of the ideal speech situation that it too merely provided an empty formalism, since an indefinitely large number of contradictory principles might be regarded as emerging from the ideal speech situation.

The deep source of these problems is to be found, I conjecture, in the ambition of theorists of autonomy to get away from the historical determination of interests and our conception of human interests, and to establish the circumstances in which a free choice can be made by persons of their life plans and projects. On this account, just as the achievement of capitalism was to free workers from the prescribed roles and statuses of serf and bondman, so the achievement of a modern political theory would be to free citizens from the historical contingencies which make them conceive their interests in terms that were too narrow. But one does not have to be a Burkean conservative to realize that this is an impossible ambition. Neither individually nor collectively do we fashion our institutional life from scratch. We make our choices, including our democratic choices, within circumstances inherited and transmitted from the past, and by extending and developing the moral and intellectual traditions we have inherited in a reflective and critical way (compare Miller, 1995, pp. 44–5). Indeed, as Peter Dews (1986, pp. 17–22) has pointed out, Habermas himself has come to accept this criticism, moving from a position in his earlier work in which the ideal speech situation could provide an account of a possible future form of life to one in which moral traditions provide the content of life-forms.

The core of truth contained in any account that stresses the importance of autonomy is that unreflective habit and the unreflective repetition of traditions is no longer an option for those who live in a modern society. We need a critical morality as well as a positive morality, and we need to be able to consider the point, purpose and rationale of the moral and political traditions that are ours. This is to say no more, however, than that modern societies are open rather than closed. What does this imply for our account of democratic autonomy, however? Since no community can live simply according to its inherited traditions, there has to be scope for democratic deliberation. These choices will concern not simply the regulation of economic activity and contractual relations, but also, since the unreflective repetition of traditions is no longer possible, choices about the political culture by which decisions have previously been taken, including such matters as the place of religion, the expression of sexuality, relations of the sexes, our place in the natural world and markers of social identity like language, ethnic group and place. But no political culture can be made afresh in one decision or even one sweep of decisions. In this sense, the notion of autonomy that is needed is what I have termed the weaker rather than the stronger notion. Autonomous deliberation does not constitute our interests, but instead operates over conceptions of interests that are previously defined, though constantly being remade.

One possible analogy here is to career choice. In a free society people will choose the careers that suit them best, and will not be obliged to enter occupations that are traditionally prescribed for them. Relations of contract will have replaced relations of status in such matters. Nevertheless, choice is not completely free, since there is only a limited, if large, range of options.

The choice is not fixed in any straightforward way. Technical change is encouraging the development of new careers and discouraging the development of others. But this is not to say that there is a deterministic process at work, providing slots into which people fit, since those who are especially imaginative, lucky or unscrupulous will be able to invent or conjure up new options for themselves, for example becoming purveyors of bad, if popular, taste in art or fashion. But some careers will be virtually impossible to pursue, like that of the village blacksmith.

The type of autonomy that is suitable for such a world is one in which persons are the best judges of their own interests, but not one in which their choices arising from autonomous deliberation constitute their own interests. Hence, I conclude that the ambition of founding a theory of interests on the idea of autonomous choice cannot provide a basis for democratic practice, any more than that the principle of autonomy at the personal level could provide a basis for sensible career choice. The principle of autonomy does find a place therefore in justificatory arguments about the ground of democracy, but in its weak rather than its strong form. Autonomous choice at the collective level is needed because there can be competing interests and unless we believed that there was a uniquely appropriate way to strike the balance between those elements competing with one another, we would not be doing justice to the character of the choice. In this sense, the practice of democracy is founded on anti-paternalist principles.

Democracy and Virtue

So far I have only considered the arguments for taking autonomy as the ground or presupposition of democratic practice. However, it is possible to turn the argument around and to treat it in a consequentialist way. This is the approach of Robert Dahl (1989, pp. 97–105), who sees the justification of democracy in terms of the capacity of democratic systems to *promote* autonomy. In this account, therefore, the principle of autonomy is not the ground or presupposition of democratic practice; rather it emerges as a valued consequence. The argument is that by participating in democratic governance citizens increase their capacity for personal moral development, since the processes of democratic discussion and debate foster certain moral capacities (compare Barber, 1984, p. 155).

The thought that the form of government should be justified in terms of the type of moral personality it produced among its citizens is one that has been advanced by a number of theorists, but was crisply expressed by John Stuart Mill:

'The first element of good government, therefore, being the virtue and intelligence of the human beings composing the community, the most important point of excellence which any form of government can possess is to promote the virtue and intelligence of the people themselves.' (Mill, 1861a, p. 226)

This is a line of argument that goes back to the Platonic–Aristotelian tradition in Greek political thought, and can be found in writers like Arendt (1958) and Tocqueville (1835, pp. 246–63).

Elster (1983, pp. 91–100) has criticized this type of argument as a justificatory strategy for democracy, objecting to the idea that the educative effects of participation could be the main or sole point of a political system. Taking Tocqueville's claim in particular that democracy is inferior to aristocracy as a decision-making system but excels it in terms of the popular energy it releases, he argues that unless democracy had a point over and above producing these psychological benefits it could not in fact produce those benefits. His argument here is dependent upon his notion of essential by-products of activity (Elster, 1983), in which certain consequences of action only follow provided agents focus on something else. (We all know of people who try to be the centre-piece of the party by telling jokes but simply end up being bores, whereas those who are unselfconsciously funny will grab attention whatever they do.)

However, as Chan and Miller (1991) have pointed out, Elster rather overstates the force of his argument against the strategy of basing a justification for democracy on its educative effects. They show that all the notion of by-products needs is the assumption that persons pursue concrete goals in politics, and that this assumption is relatively uncontroversial. Self-realization through education cannot be the sole aim of political activity, but when thinking about questions of institutional and constitutional design citizens can appeal quite properly to the educative benefits that democratic governments are supposed to bring.

The Mill–Tocqueville strategy cannot, therefore, be ruled out of court *a priori*. Provided we see politics as an arena within which people pursue certain concrete goals, it will be in principle possible to construct an argument for democratic government on the basis that it produces certain types of character and thereby promotes moral development. The question therefore turns on the issue of whether such supposed moral development is something that can be justified.

In his discussion of the issue, Dahl distinguishes two types of moral development that he believes are promoted within democratic political systems. The first type of moral development is what may be called autonomy as impartiality, 'gaining a more mature sense of responsibility for one's actions, a broader awareness of the others affected by one's actions, a greater willingness to reflect on and take into account the consequences of one's actions for others, and so on' (Dahl, 1989, pp. 104–5). The second type of development is what one may call autonomy as self-determination: 'Lacking personal autonomy, one simply could not live under rules of one's own choosing; as a result, one would be neither self-determining nor morally autonomous and to that extent could not be a moral person' (Dahl, 1989, p. 105). The argument is that democracy promotes both sorts of moral development.

The distinction between these two forms of moral development is to be found also in Mill's work, although the two principles are not as clearly separated as they are by Dahl. Asserting that the qualities of the human beings in a government are the most essential element of good performance, Mill cites the virtues of impartiality: truthfulness among witnesses, judges immune to bribes, concern for the public good among administrators, calm deliberation among legislators and a spirit of cooperation among elites (Mill, 1861a, pp. 225–6). Similarly, in citing the educational benefits of public service within a democracy, Mill notes that citizens are called to weigh interests other than their own, to be guided in cases of conflict by rules other than those of private partialities, and to apply principles and maxims that have as their concern the public interest (Mill, 1861a, p. 255). These are clearly the virtues of impartiality, and Mill's argument for democracy is that the participation it encourages and requires promote these sorts of virtues.

However, in addition to the virtues of autonomy as impartiality, Mill also cites the value of autonomy as self-determination. He contrasts what he terms the active and passive types of character, and asserts that one of the virtues of democracy is that it encourages the active rather than the passive type. The arguments for the superiority of the active type consists of a series of propositions: all intellectual superiority is the fruit of active effort; enterprise is the parent of both speculative and practical talent; and the character which improves human life is that which struggles with natural powers and tendencies, not that which gives way to them (Mill,

1861a, p. 249). How then does Mill link this notion of self-determining autonomy to the practice of democracy? Essentially he does it through an empirical generalization to the effect that persons who bestir themselves with hopeful prospects of their own circumstances are those who feel good will towards those engaged in similar pursuits. In other words, the virtues of impartiality are more likely to be attached to those types of persons displaying the virtues of self-determining autonomy and both sorts of virtues are more likely to be developed in a democracy.

Despite Mill's attempt to link these two senses of autonomy together, and to use the cultivation of both as a reinforcing consideration for each, there is much to be said for Dahl's strategy of keeping them separate and considering the merits of the argument in each case. Mill's case for linking autonomy as impartiality to autonomy as self-determination via his putative empirical generalization is not helped by the Victorian racism in which he casts the supposed evidence, which consigns orientals and southern Europeans (with whom he is quite happy to lump the French for these purposes) to the domain of sloth and envy. Only the spunky Anglo-Saxons, it would seem, have what it takes to create democracy. But even if the rational kernel of the argument could be extracted from this mythical shell, there would still be good reasons for trying to keep distinct the virtues of autonomy as impartiality and autonomy as self-determination.

The first and most obvious of these reasons arises from the argument of the previous section, namely that the notion of self-determination makes little sense in a context where irreducibly collective goods are at issue, and not much sense at all when we are talking about the pursuit of collective ideals. A sense of impartiality, of weighing the interests of others as well as the interests of oneself, on the other hand would seem to be absolutely essential if collective action is to be undertaken. Indeed, so close is the association of collective action with a sense of impartiality that I am inclined to say that it is misleading to construe the notion in terms of autonomy at all. Certainly achieving impartiality does require a certain distance on one's own plans and projects, and this attitude of mind looks at least like a close cousin of autonomy, but it may be more unhelpful to identify them by the same term than to keep them distinct by referring to one as autonomy and the other as impartiality.

Secondly, autonomy conceived in the sense of self-determination seems like a specific virtue which is highly regarded in some moral codes and not in others. (This perhaps is the rational kernel of Mill's argument.) In recent years its value has been challenged by religious conservatives, multiculturalists and feminists. Thus, just as there are some feminists who see the virtue of autonomy as being necessarily tied to a masculine ethos of individuality rather than a feminine ethos of relationships, so there are feminists who base their critique of patriarchy on its failure to achieve autonomy for women (Phillips, 1993, pp. 50–2). It is certainly not necessary to take sides in the intra-mural disputes that these challenges have fostered. Whoever is right, it would seem better if one could build a theory of democracy, which after all has to be constructed for a society containing a pluralism of moral viewpoints, on arguments that were not dependent upon particular moral judgements of this sort.

There is therefore a sense in which we do have to appeal to the supposed effects of democratic institutions in fostering a certain sort of virtue if we are to have a coherent account of the moral foundations of democracy. However, the virtue in question is not a strong notion of autonomy but the virtue of impartiality, and this in turn we can relate to the requirements of political equality. Of course it is an empirical question how far democratic institutions do have these effects, and in the chapter on participation we shall look at that evidence more closely.

Democracy and Consent

One frequently used argument in favour of democracy is that it is government by consent. If we hold to the Jeffersonian principle as set out in the US Declaration of Independence that just governments derive their powers from the consent of the governed, then democratic government will be justified if it alone can be said to be government by consent.

It may be thought that justification in terms of consent merely reintroduced the same considerations as justification in terms of the principle of autonomy, since the value of autonomy might underlay the importance of consent. But, though they are related, the ideas of consent and autonomy should really be distinguished.

As we saw in the previous section, the notion of autonomy is really an ideal of character. It connotes persons who take control of their own lives and make choices by which they are to live. The idea of consent does not carry this connotation, however. Consent might be thought to form the basis for legitimate government even in communities that conceived themselves to live by traditional moral and religious codes, since consent may be regarded as a means by which authority is passed from one person to another, and this idea does not need the presupposition that the source of the authority is autonomous.

In speaking of government by consent, we need to distinguish two distinct ways in which the idea can be used, as Bryce pointed out (1888, pp. 14–23) many years ago. In the first sense the idea is used in relation to consent to a system of government; in the second sense it can be used to refer to a system of government in which decisions taken by governments are subject to the consent of citizens. It should be clear that the distinctively democratic claim is that governmental decisions should be subject to popular consent, not that the system of government should be subject to consent. If it were merely the latter, then it would be impossible to distinguish the legitimacy of democratic and non-democratic government. After all, Hobbes's (1651) theory of political obligation grounds the authority of government in the consent of those subject to it, but the form of government may as well be authoritarian as democractic on Hobbesian premises. Hence, there does not seem to be a special connection between the requirement that the system of government be subject to the requirement of consent and the requirement that the system of government be democratic.

The conclusions of authoritarian versions of social contract theory have to rely of course upon the fiction of a hypothetical social contract, and it might be open to someone on this basis to argue that the hypothetical reasoning has been misconstrued. But, as anarchists are fond of pointing out, justifications of democratic government in terms of consent to the system also have to rely upon notions of hypothetical consent, since even within the most democratic governmental system there is never a device for expressing continuing consent over time. In some societies it is plausible to say that the inauguration of a democratic regime elicited the consent of the population, particularly in post-colonial situations or situations like that of the USA in 1787 to 1788 where there was both a constitutional convention and a series of popular votes to elect representatives to ratifying conventions. Yet, even in these cases, subsequent generations will not have engaged in explicit acts of consent to the system of government, so that any justification cast in terms of consent to the system taken as a whole will have to take the form of hypothetical or tacit consent.

Someone might argue that consent to the system of government, though only of a tacit or hypothetical kind, was more plausibly ascribed to democratic than to non-democratic systems of government, since it is only reasonable to suppose that people will consent to a system of government in which their right of authority is protected. One might say that, in a suitably constrained hypothetical social contract, consent is more likely to liberal democracies than to façade-democracies or military regimes. But does this amount to anything more than a conjecture that in the putative hypothetical situation the merits of liberal democracy would be recognized over the alternatives? To say that democracy would be preferred to that form of government in a hypothetical social contract seems to be no more than offering a metaphorical endorsement of justificatory arguments that can quite as easily stand on their own. Hence, there does not seem to be a distinctive argument for democracy cast in terms of consent to the system taken as a whole.

The claim that democracy has special merits by enabling those affected by particular policy measures to consent to those measures has more attraction. After all, through devices like elections, referendums and so on, one might say that actual processes of consent go on in democracy. So this looks to be a more promising line of argument than appeals to hypothetical consent to a system of government taken as a whole, since we can have independent evidence about what it is that people are consenting to by simply observing their choices. So on this argument one of the special merits of democratic government is that it enables citizens to consent to laws, policies and measures in the light of which they will have to constrain their otherwise free behaviour.

One issue here is whether the notion of consent is either necessary or sufficient for us to say that someone has acquired authority by virtue of an act of consent, and the answer to these questions obviously turns on the definition of consent. On one definition of consent it is to be understood as the transference of a right. The idea here is that consent forms part of a broader institutional practice of social cooperation which has its own constitutive rules. According to these rules to consent to an action is to act within the practice in such a way that a right is transferred. This was the view of consent taken by John Plamenatz in the postscript to the second edition of *Consent, Freedom and Political Obligation* (Plamenatz, 1968, pp. 163–82).

If we take this view of consent, then it seems natural to think that an act of consent is criterial for our appraisal of political institutions. By this I mean that once the condition of consent has been satisfied, the right has been transferred and no further questions need to be asked. The only problem then is whether we can find a process within the activities of modern government that functions like an act of consent in this way. One candidate for such a process is participation in elections. According to this view participation in an election is a form of consent to the outcome, and since consent is the transference of a right, participation in an election establishes the right to govern. Since elections are one of the principal devices of modern democracies, it would seem by this argument that only democracies can be classed as falling in the category of governments that rule by consent.

The obvious problem with this approach is that electorates are often divided and many people do not bother to vote. How can we say of those who have not voted or who have voted against the party or candidate who won that they have consented to the outcome, even though it is contrary to their wishes? Some people who are in the losing group may say that they are happy to see the winners get their way, but there is no reason to think that this is a widespread or usual attitude. People may have participated in an election solely with the intention of securing the election of their party or candidate, and have no reason to think that they have consented to the actual result. If we are to maintain the idea that participation in the democratic process is a form of consent, it is therefore going to be necessary to distinguish that part of the meaning of a person's act that derives from his or her intention and that part which derives from the meaning that is attached by the institutional context within which they act. Here we should need to use the institutionalist account of consent to say that participation in elections carries the meaning of transferring a right to govern to the winners irrespective of the intention of those voting.

One analogy would be with ordinary legal processes. Consider the process of making a will. If I transfer ownership of some asset after my death to a beneficiary, then I cannot circumscribe the uses to which the asset shall be put. I may intend that the transfer entail the obligation that the family house always to be maintained as a single dwelling, but I cannot impose these conditions on beneficiaries. Once they have legally acquired the asset it is theirs, and if they wish to turn it into flats they have the legal freedom to do so. So, whatever my intention in making the will, the institutional meaning of my act will trump the meaning derived from my personal intention. In just the same way, someone might argue that participation in an election carried a series of institutional meanings. It meant not simply the transference of a right to govern in the event of one's preferred candidate being elected, but also such transference in the event of any qualified candidate being elected. If consent is the transference of a right, then there would seem to be no reason why we could not construe electoral participation as such a form of consent. This would give meaning to the idea of tacit consent.

This is clearly a logical possibility, but I doubt that it can explain how the notion of consent functions standardly within liberal democracies. If we take the analogy to legal processes seriously, then it is clear that the ascription of intentions by virtue of undertaking certain legally defined acts is only possible because there has been some explicit legislative or judicial interpretation to that effect. Moreover, those who undertake legal actions like making a will would be imprudent if they did not take specialist advice on the meaning of what they were doing. The ascription of meanings independently of intentions is not arbitrary but takes place within an institutional setting in which there are well-developed and agreed techniques for working out what the meaning of particular acts is (and of course well-developed techniques for settling disputes about the meaning of acts when they are in question).

Taking the analogy to the political case reveals that there is not this hinterland of institutional provision for settling the meaning of particular acts. By analogy with everyday legal processes, we should require something like a constitutional convention or constituent assembly to define explicitly the meaning of crucial political acts like voting, as well as continuing provision for resolution of differences of interpretation. But in the political case there is simply not this rich institutional background to provide an authoritative interpretation to the acts of individuals, and a great deal of politics consists precisely in the unresolved dispute of questions about the meaning of such actions as not voting in an election, not paying one's taxes, occupying a building as part of a political protest or taking up a seat in the legislature.

The question with which I began this chapter was whether democracy could be linked intrinsically to certain values, most notably autonomy and consent. We have seen that the relevant sense of autonomy is a weak one, in which the stress is upon the idea of non-paternalism and that there is only a limited, if distinctive, sense in which democracy is government by consent. There is, therefore, a necessarily instrumentalist element essential to any justification of democracy. What consequences does this have for the competing conceptions of democracy that I identified in Chapter 2?

5 Participation and Representation

If we consider the various conceptions of democracy set out in Chapter 2, we can see that one central respect in which they vary is the extent to which they presuppose popular participation in the making of policy decisions. At one extreme are those Rousseauian theories in which popular participation is central to the very conception of democracy, since such participation moralizes citizens, thereby enabling them to form a common view of the general interest. At the other extreme is liberal constitutionalism in which the primary function of democracy is protective and popular participation, through elections, is simply seen as an ultimate control on political leaders. David Miller (1983, p. 133) plausibly characterizes the distinction between protective and participationist accounts of democracy as of 'paramount importance'. Since there are intermediate positions between a pure participationist account and a pure protective account, controversies over the nature, extent and feasibility of popular participation within democracy are going to be a central feature of any normative theory.

I have also argued in the two previous chapters that the general justification we offer for democratic government will carry implications for the particular conception of democracy that we favour. As we saw in the discussion of the principle of autonomy, there can be a very close connection between the principles in terms of which we seek to justify democracy and the form of government we envisage flowing from any particular justification. Here again, debates about political participation are likely to be important.

Although the term 'participation' is widely used within democratic theory, its meaning often remains vague. I shall follow the broad definition of Parry, Moyser and Day (1992, p. 16) and define participation as 'taking part in the process of formulation, passage and

84

implementation of public policies'. On the basis of this definition, the crucial normative question is then the extent to which there should be an institutional capacity for the public at large to have a final say on issues of public policy. This final say involves not simply voting directly on issues of public policy that come on to the political agenda, but also exercising control over which issues emerge on to the political agenda in the first place. It may also involve, as the definition suggests, questions about the role of citizens in the implementation of political decisions.

Participation and Feasibility

Among the five conceptions of democracy that I have identified, an obvious distinction in the extent of popular control occurs at the break between the direct and indirect conceptions. In a direct democracy the extent of popular control is sufficiently great to allow the public to have powers of final decision over important items on the political agenda, via such devices as the referendum and other powers of initiative. By contrast, in all forms of indirect or representative democracy, the public's power of decision is limited to choosing those persons or bodies charged with the institutional responsibility for making the final decisions. However, even within representative governments, there are substantial variations in the extent to which popular control is conceptualized as playing a role in decision-making. Thus, famously, Schumpeter wished to discourage political action by the public at large between elections, holding that a necessary precondition of any stable democracy was a willingness on the part of citizens to refrain from 'back-seat driving' (Schumpeter, 1954, p. 295). Others, by contrast, have seen the willingness of citizens to form pressure groups and to engage in political activity about which they feel intensely as a central element in the flourishing of what Dahl (1989) terms 'polyarchy', a form of representative political system in which there is widespread popular influence on government decisions on matters of public policy. John Stuart Mill's theory of representative government, as we have seen, rested in part on the claim that participation fostered certain political virtues.

As well as theoretical arguments about the desirability of greater participation within representative democracies, it is also clear in practice that representative systems contain substantial variations in what have been termed 'political opportunity structures' (Kitschelt, 1986), that is to say, institutional devices that allow members of the public to influence decision-making on public policy. In the US many states now allow a variety of devices (especially initiatives, referendums or the recall of public officials from office) that provide for some element of direct control by the public over policy decisions (Cronin, 1989). Similarly, when the nations of the European Union had to ratify the Maastricht Treaty, there were referendums held in Denmark, France and the Republic of Ireland, whereas other countries used the normal parliamentary process to make the decision. Within the UK, the referendum as a device has been used to confirm the UK's membership of the European Community in 1975, (as it then was), and in 1979 and 1997 to put the question of the devolution of power to those living in Scotland and Wales. In another context, it has been argued that there are substantial variations in the ability to influence decisions on questions of land-use planning at the stage of policy formulation, rather than policy implementation. Thus, one of the explanations for the growth of direct opposition in Germany to the development of nuclear power stations was that there was insufficient opportunity at the policy planning stage for citizens to influence decision-making and for opponents to put their case (Paterson, 1989, pp. 278–81).

Both in theory and in practice, therefore, the issue of the range of activities in which the public can engage in the formulation, passage and implementation of public policies is an important one. Not only can we distinguish the various conceptions of democracy in terms of the place they give to popular participation in the making of decisions, but we can also see that within the broad class of representative systems, there are important differences in what is expected of the public, as distinct from elected officials or the appointed bureaucracy.

In examining the arguments over participation, I shall think of them as essentially concerned with problems of institutional design and choice, where the institutional issues involve the assignment of rights to various agents (in particular, elected politicians, appointed bureaucrats or the public at large) to make the final decision on matters of public policy. The right here is to be thought of as an institutional right, rather than a moral right. The question therefore is: on what grounds can we assign an institutional right to one type of political agent rather than another, when making an allocation of decision-making responsibility within a political constitution?

In posing the question in this way, I am drawing upon the distinction between institutional and behavioural questions that I identified in Chapter 2. Institutional questions are concerned with the structure of rules, roles, norms and conventions that govern the allocation of decision-making power within a political constitution, including the rights and duties that citizens have under that constitution. Behavioural questions concern the use to which those rights are typically put by agents operating within a structure of rules, roles, norms and conventions (including, of course, the typical abuses to which constitutions may be put). Although we cannot collapse the one sort of question into the other, we should seek to answer questions about institutional design in the light of the behavioural evidence we have available to us. Thus, we need both to identify the normative arguments that relate to the institutional choices and to be aware of the behavioural evidence that bears upon those institutional choices.

The reasoning behind this methodological strategy is that intelligent institutional choice requires some knowledge of the likely behavioural patterns under a given set of institutional rules. We cannot simply depend upon normative arguments about the desirability of certain institutional rules, since that would be to confuse incentives with behaviour. Equally, however, unless we had reason to think that behaviour is constant, whatever its institutional setting, we need to relate our understanding of anticipated behaviour to questions of institutional choice. Thus, in discussing the arguments for and against more opportunities for greater public participation, it will be essential to draw upon some broadly based behavioural empirical generalizations culled from the literature.

In institutional terms it is clear that there is not one way in which participation can occur, but several. Empirical studies of political participation typically identify a range of rather disparate actions that fall under the heading of participation, including voting, party campaigning, membership and activity in interest groups, contacting or communicating with public officials and taking part in protests or demonstrations (for example, Parry, Moyser and Day, 1992, chapter 3). Some of these activities, for example voting, campaigning and party membership, are non-specific in the sense that they arise from a general interest in politics and policy, whereas others are specific, in the sense that political participation reflects some identifiable concern or interest, for example opposition to a road-building scheme or the siting of a waste disposal facility, that is non-recurrent and in the absence of which participation would not have taken place. Those participating may not always recognize their actions under the description 'political participation', but in the broad sense of the term as we are employing it (taking part in the formulation, passage and implementation of public policy), then all the activities should be included.

Although the institutional opportunities for political participation vary within existing democracies, it is clear that even the most participationist systems could increase such opportunities even further in at least three ways. Firstly, a larger number of people could take advantage of such opportunities for participation as there are. Empirical studies show that, if we regard participation as a ladder that people have to climb, very few people get above the bottom rung – which is voting – and an extremely small number indeed get above party memberships and some campaigning (Parry, Moyser and Day, 1992, pp. 48–53). Participation could thus be increased by a higher proportion of citizens using existing devices.

Secondly, participation could be increased by using certain devices across a wider range of issues. In most political systems, referendums could be used on a wider range of issues, and called more frequently. In so-called routine administrative matters, like the setting of standards for environmental protection, there could be a wider use of participatory devices like regulatory negotiation, public hearings or consensus conferences. In the supply of public services there could be greater use of consumer groups to determine the limits within which professional suppliers worked. All these are institutional devices that are currently in use somewhere within representative systems, but which are not in full use anywhere. It follows that everywhere the level of political participation could be increased above the level that currently obtains.

Thirdly, existing participatory devices could be supplemented by new institutional mechanisms. The use of referendums could be accompanied by the use of the citizens' initiative, by which a concerned groups of citizens, above some specified minimum number, could place propositions before other citizens for decision. Greater use of electronic and information technology would enable an increase in popular participation, helping modern large-scale democracies to replicate the participatory discussions that supposedly went on in the Athenian assembly. Interactive video and televised debates would, on this analysis, overcome the barriers of space and size that modern large-scale societies impose on their functioning democratic institutions. Whatever doubts one might have about the *merits* of such widespread use of electronic technology, particularly in terms of the quality of public debate it produces, the *feasibility* of some form of increased participation arising from electronic technology cannot be doubted.

The upshot of these arguments is that we can envisage, on the basis of the existing behavioural evidence, an overall increase in levels of political activity among average citizens, and we should consider the advantages and disadvantages of seeking to encourage such higher levels of activity on the merits of the individual arguments. There is no firm behavioural evidence to suggest that political communities have simply reached the limits of popular participation.

There are two obvious types of criteria in terms of which we can seek to assess the advantages and disadvantages. The first relate to the consequences of increased participation particularly for the quality of public decision-making and for the moral qualities of citizens. The second relate to the extent to which the practice of greater participation would encourage political practices that embodied certain principles thought to be desirable in themselves. I shall consider the relevant arguments under these broad headings. The implications of these arguments for the choice between our five conceptions of democracy also needs to be considered, particularly as the discussion bears upon the choice between direct and representative forms of democracy.

However, before looking at the arguments in detail, I should make one remark about vocabulary. One common way of speaking about these controversies is in terms of 'participationist' versus 'elitist' conceptions of democracy. This is a perfectly acceptable terminology, provided that it is not abused or misunderstood. In particular, the term 'elitist' is likely to be misconstrued. It does not have to carry a morally objectionable connotation, in the sense that the elite theorist of democracy thinks that only those of superior social status should be professionally involved in government.

Certainly some elite theorists, like Schumpeter, do seem to say this explicitly, and no doubt a large number of elite theorists are and were social snobs. But an elite theory of democracy could in principle come up with non-snobbish reasons for wanting to limit popular participation in the making of decisions, and we could even imagine in the limit a popular decision to limit participation.

Participation *versus* Representation?

In the varying conceptions of democracy that I identified in Chapter 2 the distinction between direct and indirect forms of democracy raises the deepest issues concerned with participation, since it touches on whether arguments about participation would incline us to favour direct over indirect democracy as a matter of principle. In other words, do the arguments in favour of greater participation suggest that representative systems are somehow less worthy as systems of democracy? Indeed, at the extreme, might we find arguments that direct democracy was the only legitimate form of government?

This question, touching on the very definition of democracy, raises the issue explicitly, canvassed in Chapter 1, of whether we should define democracy by reference to scalar or sortal categories. A proponent of the scalar approach would say that popular participation defines the ideal of democracy, and representative systems are to be evaluated by the extent to which they enable participation to approximate to the top of the scale. If democracy is good, then more of it is even better, and so direct citizen participation in decision-making is always to be preferred to representatives making decisions other things being equal. However, such plausibility as this approach possesses depends upon the presupposition that participation is an ideal, which is just the question at issue. This claim cannot simply be assumed.

Clearly, the argument that would obviously deliver the strong conclusion that participation is an ideal is the Rousseauian one of moral autonomy. If human beings are free by nature, and there is no legitimate way of constraining their freedom in the absence of their own decision to limit what they do, then the principle of self-government would be the right one. However, as we saw in the previous chapter, there are difficulties with this line of argument, both in respect of the assumptions it invokes and in respect of the conclusions that it draws. In respect of the conclusions, it would seem more logical, as Wolff argued, to favour limiting government as much as possible, and to infer that libertarian anarchy was the best institutional embodiment of the principle of autonomy. In respect of the premisses, I argued that it was simply implausible to suppose that interests could be constituted autonomously in the way required.

A weaker notion than autonomy is consent. Although autonomy implies that only those laws and rules to which citizens consent are just, the requirement that citizens consent to laws and rules need not imply a commitment to autonomy in the strong sense, since one might hold that citizens should consent in any matter that affects their interests, even though their interests were constituted heteronomously. However, again as we saw in the previous chapter, it is difficult to give as much weight to the idea of consent as this principle suggests, since there are a number of occasions on which political morality in reflective equilibrium would not take consent as either necessary or sufficient for the design of institutional arrangements or the adoption of policies.

This leaves us with the importance of participation in promoting an impartial frame of mind. As we saw in the previous chapter, this was one of John Stuart Mill's main arguments for favouring political participation and it also appears that Mill's conjecture about the effects of enlarged sympathies is borne out in practice. So, rather than consider whether participation has these beneficial effects, the question is how important it is that these effects should be produced and on what scale they are appropriately developed.

At this point it is useful to look at the question from the opposite point of view and consider the arguments *against* making participation an essential requirement of a legitimate political system. Of these there are three main variants: the time consumed by participation; the advantages that arise from the division of political labour within a representative system; and the extent to which we are entitled to assume a certain ideal of character.

Consider first the question of time. Let us suppose that communications and electronic technology have enabled modern political communities to overcome the barriers of space and size that have hitherto prevented modern large-scale democracies from replicating the participation practised in ancient Athens or the New England townships. One might then say that there was a prima facie argument for expanding the range of issues on which citizens could vote directly. Some caution is required in accepting this argument, however. No technology can expand the amount of time available to earthly communities to discuss their common affairs, and, as Dahl (1970) once showed, even a moderate amount of discussion with, say, six or seven points of view represented would quickly consume large amounts of time. Moreover, many of the most satisfying and fulfilling of non-political human activities (playing a musical instrument, writing poetry, climbing mountains, sports and dinner-table conversation, to name but a few) are also time-consuming, so that democratic political participation is likely to be in fierce competition with them for the ultimate scarce resource.

Although one should always be careful of deriving an 'ought' from an 'is', there is some significant behavioural evidence that bears upon this question. In a study of urban political participation in the US Berry, Portney and Thomson (1993) consider the increase in participation secured in five cities by efforts on the part of the local urban administration to increase popular involvement in the making of decisions. The five cities in question went to great efforts to involve their citizens in policy-making, devolving decisions to neighbourhood levels and creating a framework within which participation costs were reduced. When it came to comparing participation rates in these five cities with a sample of cities without the innovations, for the purposes of control, the study found very little difference in participation rates between those cities which had tried hard to increase participation and the control group with which they were being compared. Rates were simply low across all the sample (Berry, Portney and Thomson, 1993, pp. 73–81). There are many ways of interpreting such evidence, of course, but it is at least consistent with the claim that the opportunity cost in terms of time forgone of political participation is too great relative to the other activities in which people are involved.

If the production of impartiality is our concern, then obviously these opportunity costs of increased participation need to be set against the advantages that are claimed for participation. I do not know any empirical evidence that bears upon the question, but my own intuitive assumption (for what it is worth) would be that the gains in a sense of impartiality come pretty early in one's participation in decision-making. Thus, one does not have to spend very long on questions of public policy to realize that they are usually pretty complicated and seldom have solutions that do not require some balancing of interests. Repeated practice is unlikely to add very much to this sense, and for this reason we can expect rapidly diminishing marginal returns to increased participation.

Moreover, there are occasions when the opportunity costs of political participation can be pure loss. The sort of occasions I have in mind here are what might be called cases of 'defensive participation'. These are cases where one participates only to prevent other people damaging one's own interests. It is quite possible to find oneself locked into a series of meetings because you know that others whose interests are in conflict with yours will turn up and in your absence vote for something that is damaging to you. Unless we can be sure that the promotion of impartiality and a sense of common purpose will operate on every occasion in politics, such defensive participation is pure loss for all participants. All would be better off if none participated.

The argument for representation therefore is that citizens have a generalized interest in preserving time for the full range of activities in which they might engage, and direct democracies would erode that time. Budge (1996) argues, in favour of direct democracy, that modern communications technology renders this problem less serious than one might think. He points out that for many nowadays politics is a form of entertainment to be followed on the radio or television, and that the understanding issues is likely to arise as a by-product of following the news and current affairs that people will do anyway.

One important objection to this line of argument concerns the quality of the public debate that typically emerges from the modern forms of communication. I have said that one of the classical arguments for participation is to promote a sense of impartiality that will carry over into social life in general, but it has been urged that this can only arise if political decision-making involves deliberation, and intelligent deliberation is something that electronic forms of communication are not good at. So the implication of this view is that participation is desirable where there is an opportunity for deliberation, but it should not be pursued where deliberation is excluded (compare Fishkin, 1995, pp. 40–3). It is better in those circumstances to allow the deliberation to take place in a representative assembly.

However, at this point, the participationist can always reply that this is to make a false comparison, setting the probable functioning of electronic democracy against the ideal functioning of a representative system. In practice the quality of deliberation in a representative system is likely to depend upon such circumstances as the degree of partisanship, the historic traditions of parliamentary practice, the character of the issues being debated and the sense of responsibility of the representatives. Certainly, an Italian elector contemplating in recent years the inability of the parliamentary system to root out corruption might well be excused the thought that even a moderately well functioning system of electronic democracy would be better than a poorly functioning parliamentary system.

If time is an important consideration in the making of political decisions, the question will arise about the advantages of the division of labour in coping with the problems that shortage of time produces. Given the circumstances of political competition as I outlined them in the first chapter, the division of labour arises as a device for coping with limited attention spans and the general effects of bounded rationality. To complete a large collective task, it is partitioned among those who have to act, with each subset of participants assigned a limited role in the overall accomplishment of the task. One typical consequence of this is that few participants are likely to understand the overall process, or develop an ability to see the full implications of what they are doing.

The circumstances that give rise to these effects of bounded rationality are of particular importance in a democracy above a certain small size, since such systems will require full-time bureaucratic officials to run and implement the policies and programmes decided politically. Given the conditions of bounded rationality, such officials will come to have detailed knowledge of what they are doing. Unless they are confronted by political actors who are equally as knowledgeable, then their monopoly of information will undermine the scope for democratic control. But the most plausible way to confront this specialist monopoly of knowledge is to have political actors who themselves have sufficient opportunity to take advantage of the division of labour to acquire the specialist knowledge, and this in turn requires a system of political representation.

Hence, representation has the advantage over direct democracy that democratic authority can best be maintained in complex matters by representatives who themselves are able to challenge the specialism of unelected officials. This does not mean that they have to have the same degree of specialism as the officials (compare the way that well-trained barristers can often demolish so-called 'expert' testimony, even though they are not experts themselves). But it does require that they have the opportunity to acquire the relevant skills, and this can only come with time.

In commenting on this point, Ian Budge has pointed out to me that the argument from the division of labour, whilst it may be good against a Rousseauian conception of democracy, would still be consistent with the model of party-mediated direct democracy. Once political representatives had carried out their tasks of holding officials to account and reporting their opinion, the final decision on any matter could be put to the people, just as professional lawyers undertake the questioning in a trial, but the jury decides whether or not the defendant is guilty. This is of course true, if we think that the time cost of decision-making is primarily related to the tasks of assembling and presenting the relevant information. But there are also advantages arising from the division of labour to the people at large, since business can simply be remitted, as a whole, to political representatives. There are savings in time to be made from the need not to have to take a decision as well as from the need not to have to assemble and make sense of the relevant information. Moreover, the jury analogy is not entirely convincing, since the jury in a criminal trial is asked a very specific question about the guilt or innocence of the accused, whereas in matters of public policy the questions to be answered are rarely so well-defined.

Someone at this point might suggest that too much emphasis has been placed in the argument on what political arrangements are best for the general interests of citizens, rather than upon the role that the ideal of political equality plays in our concept of democracy. If we take the principle of political equality seriously, it might be argued, does this not imply a commitment to widespread political participation? Since no citizen is better than another citizen, according to the principle of political equality, no citizen should rule over another.

This argument moves too quickly, however. As I have defined it, the principle of political equality is that no one is to be assumed, *a priori*, to be more qualified for political decision-making than any

other. There is no privileged pool of people from who political decision-makers are to be recruited. Adam Smith was surely right to
insist that the difference of natural talents is in reality much less
than we are usually aware of, so that the 'difference between the
most dissimilar characters, between a philosopher and a street
porter, for example, seems to arise not so much from nature, as
from habit, custom, and education' (Smith, 1776, pp. 28–9).
However, equality, understood in this way, is quite compatible with
the acknowledgement that time and training is necessary to be
able effectively to challenge those who would otherwise have a
monopoly of information.

Indeed, there is an anti-participationist argument that could be
built upon the principle of equality, which runs as follows. If participation involves time, then political action is more costly, in
terms of opportunities forgone, to those who have less time. Such
people could include those with low productivity, who have to
work longer in order to secure any given income and who are
likely to be poor, and women, who may find the time costs of political participation more burdensome because of their commit-
ments to domestic responsibilities. Equal consideration of
interests, which is one of the goals of political equality, will be
more difficult to achieve in a participatory system, it may be
argued, than it would be in a representative system. Although in
principle a sound argument, this point runs up against the
difficulty that such empirical evidence as there is (for the US)
suggests that there is not so much difference in available time
between the rich and the poor as there is in the potential to make
financial contributions to political activity (Verba, Schlozman and
Brady, 1995, pp. 483–4), so it is difficult to see this argument carrying much weight in practice. However, it clearly might apply
under some circumstances and it shows how the principle of political equality cannot simply be used in a straightforward way to
justify increased political participation.

Finally, we have to consider the implications of the relationship between a participatory conception of democracy and a
belief in certain ideals of character. Ultimately, I suspect, at the
root of the participationist argument is an assumption that high
levels of participation connote excellence of character. As
Pericles said in the funeral oration reported by Thucydides's
Peloponnesian War:

'Here each individual is interested not only in his own affairs but in the affairs of state as well: even those who are mostly occupied with their own business are extremely well-informed on general politics – this is a peculiarity of ours: we do not say that a man who takes no interest in politics is a man who minds his own business; we say that he has no business here at all.' (Thucydides, 1954 edn, p. 147)

This conception of excellence of character, if it could be sustained, would of course trump the arguments about time and the division of labour that we have so far examined.

Clearly this is a perfectly coherent ideal of character and one for which I personally have a great deal of admiration. However, this is not of itself an argument for making it central to our conception of democracy, for it would make the appeal of democracy conditional upon a society having a certain sort of moral code. Consider a society, like that of Hong Kong, characterized by what Lau (1982, p. 72) calls 'utilitarianistic familism'. In this scheme of values a great deal of value is placed on the importance of individuals doing well by their own families: those who take an interest purely in their own business may have little interest in politics. To adopt as an ideal of character in a democracy a high level of public involvement is implicitly to say that such societies as Hong Kong are not fit for democracy of some sort. Of course, no democracy can exist unless its citizens are prepared to adopt at times an impartial attitude towards their own claims – even the claims of their families. But this is not to say that all well-functioning democracies have to rely upon Periclean ideals of character being widespread among citizens. Some moral codes will encourage participation whilst others will not, but that neither should be excluded from democratic practices.

So, although the arguments for increased participation are significant, they do not rule out a representative system of government as being legitimate. But what about arguments within the choice of representative system? The models described in chapter 2 and grouped together under the heading of representative systems are quite heterogeneous. There have been arguments advanced historically for favouring the least participatory of these alternatives. So we need to examine whether in adopting the principle of representation we are not taking on implicitly a series of arguments that would incline us towards one form of representation rather than another. If we favour representation, do we thereby favour its protective version?

From Representation to Constitutional Democracy?

The *locus classicus* in which to find arguments for the elite or pro-tective theory of democracy that might justify a constitutional conception of democracy is Joseph Schumpeter's *Capitalism, Socialism and Democracy* (Schumpeter, 1954). Although he does not cover all the arguments, and although some of the arguments he does cite could be better expressed, his approach has been widely echoed. The argument is often presented, as it was by Schumpeter himself, as being essentially based on considerations of feasibil-ity: elite accounts of democracy are supposed to be the only ones that can acknowledge the practical and political limitations that prevent increased popular participation. On this interpretation it will always be possible to counterpose the ideals of democracy with the practice, and to insist as did Duncan and Lukes (1963) on the impossibility of deriving an 'ought' from an 'is'. I think this interpretation substantially correct, but I should like to add one further element. It seems to me that the appeal to feasibility in Schumpeter can be treated as being within a tradition of moral discourse in which realism about what is possible is associated with the value of honest self-scrutiny, and I shall seek to bring out this element of the argument in my presentation of it.

Schumpeter's argument against increased public participation is part of his more general strategy to advance a protective theory of democracy (and of his even more general strategy of showing how centralized socialist planning might work in practice). The essence of his protective account, it will be recalled from Chapter 2, is that democracy is a method, rather than an ideal of political culture, in which certain individuals, rather than the public at large, acquire the power to decide on questions of public policy. Its principal mode of operation, therefore, is a competitive struggle for the people's vote and not discussion and decision among the people themselves. Schumpeter's contrast here is between what he calls 'classical' theo-ries of democracy and his own theory. Schumpeter's account of so-called 'classical' theory has been correctly characterized by

Plamenatz as 'ignorant and inept' with its being 'uncertain whom he is attacking, and even what beliefs he is ascribing to them' (Plamenatz, 1973, p. 96). Be that as it may, there is never any doubt what argument Schumpeter is making, even when it is aimed at a purely imaginary target.

There are in fact three arguments that Schumpeter uses against popular participation: the incompetence of typical citizens; the tendency to irrationality on the part of ordinary citizens; and the opportunities that public participation allows for special interests to pursue their own aims. Schumpeter expresses the first of these arguments as follows: 'the typical citizen drops down to a lower level of mental performance as soon as he enters the political field. He argues and analyzes in a way that he would readily recognize as infantile within the sphere of his real interests' (Schumpeter, 1954, p. 262). As this quotation makes clear, there is a theory of knowledge buried in the Schumpeterian arguments to the effect that it is only in the personal sphere that knowledge of one's 'real interests' is to be found. Indeed, Schumpeter makes it clear elsewhere that the key to knowledge of one's own interests is to be found in repeated exposure to relevant experiences. Yet, whatever the theory of knowledge in the background of the theory, its predictions about how citizens behave in political contexts seem open to empirical assessment.

The view that citizens drop down to a lower level of mental performance in politics than they display in their personal lives is, of course, the exact opposite of John Stuart Mill's assertion that political participation encourages prudence and impartiality. Clearly there is no knock-down evidence that one can point to by way of settling this dispute, in part because the evidence is not uniform and in part because there is an irreducibly evaluative element involved in assessing any evidence. However, it is possible to cite the evidence of opinion polls, which often show that, on complex issues of public policy, standards of rationality are low, with opinions being inconsistent and fluctuating randomly over time (the origin of this line of analysis being found in Converse, 1964). Such findings would appear to support the Schumpeter hypothesis. It is not a reply at this point to note that though, individual opinion fluctuates and often appears to move randomly, public opinion in the aggregate is more stable, and appears to move in rationalizable ways. That is simply to say that political systems are fortunate in being rescued from the consequences of the psychology that

Schumpeter posits. It does nothing to bestow that psychology with any claim to authority.

Against Schumpeter it might more plausibly be argued that the lower level of mental performance was an effect of the lack of opportunity to deliberate sensibly on matters of public policy. Downs (1957, part 3) speaks of the irrationality of being politically well-informed on the part of electors. With little influence on decisions about public policy arising from participation, individual citizens have little incentive to take an interest in acquiring the evidence and information that would raise the standards of their mental performance. Fishkin (1995, pp. 17–63) for example cites the problem of rational ignorance as being a reason for taking public opinion not from conventional opinion polling techniques, but from a deliberative poll in which sampled members of the public have an opportunity to hear arguments and evidence and deliberate among themselves about alternatives.

The second Schumpeterian claim is that 'even if there were no political groups trying to influence him, the typical citizen would in political matters tend to yield to extra-rational or irrational prejudice and impulse' (Schumpeter, 1954, p. 262). The implication is that the lower level of mental performance that citizens display in public affairs leads to patterns of irresponsible decision-making. This view is an echo not simply of eighteenth- and nineteenth-century fears of the 'mob', but of much longer lasting concerns, stretching as far back as Thucydides and Plato.

Here again empirical evidence is unlikely to be decisive, but it is suggestive. Cronin's (1989) review of the results of initiatives and referendums in the US does not suggest patterns of irresponsible decision-making, though this is not to say that all instances are without problems. Similarly, in the early experience of citizens' juries in the UK, where small numbers of citizens are exposed to information and evidence on a public policy topic and then asked to express their judgement, there is some evidence that juries can be particularly swayed by the personal testimony of one or two individuals, although the effect is not large. In general, most observers of citizen juries, however, have been impressed by the balance and reasonableness that jurors have brought to the task (on this, see Coote and Lenaghan, 1997). It is also an open question, of course, as to whether they would be more swayed than, say, a parliamentary committee within a representative system.

Schumpeter's third argument is expressed as follows:

'the weaker the logical element in the process of the public mind and the more complete the absence of rational criticism and the rationalizing influence of personal experience and responsibility, the greater are the opportunities for groups with an ax to grind' (Schumpeter, 1954, p. 263).

So, in the context of irrational public opinion, special interests are able to take advantage and press their own claims disproportionately. This point has been the stepping stone to a whole line of analysis in the public choice tradition that has sought to show how the public interest can be defeated by the greater activism of special interests and lobbies. The issues raised here are, however, complex, and we need to consider the logic and the plausibility of the argument in some detail.

The fear of special interests overriding a more general interest, like the fears about the irrationality and irresponsibility of the mob, has a long history. Interestingly enough, it was a prominent theme in the work of both Rousseau and Bentham, who might have as good a claim as any to be included as representatives of Schumpeter's classical theory. (This may simply show, of course, that Schumpeter was merely trying to argue from the premises of what he took to be the opposition.)

Within modern public choice analysis, there are good reasons, stemming from the theory of collective action, for thinking that the danger of special interest activity is a real one. The essence of the argument is to be found in a combination of Downs's (1957, p. 254) insight that people spend their money in many sectors of the economy but earn it only in one, and Olson's (1965) observation that groups with a small number of large members are much easier to organize for their common advantage than groups with a large number of small members. The implicit individual cost–benefit calculus that lies behind these generalizations is that for the individual the burdens of contributing time, effort or money to the activities of a group are unlikely to be recompensed profitably, since everyone gets the benefit, whether or not they have paid the cost. The implication is that geographically concentrated interests are likely to promote their interests more successfully than geographically dispersed ones, that industrial development to the profit of a few will predominate over environmental protection to the advantage of the many and that, in Adam Smith's memorable phrase, 'people of the same trade seldom meet together, even for merriment and diversion, but the conversation ends in a conspiracy against the public' (Smith, 1776, p. 145).

The problem of special interests is therefore one that should be taken seriously. The essential issue that arises in connection with Schumpeter's argument is whether the best way to counteract the privileging of special interests is by more public participation or by some other device. Schumpeter himself was critical of public participation because he thought that the irresponsibility and irrationality that it generated undermined the critical capacity of the political system to evaluate the arguments of special interest groups. But a negative argument is only as good as the alternative that it implicitly endorses, and so we need to examine what Schumpeter's alternative is to increased democratic participation, before we can evaluate what is being claimed.

In his own positive view of democracy, Schumpeter offers five conditions for democratic stability: there should be a high quality of personnel drawn from a social stratum for whom politics is a vocation, not a way of earning a living; the effective range of political decisions should not be stretched too far; the state should control a well-trained bureaucracy; the people should exercise democratic self-control and should not seek to be too much involved in the conduct of public affairs; and there should be tolerances of differences of opinion (Schumpeter, 1954, pp. 290–6).

Yet it is not clear that the assumptions necessary to sustain this alternative account are consistent with some of Schumpeter's more general views about politics. Consider his famous statement about dealing in votes:

> 'Politically speaking, the man is still in the nursery who has not absorbed, so as never to forget, the saying attributed to one of the most successful politicians that ever lived: "What businessmen do not understand is that exactly as they are dealing in oil so I am dealing in votes."' (Schumpeter, 1954, p. 285)

Schumpeter has an interesting footnote attached to this quotation. He suggests that although the sentiments expressed might seem to be cynical, there is no need to interpret them in that way. The point, he argues, is not to deny that motives of public duty and service operate in politics just as they do in the business world, but to assert that in explaining human action it is more productive to work with the assumption of self-interest. Businessmen are interested in things other than profit; but we none the less do as well as we can in explanatory terms in accounting for their actions in terms of the pursuit of profit. Similarly, politicians are interested in more than in gaining and holding on to office; but our explanations may be validly cast in terms of ascribing to them a motive for dealing in votes. In other words, according to Schumpeter, the assumption about motivation is not necessarily cynical; it is merely a methodological short-hand that we use in seeking to understand how the world works.

As an analytic device, the assumption of self-interest may have certain virtues (for example, simplicity in achieving a first approximation to an explanation), although it also undoubtedly has shortcomings, as attempts to understand even simple acts like the act of voting in self-interested terms fail, and appeal has to be made to a sense of civic obligation. However, I should like to suggest that there is an alternative interpretation of this approach in which ascribing self-interested motives is neither unduly cynical nor a mere methodological short-hand. According to this third interpretation, we should see the ascription of self-interested motivation as an attempt to render human activity open to serious moral scrutiny. There is a tradition of moral discourse (to be found in writers like Pascal and La Rochefoucauld) in which the need to be scrupulously honest about human motivation acquires considerable importance, and in which one of the greatest moral faults is a high-minded lack of honesty about the role of self-interest in human motivation. When La Rochefoucauld (1678, pp. 39 and 42) writes, for example, that the clemency of princes is often nothing but a policy to gain popular affection, or that our promises are made in proportion to our hopes, but kept in proportion to our fears, he is writing within this tradition. Moreover, within this tradition, an important strand is always to draw a contrast between the way that things seem and the way they are, and to point out that to confuse appearance and substance can lead to worse consequences than ignoring the discrepancy. On this interpretation, then, to see politics as a sphere of human activity in which self-interest has a powerful hold is not to abandon a political morality, but rather to adopt one form of political morality.

Putting the matter in this way in part rescues Schumpeter's account from the apparent inconsistency of both asserting the importance of self-interest and also asserting the importance of an ethic of restraint on the part of the populace. The argument then becomes a complex one to the effect that if a populace favours democracy as a form of government it should be honest and recognize that the best it is likely to do is to have a system in which there is still an admixture of considerable self-interest, but this fact alone should not lead to an abandonment of the principle of democracy. Instead, it should be seen as an honest recognition of the limits of human institutions.

This is, I think, a plausible reconstruction of the Schumpeterian position, which otherwise might seem to be involved in a straight contradiction. The difficulty is that without rather special empirical premisses, this line of argument is entirely neutral between the Schumpeterian/Whig account of political representation and more participationist accounts of representative government in which citizens are encouraged to articulate their interests through various participatory devices. After all, if self-interest is such a powerful motive, then a socially exclusive stratum is likely to find it difficult to escape from its operation. After all, in the late 1920s Hitler received money from industrialists with anti-democratic inclinations (Bullock, 1962, p. 149). So, on the basis of an assumption of self-interest, combined with suitable and quite plausible premisses, one can draw the opposite conclusion from Schumpeter, and assert that public decisions cannot be trusted to the hands of a small and socially unrepresentative elite.

Choosing among Systems

What conclusions are we entitled to come to on the basis of this review of the arguments for and against representation as opposed to participation? The first point arises from the discussion of feasibility, namely that it would be possible to increase substantially popular participation in the making of decisions in matters of public policy. The chief arguments against this derive from the advantages of the division of political labour in allowing citizens time to develop their other interests and in enabling elected representatives the opportunity to develop the skills and expertise necessary to challenge unelected public officials who would otherwise monopolize relevant knowledge.

These arguments concern the ways that members of a political community balance their competing interests against one another, when they consider themselves as partners engaged in cooperative action to promote common interests. There are thus no grounds of political morality on which it would be possible to say that a political community was wrong to adopt representative institutions so that its members could have more free time to do other things. By the same token, however, it is not possible to state a principle by which it would be wrong for the members of a political community to sacrifice a great deal of their other interests to achieve participation. I myself would not want to live in such a community, but that is a far cry from saying that it would be wrong to press for more participation. I simply think that, considering the all-round nature of potential human achievements, it would be a pity to sacrifice too much to the mundane business of politics. If we accept the case for a representative system of government, however, what form should it take? To that question I now turn.

6 Forms of Representation

If we accept that there has to be some division of labour in politics and that there are limitations to public participation in decision-making, then we need a theory of political representation. That is to say, we need an account of what representatives should do, what sort of people they should be and how they should discharge their duties. Representatives will undertake those tasks that citizens lack time or opportunity to undertake. But upon what understanding of representation should the design of a system of representative government be based? On the answer to this question hangs the issue of how we evaluate the competing models of indirect democracy that we have identified.

These various models of representative government were in part distinguished from one another by the extent to which they offered competing accounts of representation. Within the Westminster conception of democracy the emphasis was placed on the importance of governing political parties being accountable to the electorate. This in turn involved relatively few political parties competing for office, with parties in office enjoying the conditions that would enable them to govern effectively, in particular a secure parliamentary majority and control over the legislature. We can call this the 'responsible government' model of representation. In the representational model of democracy, by contrast, the emphasis was upon seeing the legislature as broadly representative of varieties of political opinion. In consequence, representational systems typically have a relatively large number of political parties competing for office, shared executive authority, broad representation on legislative committees and an emphasis upon compromise among competing opinions in the construction of governing coalitions. The distinguishing characteristics of these two conceptions, therefore, turn on the competing conceptions of representation that each contains. Moreover, it is clear that these conceptions are also related to the role that the electoral system is expected to perform.

As Lijphart (1994, p. 10) has noted, there is broad agreement among electoral system experts that the two most important dimensions of electoral systems are the electoral formula and district magnitude (that is the number of representatives elected per district). The two main varieties of electoral formula are the winner-take-all, first-past-the-post system and various systems of proportional representation. In the former, candidates win office by securing the single largest share of the vote, whereas in the latter candidates are elected in proportion to the votes they receive. However, it is also clear that the exact effects of the different formulae interact with the size of the typical district, with a larger district for example reinforcing the trend in first-past-the-post systems towards disproportionality. Thus, in the limit, in an at large election covering the whole country the simple plurality formula would give all the seats to the party with the largest share of the votes.

If we focus simply on the electoral formula, thinking of single-member district systems, then the 'mechanical effect' of the first-past-the-post system alone will create conditions in which there is a tendency towards the under-representation of smaller parties in the legislature. Moreover, there is also a 'psychological' effect arising from the desire of citizens not to waste their votes, which will reinforce the original mechanical effect (Duverger, 1964, pp. 216–28). Thus, a central feature of the responsible government model of democracy is the first-past-the-post electoral system in which winning parties acquire the right to govern, but are held accountable for their performance at election time. Conversely, the emphasis with the representational model of democracy on the importance of having a broad sweep of public opinion influencing the making of law and public policy is naturally associated with proportional representation schemes of elections, giving rise to the large number of political parties many of which will represent only small segments of public opinion.

The constitutional model of democracy shares with the Westminster model the notion that governing parties should be made accountable to the electorate, and in this respect the two models possess similar conceptions of political representation. Where they are likely to differ from one another is in relation to the interpretation of the act of voting. Proponents of constitutional democracy, like Riker (1982), criticize the Westminster model for resting on the false notion that it is possible to identify a popular will to which public policy should conform. Instead, according to Riker, the key function of elections is to provide the opportunity to 'throw the rascals out'. On this view, therefore, the electorate does not mandate a prospective political programme, but rather makes a retrospective judgement about the tolerability of past performance. The relevant notion of political representation is then one of retrospective accountability rather than of prospective accountability operating through the influence of the dominant strand of public opinion on the election of a governing party.

Although electoral laws are crucial in distinguishing different models of democracy, the evaluation of their relative merits in full raises more issues than can be considered here (see Grofman and Lijphart, 1986). Accordingly, rather than consider the case for and against proportional representation as such, I shall simply consider the merits of alternative views of political representation that fit, to some extent at least, different types of electoral law. It is clear that a general theory of political representation will have implications for the way in which we evaluate electoral rules, for on some accounts of representation the effects of the first-past-the-post electoral system are seen as desirable, whereas on other theories of representation the more broadly based view of representation is seen as preferable. But how far are we able to make a principled choice among the competing conceptions of representation?

Representing Interests, Opinions or Characteristics?

Before looking at competing conceptions of representation, it will be useful to consider the concept of representation itself. The general concept of representation is that one thing 'stands for' another. Contour lines thus represent hills, in the sense that they stand symbolically for the hills on the map. Similarly, plastic pieces on a board can represent armies, navies and the like. In cases where one physical system represents another, the only thing that needs to be established, by convention, is a one-to-one correspondence between selected elements of the represented system and the elements in the representing system that are designated to correspond. Provided we know that the lines are supposed to be contours standing for points of equal height above sea level on the land, we shall not mistake them for footpaths.

When we turn to representation in politics, however, the situation is more complicated, since the notion of 'standing for' is ambiguous. If we seek to remove the ambiguity, we can identify at least three different senses of representation. The first we can think of as 'standing up for', that is representing the interests, either of a constituency of electors or of the country as a whole. On this account of representation, for example, political representatives, like political parties, are seen to represent interests, and the model of the representative is assimilated to other examples where, according to the principles of the division of labour, somebody acts on our behalf, as when a lawyer represents us in a legal dispute.

The second type of political representation we can think of as 'standing out for' in the sense that a person might stand out for a particular belief or view. Here we have the notion of representation as being about the putting of opinions, rather on the model of someone who attends a meeting to put our point of view and vote on the business at hand.

Thirdly, we can think of representation as 'standing in for' in a strict statistical sense, and conceive of political representation not as something that is carried on by individuals, but rather as a feature of a certain sort of institution, one in which the composition of the institution mirrors society at large. If a representative body is an exact microcosm in this sense, it could be said to stand in for that which it represents.

It should be clear that these three conceptions of representation will not always coincide in their practical implications. The best advocate of an interest will not always be the person who is drawn from the most typical sample of a group. Indeed, if we are looking for vigorous proponents of our interests, we would rationally expect to find them among people who were rather untypical, for example with a higher propensity than average to be good bargainers. Similarly, those who are the best exponent of an opinion may not always be the best people to bargain over the compromises that are usually necessary in politics.

How then should we choose among these differing conceptions of political representation? It will highlight the issues involved in making this choice if we contrast the interest and opinion theories of representation with that of the mirror conception.

Suppose we wanted a parliament or legislative chamber to be a mirror or microcosm of the political community, and so be representative in that sense. The simplest way to do this would be to have a representative sample of citizens chosen randomly or by chance to stand for the community at large. Such a random sample would represent the range of major social characteristics (age, sex, occupation, race, religion, family circumstance and so on) that one finds in a community. Moreover, the members of such a representative sample would also be similar to the community at large in the sense that they could be expected to have a wide range of views about the importance of politics, whereas political representatives who compete for office in elections are presumably unrepresentative of the population at large in the interest they display for public affairs.

The notion that ordinary citizens, chosen by lot, should undertake major political tasks is an old one, and was an important part of the practice of ancient Athens. Indeed, Manin (1997) has argued that modern methods of election and principles of government by consent evolved from practices and theories that were originally opposed to democracy. When representative government came to replace direct democracy, there were still those who argued that the legislative body should be a microcosm of the community at large (see the anti-federalist arguments cited in Fishkin, 1995, pp. 60–3). More recently, Burnheim (1985, pp. 110–13) has argued for representation by randomly selected volunteers put in control of functionally specific organizations. Yet, what is striking about the notion of representation in this statistical sense is how distinct in logical terms it is from notions of representation resting on ideas of accountability or even the representation of political opinions.

In what sense would political representation be inadequate if we simply allowed a random sample of the electorate to stand for the whole? The most obvious source of inadequacy would be that there was no mechanism of accountability linking the representatives with those whom they are supposed to be representing. Since the standard form of accountability is given by teams of putative representatives standing as political parties and seeking office by standing for election, there would be little institutional capacity or incentive among randomly selected citizens to explain or account for their decisions. The price of social representativeness would be a loss of accountability. In being a substitute for the community, the sample would not have to be accountable to the community.

A parallel point can be made with respect to the representation of opinion. To represent an opinion is more than simply to hold an opinion. It is a process of engaging in argument, criticism and exchange of opinions with those who hold a different view. This too requires the organization of opinion into broader programmes or at least principled understanding of what is involved in politics. The organization of political opinion in the form of political parties certainly narrows down the range of views that are standardly expressed in politics, and in this sense politics is always the mobilization of bias. But it is this narrowing down of all the possible opinions that could be expressed that is the condition under which any coherent opinion can be expressed at all. One way of seeing this is to note the importance of political parties in reducing the weight of information with which the individual has to cope. The form of proportional representation favoured by J. S. Mill was the Hare scheme under which voters would be allowed to vote for any candidate who might be standing in the country. Clearly, under such a scheme, there could be hundreds of candidates, and it would be almost impossible for even a committed voter to make an intelligent choice among them. Since politics is about choice, this is a severe limitation, and so conversely the narrowing of the range of possible opinions by party systems should not of itself be considered a disadvantage.

Someone may urge at this point that accountability and the representation of opinion are unnecessary, since the microcosm of society that is the representative sample can simply stand for society as a whole. There simply would be no need for the members of the sample to explain their decisions to citizens at large, as current political representatives attempt to do, since the statistical basis of selection means that any decision that is taken just would, by definition, emerge from a body that was representative of society taken as a whole. The problem here is that such a body would be taking decisions not simply for itself but for society as a whole. Its choices would therefore be binding on those who were not party to the process, and it is difficult to see how those who were not party to the decision would feel obliged to accept it, if there were no explanation or account forthcoming at all.

If these arguments are right, they establish that, although political representation arises from the need for a division of political labour, its existence means that it is not purely a matter of the division of labour. Instead, its existence calls into being the need for distinct principles of evaluation and assessment. One of these principles concerns the extent to which the political system is representative in the sense of being authorized by the people. As well as 'standing for', in its three variants, there is also a sense of representation which is that of 'acting in the name' of someone, and in a democratic community such acting by one person in the name of someone else requires processes of authorization through mechanisms of accountability.

If we cannot see political representation on the model of a statistical sample, how should we assess the alternative competing models that stress, respectively, accountability for the representation of interests and the representation of opinion? As we have seen, this distinction is in turn related to the differences between the Westminster system, where the notion is that of responsible government, and representational systems in which a representative assembly is seen to contain a large number of political parties expressing a range of public opinion. Thus, in evaluating the competing conceptions of representation, we are in effect evaluating competing models of government.

In comparing these two conceptions of political representation, we need to look at a range of questions that are at issue between the two views. How far do we conceive of the activity of legislation as deliberation to a common point of view, versus bargaining to an agreed outcome? How far do interests, opinions and social characteristics coincide? What is the appropriate notion of accountability in looking at political representation? And how far should we aim at inclusive representation?

The notion that legislation is about deliberation to a common purpose was famously expounded in Burke's account of the function of the political representative. As Birch (1972, pp. 37–40) has pointed out, it was a Whig theory of representation that found clear expression in Burke's address to the electors of Bristol in 1774, when he said that representatives owed electors not merely their industry but also their judgement. On this account, representatives are not delegates, but persons whose function is to deliberate about the good of the whole. This view came to be widely accepted during the nineteenth century as stating the correct view of the functions of parliamentary representatives, as is partly illustrated by the fact that Sidgwick (1891), who was the epitome of progressive, but moderate, common sense, defended it in his account of democracy. Even Schumpeter can be read as endorsing something like this theory in his five conditions for democratic stability, identified in the last chapter: a high quality of personnel drawn from a social stratum for whom politics is a vocation; a small effective range of political decisions; state control of a well-trained bureaucracy; democratic self-control by the people; and tolerance of differences of opinion (Schumpeter, 1954, pp. 290–6). There are various ways of understanding these conditions, but taken together they bear a remarkable resemblance to the Whig theory of representation as it emerged in Britain in the eighteenth century.

If we take this line, it would seem that we have the rationale for either the Westminster or the constitutional account of democracy, but not the representational account. However, the jump to this conclusion moves a little too quickly. Burke in effect draws two contrasts: that between deliberation to a common good and the pursuit of interests on the one hand; and that between representatives as delegates and representatives as having some independence on the other. It is important not to confuse these two sets of categories if we are to understand their implications clearly.

It may seem that the representational theory of democracy went along with an interest bargaining account of democracy, but as I pointed out when discussing the models, all accounts in fact had to leave scope for deliberation. The notion that any democratic political system can simply operate without some internalization by major social groups of the common interest – even if that interest is only a high-level one in the maintenance of procedural rules for settling group conflicts – was seen to be a myth. Conversely, however, the notion that political decision-making can entirely dispense with bargaining, substituting only deliberations orientated towards the common interest, is also a myth. The practical context of political decision-making will impose constraints on how far political decisions can depart from the articulated interests of major actors. In short, all forms of representative democracy will have to perform both the deliberation function and the interest aggregation function.

Turning now to the second distinction, that between representatives as delegates and representatives as exercisers of independent judgement, we can also see that this does not map straightforwardly on to the different types of model of representative democracy. To be sure, it seems more plausible to think of representatives in the broadly based representational system as being delegates than it does in the Westminster system. After all, with a large number of political parties, each political party can be thought of as representative of a distinct segment of opinion, perhaps related to a particular interest or perspective of different social groups. With this institutional arrangement, it might then seem natural to think that constituents might wish to bind their representatives rather closely as delegates. However, such an approach does not seem to be *entailed* by a representational account of democracy. Constituents might hold that for a number of reasons it was better to allow their representatives some freedom of manoeuvre in order to achieve agreed goals. Thus, while it would be possible to hold a delegate view alongside a representation account, there is no logical necessity to do so. The merits of delegation, such as they are, are independent of the merits or otherwise of having representatives who are broadly reflective of the population in some sense.

However, someone at this point might argue for an asymmetry between the Westminster system and the representational system on the issue of delegation. There is this important difference between Westminster and representational systems: whereas, tight control cannot be exercised by electors over their representatives in the Westminster system, representational systems will at least allow, even if they do not require, the possibility of delegation. So, although it does not follow that a commitment to representational democracy is *ipso facto* a commitment to a delegate theory of representation, it is still true that if the delegate theory were the most plausible, then a representational system is the one that would be needed.

Are there independent reasons for having a delegate theory of democracy therefore? It is difficult to see that the case is a strong one if deliberation is to play a role in policy-making. A delegate goes to a meeting to state a position and register a vote, not to be influenced by the debate (compare Pitkin, 1972, p. 151). Once the notion of deliberation is introduced, it follows that representatives ought to be able to listen to what is being said, and make a final commitment in the light, partially at least, of the arguments that are advanced. At a more empirical level, it can also be argued that the closer systems approximate to ideas of delegation, the less good they are at dealing with the collective problems that legislation is needed for in the first place. King (1997) has shown, for example, that as US politicians have had to become more responsive to every modulation of their constituents' concerns, so their ability to deal with long-standing collective problems (economic policies, budget deficits and crime) has been undermined.

If the notion of delegation is not much help in choosing between competing models of representation, how far can we get by considering the distinction between interests and opinions? After all, one thing is clear in a democracy. There can be no ultimate distinction between the representation of interests and the representation of opinion. That is to say, whilst, given the division of political labour, political representatives will typically be more familiar with the considerations that bear upon the choice of political alternatives, the way in which they seek to advance common interests must be subject to a test of public opinion. Indeed, this requirement was built into our very definition of democracy.

If we allow that, even on an interest theory of representation, there has also to be a test of public opinion, then the choice of interests versus opinions in fact again relates to the question of how much latitude representatives should be allowed in the representation of their constituents' interests, and hence brings us back to the objections to a simple delegate account of representation.

However, we can go beyond this point, and say that if a democracy is founded on the idea that it is a mechanism of collective choice about common interests, then opinion should play a central part in our concept of representation. To put forward a conception of the common interest is to put forward a particular view or opinion. Naturally, in advancing an opinion, any elector or group of electors hopes that the view advanced will come to seem the right one. However, at the stage at which it is advanced, all such views will be one opinion among many. It might seem from this perspective that the representational view were more suited to this understanding that the responsible government model.

In fact, it is more difficult to move from considering the idea of democracy to favouring one particular account of representation than this argument suggests. It confuses a necessary condition for a practice with the most important feature of such a practice. It is certainly true that the test of public opinion is one that governments in a democracy need to face. But the form in which they should face it is not resolved simply by appealing to the bare idea of democracy. As I shall argue in the next chapter, in choosing between the different forms of representative government we are in effect choosing what meaning we assign to the notion of majority public opinion. Only when that argument has been developed shall we be in a position to choose between competing conceptions of representation.

In making notions of the accountability of governments and the representation of public opinion central to the idea of representation, I have contrasted what these notions share with the social characteristics view of statistical representation. However, at this point we meet the argument that the best people to express an opinion are those who actually share the social characteristics of those who are being represented. Does this lead us back to social characteristics and, if so, how?

Back to Social Characteristics?

I have argued that there are problems with the idea that it is only social characteristics that we care about in political representation, and that we need to insist that opinion is an essential element of democratic accountability. But to say that it is not only social characteristics that we care about is not to say that we do not care about social characteristics at all. There is a way of understanding opinion such that the best expressions of opinion will only come from certain sorts of people. If this is the approach taken, what is the implication for the relationship between the representation of opinion and the representation of social characteristics?

Clearly, the representation of opinions need not entail that those doing the representing share the same characteristics as those whom they represent. You do not have to be sick to speak up for those who favour more spending on hospitals, nor old to think that retirement pensions are too low. However, it may be that without there being some political representatives who share certain interests, certain points of view will simply be ignored. John Stuart Mill put the point well back in the 1860s:

'In this country, for example, what are called the working classes may be considered as excluded from all direct participation in government. I do not believe that the classes who do participate in it, have in general any intention of sacrificing the working classes to themselves ... Yet does Parliament, or almost any of the members comprising it, ever for an instant look at any question with the eyes of a working man?' (Mill, 1861a, p. 246)

Some years previously, Tocqueville had had a similar thought, arguing that though the ruling English aristocracy was perhaps the most liberal that had ever existed, under its government it 'cannot escape observation ... that in the legislation of England the interests of the poor have often been sacrificed to the advantages of the rich' (Tocqueville, 1835, p. 250). So while it may be true that to represent someone's opinions you do not have to share their social characteristics, there has to be some assumption that it helps to have patterns of political representation that broadly reflect that statistical distribution of politically salient characteristics in the population.

In effect, this is a sort of negative conclusion. It amounts simply to the thought that political representatives who are drawn exclusively from a limited social stratum are unlikely to be able to represent all points of view fully. In a way, it is a sort of protective argument, akin to our earlier assumption about political equality, that no one group of people can be guaranteed to be politically competent on behalf of others. Is it possible to go beyond this rather negative statement of the case to a more positive view, which says that there is a definite virtue in having a representative chamber that contains the representatives of a wide variety of social groups, and in that sense represents the distribution of social characteristics within the community? As Anne Phillips (1995) has put it: how far do we need to complement a politics of ideas with a politics of presence?

The question is pertinent because representative chambers are often highly unrepresentative in a statistical sense of the populations from which they are drawn: they are more male, better educated, from more prestigious and better paid occupations and older than the average. John Stuart Mill argued for the extension of the franchise to women and working-class men as a way of ensuring that certain points of view were articulated within parliament.

Subsequent experience would appear to show that the mere formal inclusion of groups in the process of electoral competition is insufficient to secure the representation of those groups in the process of legislation. Thus, even in systems of proportional representation, which are better than first-past-the-post systems at securing the presence of women in parliament, it has proved necessary to supplement the voting rules with rules about the party selection of candidates to increase the number of women MPs. Similarly, in the US redistricting has been necessary in order to ensure that African-Americans could be represented by members of their own ethnic group (Tribe, 1988, chapter 13). But, of course, these extra rules would only have a justification if there really were a case for the politics of presence.

One argument that can be advanced at this point that political presence may be necessary in order to establish a symbolic move away from exclusion. Seeing members of one's own social group participating as representatives in the process of government is a way of enhancing one's own sense of dignity and political status (Phillips, 1995, p. 40). Where previously social groups have been denied the vote or effective political representation, then it seems right that great importance is attached to members of those groups seeing people like them exercising political power.

Phillips cites three closely related arguments supporting this point of view. The first is that those representatives who share the social characteristics of their disadvantaged constituents are likely to be better advocates on their behalf, particularly under conditions of deliberation in which delegative mandates are weak or inoperative. The second is that such representatives are also needed to see beyond the limitations of the present political agenda, by raising issues that are not salient to those who are used to exercising political power. And the third is that groups need to be explicitly represented because the coalition of groups within political parties may form around clusters of opinions that are only partial.

An example may illustrate this last point. Suppose working men and women as a group share an interest in high standards of working conditions. They would naturally then support a political party that campaigned on that issue. However, they might not share opinions on another set of issues (say, abortion). Since a political party will only be built on a subset of opinions of its supporters, there will be issues that some supporters would like pursued but which will be marginalized or ignored by the party in question. Thus, any party mandate is partial, and group representatives are necessary to put the claims that would otherwise be ignored.

The logic here is that parties have to campaign on combinations of issues. But since there are many issues, and only few parties, the combinations of issues that are actually represented in the political system at any one time will only be a small subset of all the issues that could be represented. Political parties, even in representational systems where they may be present in relatively large numbers, will substantially narrow down the range of views represented, since political parties may be regarded as organized bodies of opinion. The only way to overcome this organizational bias, it is said, is to have broader group representation within political parties, say by a system of quotas.

Notice, however, that, though the above are arguments for a politics of presence, they are arguments for there being some representatives who share the social characteristics of the previously disadvantaged, not arguments for statistical representation in the sense we have previously discussed. Indeed, as Phillips (1995, p. 67) points out, the upshot of these arguments may well involve non-proportional representation in the statistical sense. Certain groups may be under-represented statistically in the population, but may still need to have threshold representation in the political process if the need for symbolic representation and associated advantages is to be addressed. If these arguments are accepted, they become reasons for favouring certain practices in the selection of representatives, most notably the use of quotas for women and ethnic minority groups in the selection of parliamentary candidates and the arrangement of districts in single-member constituency systems that ensure that certain designated groups are able to elect members who represent them in certain respects (on this see Rogowski, 1981).

The problem with these conclusions, as Phillips herself notes, is that such practices appear to cut across the formal principle of political equality, to the effect that members of all groups should compete for political office on the same terms. If political equality is to be taken seriously as a value, how is it possible to allow one group or set of groups an advantage in the selection of members? For example, if quotas for women are used in the selection of parliamentary candidates, does this not mean that men are placed at a disadvantage when they run for office, and, if so, is this unfair? In reply to these sorts of questions, Phillips argues that we ought not to take the principle of equality in an abstract way and that we cannot deduce a politics of presence directly from the principle of equality. Instead, 'the core of the argument lies in a more historically specific analysis of existing structures of exclusion and existing arrangements for representation' (Phillips, 1995, p. 31).

Let us agree that the formal interpretation of the equality principle is not much help here, as it is often not much help in many situations in which original disadvantage has to be overcome. Even treated as a procedural notion, the rule that everyone should be treated the same is at best a defeasible concept, which can easily be shown to be inappropriate given some initial inequality (Weale, 1978a, pp. 16–17). Where there is no clean sheet, clean sheet non-arbitrariness is not applicable. However, it is not clear that the relevant alternative is to place so much weight on the notion of 'an historically specific analysis', not least because no matter how historically specific one is, this will not decide the principles that should determine choice.

Suppose someone were to say that the objection to the practices implied by a politics of presence was that it violated a principle of impartial or non-arbitrary treatment. What could be the reply to this question? One obvious reply is that the practices were necessary to overcome existing discrimination or disadvantage. But one reply in turn to this view is that part of the lack of representation may arise from the failure of members of certain groups to put themselves forward, and that empirical research shows that there is less discrimination in, say, party selection procedures than the assumption appears to warrant. For example, Norris and Lovenduski (1993) show that it is supply-side factors (the absence of women putting themselves forward) rather than demand-side factors (prejudice and bias on the part of selectors) that accounts for the low number of women party candidates.

Would it follow from this observation that arguments from presence had no force? Arguably not. One could still hold that systems that promoted presence had advantages over systems that did not. To see how this might work, consider the following. Suppose we say, for all the reasons that we have already considered, that arguments connected with the politics of presence have force. This means that if a purely formal application of the equality principle was consistent with an adequate representation of some group, then we would count this a better situation than if application of the same principle led to less representation. But if representation of this sort has independent value, might it not lead us to modify the application of the purely formal equality test? Even if under-representation does not arise from discrimination, we could still judge it to be worth some sacrifice of the formal equality principle to achieve greater representation.

Why favour the representation of certain sections of the population over the proportionate representation of views that would be implied by a system that dispensed with any quotas or other special arrangements? One answer here is that it is people with interests that need the protection of the political system, not any particular set of political opinions. To be sure, if certain opinions were associated with certain groups, one would be concerned, according to the principle of equality, with the exclusion of that opinion, but this would logically seem to arise from a concern lest the interests of that group were being neglected.

Social disadvantage may be the relevant test here, but it does not have to be. One argument that bothers Phillips is what we might term the 'open-list' argument. If we make efforts to ensure that certain groups, like women and ethnic minorities, are included in the process of representation, what is there to stop us saying that people with red hair or blue eyes ought to be represented in their own right? But the answer to this question is that there is no plausible basis of interest on which such groups would organize politically, whereas the characteristics that have been picked out in quota systems for European political parties or applied in the case of congressional districting in the US do reflect clear sections of organized interests.

What is clear is that there is no single criterion of the form 'this group is identifiable by this test, therefore it ought to be represented', but this is true given the nature of the argument. Consider a parallel case. Suppose we thought that there was a public interest in having more people with a training in the natural sciences in the legislature. We might have a number of reasons for thinking this, and we might also note that at present natural scientists are under-represented. Should we be worried by the thought that someone else might point out that water engineers, rat catchers and dentists were also under-represented? After all, there is no general criterion that distinguishes the one group from the others, except a substantive judgement in each case about the contribution to public deliberation that each group could make.

Moreover, the argument about the representation of specific groups is as much related to concerns about diversity as it is to concerns about disadvantage. One reason for this is that the disadvantage argument would seem to imply only a limited period of time within which rectificatory measures should be taken. If the presence of certain types of representatives is justified in terms of overcoming historic disadvantage, then after a period, which may extend over some time of course, it would seem logical to remove the policy of preference as the legacy of disadvantage is worked out of the system. However, where there are distinct social groups, whatever their relative position in relation to others, then there appears to be a case for a policy of distinct representation.

Conclusions

Where do these arguments leave us in terms of the competing theories of representative government with which I started this chapter? I have argued that a theory of representation cannot simply be based on the notion that key political decision-makers should be statistically representative of the community of which they are a part. Political representatives must also stand in a relationship of accountability to those whom they represent, as well as exercising deliberative skills and engaging in the development of political principles and policy positions.

However, although simple statistical representation is not enough, too narrow a social composition among representatives is unjustified. In part, this is for protective reasons: members of unrepresented groups have their interests undervalued or ignored. Just as important, however, is the symbolic affirmation of political equality comprised in a system of representation that is not exclusive. Moreover, insofar as interests and opinions run along the same lines, considerations of both protection and equality would suggest what Steiner (1971, p. 63) has called the 'proportional' principle of representation, namely that all groups should influence a decision in proportion to their numerical strength. The one caveat to this conclusion is the recognition that some very small groups may need to be over-represented in order to exercise fair influence.

The proportionality principle contrasts, of course, with the Westminster pluritarian principle, based on a winner-take-all conception of political power. In practice, the sharp edges of this principle have often been blunted in the UK through such extra-electoral devices as broad political representation on various advisory or consultative bodies. When these modifying conventions have been absent in the Westminster system, however, the results have been disastrous, as the experience of Northern Ireland goes to show, where the history is one in which neither protection nor equality has been guaranteed to all citizens.

However, although there is a strong case from first principles for a proportional notion of representation, it is by no means absolute. Broad proportionality is at odds with accountability, as critics of coalition government have often alleged (for example, Downs, 1957, pp. 146–56). Moreover, there may well be circumstances in which the political fragmentation that proportionality induces threatens the functional effectiveness of the political system, as was arguably the case with the Fourth French Republic during the war in Algeria or with Italy throughout the post-war period. Even so, it seems plausible to suggest that some principle of proportionality be used in extra-electoral contexts at least.

7 Unanimity, Consensus and Majority Rule

Democratic political action is collective action. This means that it is both about determining the collective conditions of a society and about making choices binding on all in connection with those conditions. However, under the circumstances of politics I identified in chapter 1 (partial cooperation and conflict in situations of confined generosity and bounded rationality), these choices will exhibit difference and diversity. Even with goodwill and social awareness, citizens are likely to disagree in their political opinions and judgements. Differences of interest as well as of perception and values will lead the citizens to divergent views about how to direct and use the organized political power of the community, in order to promote and protect common interests. If political representatives reflect this diversity, then there will be as much disagreement in the legislature as there is in the population. At both the level of citizens and of their representatives we have the problem of how disparate views are to be aggregated into the single choice that governments must make.

In standard analyses of this problem, such differences of view are often called 'preferences'. This is an unfortunate term. It suggests that the problem of aggregation is one about how to satisfy conflicting wants. In some social situations, thinking about the problem of aggregation as one about satisfying wants makes a great deal of sense. If you and I are going out together to eat, and I know you like traditional food but hate nouvelle cuisine, whereas I am happy with either, then there is a clear case for giving you a veto on where we go, because your want satisfaction would be much lower than mine if the wrong choice is made. As Peter Jones (1988) has pointed out, however, it is a mistake to regard political choice in this way. Political choice is more like a jury deciding whether the verdict should be innocent or guilty than it is like satisfying

124

competing wants within a group. Certainly within a theory in which citizens are thought of as having to make decisions on matters of common interests, we are better thinking of their views or opinions as judgements rather than as the expression of their own wants (compare Sunstein, 1991, pp. 6–14).

Despite the force of this argument, the notion of preferences has found a place in the literature on aggregation, and it is difficult to avoid, particularly when we consider the possibility that people may be able to rank-order their views across a range of alternatives. In what follows, therefore, the term 'preferences' will sometimes be used, but it should be taken to mean the ordering of alternatives according to some standard of value that citizens or their represent-atives advance in the process of political choice.

The most common rule of aggregation is majority rule, which makes the collective choice depend upon the agreed view of a majority of those voting. However, many institutions of govern-ment use other rules of social choice. One modification is to have weighted majority voting, so that some voters are given more influence than others. For example, in the EU's Council of Ministers, the votes of each minister are weighted by a formula related to the population size of each member state. Another variant is to use super-majorities, in which the criterion is not a simple majority of those voting but some specified proportion above the simple majority. The Council of Ministers also incorporates this modification by requiring a super-majority of the weighted votes to adopt a policy. Finally, among many other possibilities, one could require a rule of unanimity, so that all those affected by a policy had to agree to its implementation before it was adopted. This is the rule adopted by some religious groups in the making of decisions as well as by many radical communitarian groups. It is also, in effect, the rule at work in the standard form of international agree-ments. The unanimity rule is thus invoked in a variety of circum-stances, and as Mansbridge (1980, pp. 252–69) has pointed out, it can thus be an expression of social unity or a device of self-protection.

The normative issues raised by the problem of aggregation are essentially concerned with assessing the merits of rules like unanim-ity and the majority principle. They also involve the question of whether we can meaningfully speak of a 'popular will'. On some theories of democratic government, the function of government is to enact the popular will. In terms of the models we are discussing, this idea is at the heart not only of direct accounts of democracy but also of representational and Westminster models of democracy. However, the claim that democracy requires a notion of the popular will has not gone unchallenged. In a famous passage Schumpeter wrote in criticism of what he termed the classical doctrine of democracy:

> 'There is, first, no such thing as a uniquely determined common good that all people could agree on or be made to agree on by the force of rational argument. This is due not primarily to the fact that some people may want things other than the common good but to the much more fundamental fact that to different individuals and groups the common good is bound to mean different things.' (Schumpeter, 1954, p. 251)

Schumpeter went on to argue that in the absence of a definite determination of the idea of the common good, the notion of a general will collapses and that though we may detect a common will or expression of public opinion 'from the infinitely complex jumble of individual and group-wise situations, volitions, influences, actions, reactions of the "democratic process," the result lacks not only rational unity but also rational sanction' (Schumpeter, 1954, p. 253). The inference was clear. We cannot use the idea of the popular will to form the basis for government action and public policy. A theory of democracy should therefore fulfil the negative function of protecting citizens from the tyranny of government abuses of power through the mechanism of political competition, and not the positive function of implementing or responding to popular opinion. In such protective theories of democracy there is typically a great emphasis upon what we can call counter-majoritarian constitutional mechanisms (for example, constitutional restrictions on legislative decisions) that limit or slow down the implementation of majority views. If the constitutionalist case is pursued to great lengths, it can lead to a position requiring the principle of unanimity before any political decision is made. Is the logic of this position justified?

The Principle of Unanimity

Some theories of constitutional government urge very strict limits on the operation of the majority principle. The worry is that

majorities represent only sectional interests, and will pursue policies at odds with the public interest. Using super-majoritarian
devices is seen as a way of constraining this sectional interest. For
authors like Buchanan and Tullock, the principle of unanimity is
the obvious way of preserving individual freedom from majority
coercion: in one sense it makes the collective choice voluntary
(Buchanan and Tullock, 1962, p. 90). Unanimity can thus be urged
as a principle of collective choice on grounds of freedom. The fundamental idea is that if decisions are taken according the principle
of unanimity, then individuals will not be coerced into public
policies with which they fundamentally disagree or which impose
disproportionate costs on them.

Despite this rationale, there are some obvious problems with
using unanimity as a principle of decision, which include the following: it is time-consuming to implement, thus raising the transaction costs associated with decision-making; it privileges the status
quo; it can lead to 'pork barrel' politics; and it is difficult to believe
that preference convergence will take place, so that everyone will
agree after discussion (compare Rae, 1975). Buchanan and Tullock
(1962, pp. 97–116) acknowledge the problems of decision costs
associated with this position, and argue in favour of various super-
majoritarian rules as a second-best. But it is clear from their discussion that the unanimity principle is still the position that is
normatively the ideal.

The problem with the line of argument is a familiar one, however,
namely that super-majoritarian systems create their own decision-
making pathologies. The most important of these is a tendency
towards 'pork barrel' allocations in public finance, by which spending
is concentrated upon certain groups in the population above some
notional optimal level, because that group can veto any change. Tax
loopholes, subsidies to 'strategic' industries and price supports to
farmers provide examples of such pork barrel expenditures.

In their discussion Buchanan and Tullock confuse this issue, by
suggesting the opposite, arguing that the pork barrel is a phenomenon of majoritarian politics. The plausibility of the argument was
not helped by the fact that such empirical support as Buchanan
and Tullock bothered to muster came from the United States,
which is hardly a paradigmatic example of a majoritarian system.
However, more important than this point is the fact that on theoretical grounds the expectation that majoritarian systems will

produce the pork barrel seem ill founded, as Brian Barry pointed out many years ago: 'The nearer a system comes to requiring unanimity for decisions, the more prevalent we may expect to find the "pork barrel" phenomenon' (Barry, 1965, p. 317). The argument here is that with perfect information and low transaction costs, rational egoists have an incentive to misrepresent their preferences to get the bribe of coming in late, and under imperfect information, log-rolling will produce specific and visible benefits since these are the items that are traded.

Inductive support for this general theoretical line comes from Scharpf's (1988) analysis of the 'joint decision trap'. The joint decision trap arises when there have to be a range of different actors, amounting to more than a majority, to agree to a measure in order for it to pass. Buchanan and Tullock's expectation that such super-majoritarianism will reduce exploitation and over-expenditure ignores the fact that there may already be a built-in dynamic towards certain forms of expenditure within the political system. As Scharpf points out, an example of just such a built-in dynamic is provided by the Common Agricultural Policy of the European Union. The virtual unanimity rule that has operated in this area has made it extremely difficult to reform the system, even when it was clear to informed observers that it was producing unwanted surpluses at high prices. As long as a minority of countries could use their effective veto to block reform, the pork barrel could not be eliminated.

Super-majoritarian justifications have not always turned on questions of public expenditure, however. The most notorious case is the claim for super-majoritarianism to protect the 'peculiar institution' of slavery in the southern states of the ante-bellum US. In this case, Calhoun (1853) argued for a system of 'concurrent majorities', by which a majority of every state in the union would have to vote in favour of a constitutional change for it to be legitimately adopted. There is no argument in democratic theory for such a proposition within a system like that of the US in which the federal government has direct powers over citizens. True, such arrangements may protect historically negotiated compromises in the formation of federal unions, but the proposal for such protection is simply a way of preventing a change that is not only called for by considerations of justice, but also pose a direct challenge to democratic values.

So far I have taken the unanimity principle in the version in which it is motivated by a distrust of others. However, following Mansbridge, we can also think about it as an expression of social consensus. I delay discussion of the merits of this view, however, until after considering some of the advantages and problems associated with the simple majority principle.

The Properties of Majority Rule

Of the conceptions of democracy I identified in chapter 2, all but the liberal constitutionalist suppose that the proper principle of collective choice is that the will of the majority should prevail on matters of public policy, usually across a wide range of issues. Is this just an intellectual curiosity or can it be given a principled rationale? Here it is useful to turn to the results of social choice theory (compare Ackerman, 1980, pp. 277–93).

Kenneth May (1952) has shown that the simple majority principle can be characterized in terms of a few logical properties. It is the only principle of collective choice to be simultaneously universal, positively responsive, anonymous and issue neutral. A universal rule is one that is able to deal with all preference orderings. A positively responsive rule is one that makes a collective choice in favour of an alternative more likely as opinion moves in favour of that alternative. However, the important conditions within the present context are neutrality and anonymity, both of which need some explanation.

Issue neutrality means that no one person's conception of the good weighs more heavily in the balance than any other person's. If I favour the public subsidy of pushpin over poetry for low-minded reasons of the fun that pushpin gives, and you favour the public subsidy of poetry over pushpin for the high-minded reasons of the qualitatively superior pleasures that poetry prompts, our preferences will be counted equally. More importantly, majority rule will operate in exactly the same way no matter what the type of issue is that is being considered. The counting of votes in a referendum over whether or not to require dog owners to hold dog licences will be exactly the same as the counting of votes in a referendum as to whether or not to phase out nuclear power, despite the obviously greater significance of the latter vote than the former. I take this property to imply that when we are using majority rule, we are prepared to accept that the decision could go either way and that we do not think of it as an issue that raises problems, for example, about the basic human rights of minorities.

The property of anonymity is more important, however. Anonymity means that no one person's preferences weigh more heavily in the balance because of who that person is. In other words, if we simply swop the names of individuals leaving the preferences intact, then the collective choice will remain unaffected. The views of dockers and dustmen thus count the same as those of dukes and directors. In a sense, we can say that anonymity embodies the principle of democratic equality, at least if that means everyone should count for one and no one for more than one. Since the majority principle is the *only* decision rule to satisfy all four conditions, including anonymity, we seem to have some ground for saying that its widespread adoption in different conceptions of democracy is more than an accident.

It can be argued, however, that thinking about majority voting as an expression of the principle of equality is misleading, because it ignores what can happen over a sequence of votes. Peter Jones (1988) asks us to consider three votes on three issues, where in each case the same two-thirds majority lines up against the same one-thirds minority. Considerations of fairness and equality might suggest a proportionality principle, by which the one-third minority secured its preference on one-third of the votes. In principle, where there are such persisting cleavages, the proportionality principle seems unassailable, viewed from the viewpoint of fairness, and indeed in consociational systems it is often implemented either in the way that resources are allocated or in terms of the rotation of office holders (compare Steiner, 1971). However, that still leaves the problem of why we should ever prefer the rule of the majority and as I shall seek to show in what follows, the problem is that all too often it is difficult to know what the majority view is at all.

To place this problem in context, consider the straightforward case of a binary choice, where it is a matter of whether a set of voters is in favour or opposed to an alternative. In this case the principle of majority rule gives a clear result. Many people have thought that such situations were typical of politics. Schattschneider (1960), for example, thought that the tendency of people to gather round one of two parties was quite natural, just as it was natural for people to take sides in a fight. In a slightly more high-minded way, Macaulay (1906, p. 82) traced the origins of the two parties in the Westminster system back to opposing tendencies in human nature, one favouring change and innovation and the other favouring conservatism. Yet, despite this impressive support, it is clear that there are often choices in politics that cannot be represented in a simple binary way, and the question is what implications this has for our understanding of majority rule.

In order to examine this question, and the normative and logical problems to which it gives rise, I shall work with a simplified example. I shall assume, in particular, that the members of a community are divided over two sets of issues. One set of issues concerns the extent of government intervention in society and the economy to maintain a 'welfare state', where some people are in favour of an extensive welfare state whilst others are against. The second set of issues concern nuclear power. Here too people can be grouped into two broad camps: those who favour nuclear power and those who do not.

Suppose, then, for the sake of simplicity, that the members of society can either be for or against a 'welfare state' or for or against 'nuclear power'. Suppose also that opinions on these two sets of issues are not perfectly correlated, so that, for example, some who are in favour of the welfare state are also in favour of nuclear power, whilst others who are in favour of the welfare state are opposed to nuclear power. Similarly, some who are in favour of nuclear power are also in favour of the welfare state, whereas some of those opposed to nuclear power are also opposed to the welfare state. There are thus four logically possible political positions that members of the community can adopt: pro-nuclear power and pro-welfare state; anti-nuclear power and pro-welfare state; pro-nuclear power and anti-welfare state; and anti-nuclear power and anti-welfare state. Imagine, for the sake of the example, that the members of the community are divided among these alternatives according to the distribution of their first or ideal preferences as given in the matrix in Table 7.1. We can think of the cell entries either as party positions in a legislature or as the proportions of the electorate who support each of the positions.

Table 7.1   *Two-Dimensional Political Choice*

Welfare State

		For	Against	
	For	*w* (25)	*y* (40)	65
Nuclear Power				
	Against	*x* (30)	*z* (5)	35
		55	45	100

Party A (25 per cent): *w x y z*
Party B (30 per cent): *x w z y*
Party C (40 per cent): *y w z x*
Party D (5 per cent): *z x y w*

We can also suppose that members of a political community can identify not only their first preference for public policy measures but also second and subsequent preferences. These lower ranked preferences become important, for example, when parties are contemplating with whom they might form parliamentary coalitions, or voters are wondering whom to vote for when a candidate of their first preference party is not standing in an election. In Table 7.1, in addition to the matrix of ideal positions, I have also set out an hypothetical set of preference orderings over all four logical alternative positions for all four imagined political groupings. (It should be noted that there are many more logically possible orderings than those represented – but I have simply put down four for the sake of simplicity.)

When considering political preferences over two alternatives, we are able to assume that one of the alternatives secured a clear majority (at least 50 per cent plus one) over the other. In such a case the principle of majority rule could be given a clear meaning. Of course, there might be moral or practical objections to what the majority wants, but at least it would be clear what it was that the majority wanted. Once we consider three or more alternatives, however, this supposition breaks down as a general rule, as illustrated in the example in Table 7.1, where no one political grouping contains a clear numerical majority. Although party C represents 40 per cent of the political community, and it is therefore the single largest grouping, it is obviously not a majority in a straightforward sense. How then, if at all, can we give sense to the idea of majority rule in this sort of case? The question is not an idle one. In parliamentary systems of government no political party typically wins as much as 50 per cent of the vote, and in countries like the UK, where single-party government is the norm, no government elected since 1935 has rested upon the support of at least 50 per cent of the those voting.

Two criteria have been most commonly offered in response to this dilemma (Dahl, 1989, pp. 144–6): the plurality rule and the principle of the Condorcet-winner (named after the Marquis de Condorcet, a distinguished eighteenth-century theorist of voting – see McLean and Hewitt, 1994). Of the two, the plurality rule is the simpler to explain, since it merely substitutes the concept of the single largest group for that of the majority. Thus, in the example, party C with 40 per cent support within the community would be regarded as the majority alternative. Although the combination of nuclear power and opposition to the welfare state does not secure a numerical majority in the population, many people would regard it as the next best thing to a simple majority. Indeed, in the UK where candidates are elected on the first-past-the-post rule 'the support of a plurality of voters for the government party is taken as the expression of the popular will' (Hofferbert and Budge, 1992, p. 152).

The alternative option is to take the Condorcet-winner as the majority preference. The Condorcet-winner is that alternative that could defeat every other alternative in a pair-wise contest. If we take the preference profile recorded in Table 7.1 and consider the orderings by the different political groupings, we can see that the Condorcet-winner is position w rather than position y. When considered against w, y is defeated by a majority, since parties A and B (representing 55 per cent of the community) prefer w to y, whereas only parties C and D, representing 45 per cent of the community, prefer y to w. Similarly, w is preferred to x by a majority (65 per cent to 35 per cent) and w is preferred to z by an even larger majority (95 per cent to 5 per cent). Hence, w is the only alternative that can beat each of the other alternatives when placed against them in pair-wise comparison.

From the example in Table 7.1, it is clear that the plurality principle and the Condorcet-winner principle can yield conflicting and
discrepant conclusions in those cases where there is no alternative
that commands a clear numerical majority. Are there any reasons
for favouring one principle rather than the other?

At first sight it might appear that there was an advantage in the
plurality principle. One argument in its favour is that it is relatively simple to operate with, since we can normally identify in a
straightforward way the largest group from a set of groups each of
whose members has ideal preferences. By contrast, the criterion of
the Condorcet-winner would seem to require us to know something
about second and third preferences as well as ideal preferences. So,
if simplicity is an important test, then there is something to be said
for the plurality principle.

A further reason for the plurality rule stems from the relative
sizes of the four political groupings. A plurality is just the largest
grouping around an ideal preference. With four alternatives this
could be as small as 25 per cent plus one, with five alternatives 20
per cent plus one and so on as the number of alternatives increases.
Nevertheless, no matter how small it gets, the plurality will always,
by definition, contain the single largest grouping of the electorate.
There is no equivalent guarantee with the Condorcet-winner. In
the example in Table 7.1 the Condorcet-winner is the ideal preference of only the third largest group. If one feels uneasy about
allowing 40 per cent of the population to decide a series of issues,
should one not feel much more uneasy with adopting the preference of only 25 per cent of the community? Indeed, the problem is
even more serious than this example would suggest. It is logically
possible, under some circumstances, that the Condorcet-winner
was that alternative that was the ideal preference of no one at all!
So, if one has doubts about allowing that minority which is the plurality determining the collective preference, it seems as though
these doubts would be overwhelming were one to follow a rule that
selected that alternative that was favoured by no one at all.

Despite appearances, this last point can be turned to the advantage of the Condorcet rule. Consider the following question: how
does it come about that an alternative less popular in absolute terms
than the plurality ideal preference can nevertheless be a Condorcet-
winner? The answer to this question is that where there are more
than two alternatives the Condorcet-winner is that alternative

around which a majority of people in the community are most able
to compromise given that others in their political community have
differing preferences. Where there is no majority ideal preference,
the plurality winner is that alternative that can secure the single
largest group of supporters, but there is no guarantee that the plurality alternative offers a balanced compromise for the majority.
Indeed, under the plurality rule a reasonably large and fanatical
minority may well be able to impose its will against the opposition
of a clear majority. Thus, in Table 7.1 the majority against y and in
favour of w is fifty-five to forty-five, but the simple plurality rule
will secure the choice of y. Even in the extreme case where the
Condorcet-winner is the ideal preference of no member of the community, it will still typically represent the agreed-upon second-best
of a majority who are otherwise antagonistically opposed on their
first preferences. Hence, given the existence of preference diversity, the Condorcet-winner may be said to be that alternative
around which a majority of the electorate can converge once they
realize that not everyone can secure his or her ideal preference,
and that some give and take is necessary.

However, the question of simplicity is still left. The plurality rule
requires relatively little information to implement. All we need
know are the relative sizes of the political groupings united by their
ideal preferences. The Condorcet criterion, by contrast, appears to
be more demanding in informational terms, since it requires
knowledge of complete preference rankings rather than an indica-
tion of most preferred alternatives. Yet here too appearances are
deceptive. It is possible to identify the Condorcet-winner without
requiring information on complete preference orderings for
members of a political community. If we take a majority vote on
each issue separately, then the Condorcet-winner will be found by
taking the intersection of the majority preferences in each issue
dimension.

The simplest way to see this is by considering the example in
Table 7.1. If we allow the voters or their representatives to vote in
sequence on the two sets of issues, then the combined consequences of that vote (known technically as the issue-by-issue
median, see Ordeshook, 1986, pp. 245–57) will coincide with the
Condorcet-winner. Thus, in Table 7.1 65 per cent of those voting
are pro, rather than anti, nuclear power, so taking a majority on
the nuclear power issue alone will lead to a collective preference in

favour of nuclear power. On the second dimension, since 55 per cent are in favour of the welfare state, that too would be the majority outcome. Putting both these votes together to form the issue-by-issue median will lead to w (the alternative that combines nuclear power and a strong welfare state), which is of course the Condorcet-winner. Hence, the Condorcet-winner will be chosen by the issue-by-issue median, which may be defined as that alternative that would be chosen by a sequence of votes on the majority principle in each of the relevant dimensions of choice.

This association between the issue-by-issue median and the Condorcet-winner is not accidental: indeed, there is a logical connection between them. A Condorcet-winner is defined as that alternative that can beat all others when pitched against them in pair-wise comparison. If the issue-by-issue median did not coincide with the Condorcet-winner, that would mean that, in some dimension of collective choice, a majority of voters would prefer an alternative which lacked one of the essential properties of the Condorcet-winner. But, if that were to happen, the putative Condorcet-winner would no longer be able to beat it, and so it would not be the Condorcet-winner. Hence, there is a contradiction in supposing that the issue-by-issue median and the Condorcet-winner do not coincide. Put another way, issue-by-issue voting separates all the alternatives into sets by reference to whether their separate features (for example, attitudes on nuclear power or the welfare state) are preferred by a majority or not. The intersection of these majority preferred sets defines the issue-by-issue median.

Implicit in this coincidence of the issue-by-issue and the Condorcet-winner is the requirement that the different dimensions of each alternative are separable from each other. Separability here means that the choice in one dimension does not depend upon the choice made in another dimension. A simple example with which to illustrate this condition is provided by altering slightly the dimensions of choice in Table 7.1. Suppose that one dimension remained the welfare state, but the other dimension involved not nuclear power policy but a choice between high and low taxation. It is quite possible that issue-by-issue voting would lead to that alternative representing the combination of a strong welfare state and low taxation. Although not contradictory in strict logic (since someone might hold that public expenditure savings to maintain low taxation could be secured from elsewhere – perhaps nuclear power), there is clearly a pragmatic contradiction between these two positions. Each choice has in practice implications for the other, so that treating them separately neither makes sense in itself nor could it be expected to lead to an alternative preferred by a majority when placed against all others in pair-wise comparison.

The conclusion I derive from the above arguments is that, if we have to choose between the simple plurality criterion and the Condorcet-winner, then the latter has a better claim to represent the idea of majority preference, when there is no outright numerical majority, than the former. It both captures the idea of a majority converging around a compromise solution where there are divergent ideal preferences and it can be construed as the outcome of a procedure by which members of a political community take issues one by one (where it is sensible to do this). However, there is one other consideration relevant to choosing between these two criteria which leads us into complex considerations. This is the question of whether we can always identify either the plurality winner or the Condorcet-winner, and this in turn depends on whether each always exists. Clearly a plurality winner will always exist, since, in any group of people distinguished into sets by reference to their ideal preferences, there will always be a largest group (except in the trivial case where two or more groups are of exactly equal size). The same cannot be said of the Condorcet-winner, however, and in the next section we explore the ramifications of that fact.

Condorcet Cycles and the Paradox of Voting

When there are three or more alternatives a Condorcet-winner may not exist under the rule of majority voting. An example of how this might arise is shown in Table 7.2. This adapts the example from Table 7.1, but assumes that there is a different distribution of preferences. With this preference profile there is no Condorcet-winner. This can be checked by considering a sequence of pair-wise votes: w will be preferred by a majority to both x and y, but it will not be preferred by a majority to z, even though both x and y are also preferred by a majority to z. Hence, the outcome of a sequence of pair-wise votes is not a unique winner but a cycle, as w beats x, which in turn beats y, which in turn beats z, which then beats w.

Put another way, for any alternative that may be selected, there is bound to be some other alternative that beats it in a pair-wise comparison. If there are good reasons, as I argued in the previous section, for taking the Condorcet-winner as the second-best alternative to the straight application of the majority principle where there was no outright winner, then they seem entirely to lose their force in the present case, since the phenomenon of majority rule cycling deprives one of any sense of what the majority collective preference might be. In any particular case where one would take a vote, the outcome seems only to depend on the arbitrary fact of the point at which the voting stops. This problem of the absence of a clear winner with three alternatives is known as Condorcet's paradox, to recognize Condorcet's discovery of the problem (see McLean and Hewitt, 1994, pp. 40–2).

It is worth noting in this connection that the preferences of individuals may be perfectly coherent, even when there is cycling at the collective level. Looking at the ideal preferences of individuals in Table 7.2, it is easy to see how the individuals holding those ideal preferences would have the preference orderings that they do. In particular, we may note that there is no 'extremism' in the individual

Table 7.2   *Two-Dimensional Political Choice without a Condorcet-Winner*

Welfare State

		For	Against	
	For	w (40)	y (20)	60
Nuclear Power				
	Against	x (20)	z (20)	40
		60	40	100

Party A (40 per cent): $w\ x\ y\ z$
Party B (20 per cent): $x\ z\ w\ y$
Party C (20 per cent): $y\ z\ w\ x$
Party D (20 per cent): $z\ x\ y\ w$

preference orderings. In each case the individual starts with an ideal preference, and then chooses second or third preferences by holding on to a dimension that is more important, placing last the alternative that fails in *both* dimensions. Thus, we seem to have a case where the 'irrationality' resides not in the individuals who compose society but in the way that their individually rational preferences are amalgamated.

It is this potential of a move from individual rationality to collective irrationality that has led some theorists to reject the majority principle altogether, saying that if it is compatible with there being no Condorcet-winner, we really cannot attach any sense to the idea that majority collective preference should have any sway over us. For example, Robert Paul Wolff writes in the light of the paradox that 'majority rule is fatally flawed by an internal inconsistency which ought to disqualify it from consideration in any political community whatsoever' (Wolff, 1970, p. 59). Individuals might be willing to sacrifice their autonomy if there was a clear idea of the collective interest to which they should subject their judgement, but the paradox of voting shows that no real meaning can be attached to the idea of collective preference or choice. From another point of view, we seem to be back to Schumpeter's claim that the result of populism 'lacks not only rational unity but also rational sanction'.

The existence of Condorcet cycles also casts doubt upon the justification of the Condorcet-winner criterion offered in the previous section. There I argued that the Condorcet-winner incorporated the virtue of political compromise, since it represented that alternative around which a majority could converge if they could not secure their first preference. But where there is no Condorcet-winner, this justification loses its force. Someone might argue that these problems merely reflected the logical peculiarities of the majority principle. But in his justly famous result, Kenneth Arrow (1963) showed that this was not true. There was no way of making social choices that could avoid the paradox of voting and satisfy otherwise intuitively attractive conditions, most notably that social choices should not simply track the preferences of one particular individual in society.

The potentially negative implications of social choice theory for populist accounts of democracy was noted by Dahl as long ago as 1956:

'Arrow shows that if there are more than two alternatives, any method for making social decisions that insures transitivity in the decisions must necessarily be either dictated by one person or imposed against the preferences of every individual ... This brilliantly developed and quite startling argument has, unfortunately, so far been totally ignored by political scientists.' (Dahl, 1956, pp. 42–3)

By 1982 Riker was able to build not only on Arrow's own work but also on a whole raft of subsequent results in the same tradition, and on the basis of his review concluded that any attempt to construct a theory of democracy on the idea of a popular will was doomed to failure:

'Populism as a moral imperative depends upon the existence of a popular will discovered by voting. But if voting does not discover or reveal a will, then the moral imperative evaporates because there is nothing to be commanded. If the people speak in meaningless tongues, they cannot utter the law that makes them free. Populism fails, therefore, not because it is morally wrong, but merely because it is empty.' (Riker, 1982, p. 239)

Earlier Runciman had put the point rather more bluntly: 'Put crudely, what Arrow has done is to show that strict democracy is impossible' (Runciman, 1969, p. 133).

This stress on the meaninglessness of popular rule might seem to echo familiar conservative objections against democracy, going back to Plato's *Republic* or Thucydides's *Peloponnesian War*, and invoked subsequently by *The Federalist Papers*, that popular passions were unstable and shifted in unpredictable ways, so that no coherence could be expected from popular participation. But the elegance of formal social choice theory is that it does not depend upon these contentious empirical premises. Arguments about the difficulties of aggregation drawn from social choice theory have been built up on the assumption that popular preferences remain constant and the emphasis of the analysis has been upon the different, and inconsistent, ways in which a given body of preferences can be aggregated into a collective choice. Thus, someone arguing an anti-populist case on the basis of social choice theory is potentially on strong grounds, since it can be said that an assumption relatively favourable to majoritarianism is being taken and shown to yield inconsistencies or incoherence. If this line of argument can be made to work, it thus promises to be a powerful one.

Yet how powerful are the anti-populist inferences that can be derived from the tradition of Arrowian social choice theory? Does Arrow's impossibility theorem and the raft of results that have been proved in its train justify the strong conclusions of Dahl, Riker and Runciman?

One response to Arrow's impossibility theorem has been to say that it is logically watertight within its own terms, but that its terms are too narrowly construed. In particular, it has been argued that because the impossibility results relate solely to the problem of aggregation, they ignore the problem of preference formation. I have already noted that one of the apparent strengths of Arrowian social choice theory is that it does not invoke the familiar anti-populist point that popular preferences are inherently unstable and therefore cannot form the basis for a responsible public choice. By taking the seemingly hard case of stable, well-formed individual preferences and showing how it may not be possible to assign a meaningful interpretation to the collective decision, it seems to put the populist at a disadvantage. But this seeming strength of the social choice approach can be turned to its disadvantage, according to some critics. Barry Holden has put the point with great clarity:

'... if the assumption that preferences are *fixed* is challenged one can take on board differing preference intensities *and* moreover one can build on the notion of bargaining and reconciliation, and the alteration of preferences in the face of divergencies, to arrive at the idea of unanimity. This avoids all the difficulties associated with trying to aggregate diverse fixed preferences ... If we push these ideas further we get to the crucial point of recognising that people have (sometimes complex) views rather than mere 'preferences'; and the process of interaction involves *discussion* and the bringing together of views.' (Holden, 1988, p. 42)

Holden goes on to suggest that we must look to the tradition of Rousseau and Idealist political theory to understand the notion that decisions by people emerge out of a process of discussion.

A similar appeal to Rousseauian ideas can be found in other defenders of populism against the attacks based on social choice theory, particularly in the form in which they were mounted by Riker. Thus Coleman and Ferejohn (1986, pp. 15–16) define an epistemic populist as someone who thinks that voting over issues requires judgements rather than preferences and who treats the outcomes of voting as evidence of what the general will is. Similarly, Cohen (1986, p. 29), though he dissents significantly from the analysis of Coleman and Frerejohn, also argues that votes can be treated as expressions of opinions or judgements about how best to advance the common good. David Miller has summarized the conclusion as follows:

> 'The upshot of this argument is that we have good reason to expect the deliberative process to transform initial policy preferences (which may be based on private interest, sectional interest, prejudice and so on) into ethical judgements on the matter in hand; and this will sharply curtail the set of rankings of policy outcomes with which the final decision procedure has to deal.' (Miller, 1993, p. 84)

In sum, we need to distinguish between a liberal account of democracy which sees the political problem as one of preference aggregation to a deliberative account of democracy which sees the political task as establishing forums for public discussion.

I suggested right at the beginning of this chapter that the language of 'preferences' is unfortunate in the context of the problem of aggregation, but that is not to say that transforming the language into one of ethical judgements solves the difficulties, unless we think that consensus is always the outcome of discussion. But why should we assume that the higher the level of discussion the greater the level of consensus? It would be just as possible to argue the other way and to say that discussion provides the catalyst for people to realize how much they are in disagreement. Unlike many who simply assert that discussion will lead to consensus (but see also Mansbridge, 1980, pp. 272–3), David Miller does have a go at presenting evidence to support the contention. However, quite apart from the fact that the figures cited do not show a convergence to unanimity, it is not clear that it is even the right sort of evidence to quote, since it comes from small group experiments mimicking, for example, the behaviour of juries. There are well-known normative pressures within such groups leading to the phenomenon of 'groupthink' (Janis, 1982), which is a form of premature consensus. It is far from clear that the results of such experiments can be transferred to the level of macro-politics, or how far they count against the historical and comparative evidence that political agreements are often founded on differences papered over by compromise. Moreover, it is clear from Miller's discussion that when differences do remain they cannot always be regarded as the lingering remnants of self-interest or sectional interest but are composed of differing conceptions of the public good based on logically distinct dimensions of appraisal. As we have seen, this is the crucial reason why the paradox of voting arises.

Moreover, we should not assume that consensus is good in itself. Quite apart from the problems of 'groupthink', which can often lead to policy fiascoes, there is the danger that too great an emphasis upon consensus will lead to pressures to create artificial agreement. Douglas Amy (1987), for example, has raised the question of whether the use of consensus techniques in discussions of environmental policy does not put pressure on some of the weaker parties to concede too much. One of the great merits of saying that a system of voting is simply a way of coming to a conclusion is that you can say to a minority that, in losing the vote, it has not necessarily lost the argument. We do not have to go as far as Warren (1996) and say that politics always emerges from 'social groundlessness', that is an incomplete ability to be able to justify any position, to see the force of the point that sometimes the preservation of dissensus is valuable. There is also a line of argument going back to J. S. Mill's defence of free speech (Mill, 1859, chapter 2) that, even if a consensus did exist, there would be benefits all round in disrupting it. In other words, if we take the fallibility of human institutions seriously, we would be sensible to ensure that critical rationality was always present in the course of political decisions. Unanimity ought not always to be treated as a sufficient condition of choice.

Voting Cycles and Institutional Rationality

Where does this leave us in the face of Arrow's theorem and its extensions? In order to see whether we necessarily have to abandon a popular will conception of democracy in the light of the paradox of voting, let us consider more precisely what Arrow's impossibility theorem shows. The theorem says that there is no process of social choice that simultaneously satisfies the conditions of transitivity, universal domain, respect for the Pareto principle, the independence of irrelevant alternatives and non-dictatorship (see Table 7.3). Since majority rule satisfies all but the condition of transitivity, the rationale for requiring this condition of an aggregation procedure needs to be explored. One reason for wanting to impose the condition of transitivity is to make the final social choice independent of the order in which the alternatives come up for decision. As Arrow himself put it, the importance of the transitivity condition is to ensure 'the independence of the final choice from the path to it' (Arrow, 1963, p. 120). Moreover, the property of path-independence is closely associated with the condition of the independence of irrelevant alternatives, since that condition requires that, for fixed individual preferences over identical alternatives, the social choice should remain the same. Thus, both the transitivity condition and the independence condition are intended to ensure that social choices depend only upon information about preferences and not on the contingent workings of the process by which preferences are amalgamated.

Table 7.3   *Relation between Arrow and May Conditions*

May conditions	Arrow conditions
Unrestricted domain: Any preferences accepted.	Unrestricted domain
Neutrality: Choice rule insensitive to issues.	Independence of irrelevant alternatives: Choice rule always gives same result for same alternatives.
Anonymous: Identity of preference holders irrelevant.	Non-dictatorship: No one individual always decisive.
Positively responsive: Choice will change in direction of preference changes.	Pareto responsive: Choice will always coincide with what everyone wants.
Transitivity can be violated.	Requires transitivity.

The obvious question to ask at this point is whether this attempt to detach outcomes from the processes that led to them is so important. In fact, in a number of social choice processes, this requirement is regularly violated. The obvious example is the market. Traders in a market will typically have divergent views about which the various equilibrium outcomes they would most prefer. Which view predominates in practice will depend on the initial endowments that each brings to the market. Markets therefore do not meet the condition that the final choice is independent of the path to it. This is partly because all social institutions work by establishing pathways of choice and then processing decisions according to those established pathways. Indeed, the dependence of the final choice upon those pathways is what gives many institutions their legitimacy.

Within voting systems the relevant pathways of choice function in part by breaking down complex alternatives into their component parts. To illustrate this point consider the choice between policies in the running example of this chapter. The combinations of alternative welfare state and nuclear power policies represent descriptions of four possible social alternatives. Treated as a whole that alternative might be vulnerable, under majority rule, to some other combination of policies. But how would we know whether there was some other combination of policies that would defeat it? The examples I have been considering are highly simplified. We are only looking at two dimensions of policy and two possible stances within each dimension. In practice, there is likely to be so much complexity that it is impossible to look at whole alternative sets of policies pitched against one another. Thus, in practice, even if a society were confronted by a pattern of cyclical majorities along the lines of that presented in Table 7.2, it would be extremely unlikely to know that this was the case. It is certainly true, as William Riker so brilliantly demonstrated in a series of works (Riker, 1982 and 1986), that a central dynamic of political competition can be to find and exploit the contradictions inherent in out-of-equilibrium majorities. But if we ask how frequent in practice is the turbulence associated with majority-rule cycling, the answer appears to be surprisingly little. Thus, in the archetypical majoritarian system (Lijphart, 1984), namely New Zealand, the constant flux that one would associate with out-of-equilibrium majorities is not a feature of its political history. Instead, one finds long periods of one-party dominance, in large part associated with ideological constraints (Nagel, 1993 and 1998).

As well as these cognitive and ideological constraints on political competition, there are also strong institutional pressures to prevent a synoptic evaluation of alternative policy combinations. The principal means by which this is accomplished in functioning democracies is by political parties, which reduce the many dimensions of potential competition down to two or three. Moreover, policy-making is in practice highly sectorized. Policy communities are an established feature of different fields of policy, forming intellectual and political reference-groups for different issues. Of course, this can lead to a lack of coordination on problems where actors need to cooperate across sectors. But even with greater co-ordination across three or four policy sectors, we would still be a long way short of the synoptic rationality implicit in Arrow's condition that the final choice should be independent of the path to it.

Conclusions

Suppose we acknowledge that democratic decision-making typically does not take place over complete combinations of policies, and that instead representatives compete on a subset of issues in indirect democracies and electorates decide questions issue by issue in a direct democracy. Then we are saying that the final choice of policy is not independent of the pathway to that choice.

In the first place, if political questions are decided issue by issue, in accordance with the principle of majority rule, then, if there is a Condorcet-winner, issue-by-issue majoritarianism will select it. Since, as I have argued earlier, the criterion of the Condorcet-winner yielded the most acceptable interpretation of the majority principle when no one alternative commanded a simple numerical majority, this tendency of issue-by-issue decision-making is to be welcomed.

Secondly, there may be no Condorcet-winner among a set of alternatives given the preference profile of those voting. In these circumstances, issue-by-issue decision-making will still yield a result. Moreover, provided that the issues are separable, in the sense that voters' preferences on one issue do not depend on how the voting turns out on another issue, then the outcome of the issue-by-issue voting will be stable, with no voters having any rational incentive to unpick the final result (see Ordeshook, 1986, pp. 245–57, for this result). This is sometimes known as a structure-induced equilibrium, and the essential point about it is that the pattern of institutional decision-making fixes the outcome in such a way that there is no tendency for a political community deciding issues in sequence to go round in circles. Thus, issue-by-issue majoritarianism will never eliminate from choice a Condorcet-winner if there is one, but it will produce a definite answer when there is no Condorcet-winner to be found.

Of course, where there is no Condorcet-winner, the issue-by-issue median is vulnerable to defeat by at least one alternative when the situation is viewed from a synoptic point of view. Institutional and procedural constraints will inhibit the identification of that alternative and it cannot be reached by sequential voting. Nonetheless, there is in theory a combination of policies that a majority would prefer (this simply follows logically from the definition of a Condorcet-winner). But there should not be a normative worry about selecting the issue-by-issue median in this case. Although the community has chosen an alternative that is less preferred than another alternative, the problem is generated by the cyclical structure of the preferences. Since one alternative has to be selected, there is bound to be one alternative that will defeat it.

In terms of the alternative conceptualizations that I identified in Chapter 2, arguments surrounding the problem of aggregation go only a little way towards helping us with an intellectually defensible evaluation. I have tried to show that the paradoxes of social choice need not incline us towards the anti-populist liberal end of the spectrum in the way that Dahl, Riker and Runciman suggest. In one sense, no doubt, Riker was right: it is not possible to identify with confidence the popular will as it is revealed in the selection of one alternative outcome rather than another. But this is partly because the demands of synoptic rationality involved in a comparison of alternative policy packages cannot be met in any but the most simple world. Outside very small situations citizens do not choose over logically integrated political programmes. Issue by issue we may know what the majority wants, but there is typically no way of knowing whether the intersection of these majorities, in relation to all issues, expresses a popular will. Nevertheless, the issue-by-issue median is the best approximation we shall have to a popular will.

8 Inclusion

So far we have defined democracies as political systems in which important decisions of public policy depend, even if only indirectly and at one remove, on public opinion. However, this definition implicitly leaves one major question unanswered. How should we define the relevant public? Clearly, it is possible to define the public narrowly or broadly, with quite different implications for our understanding of the character of the political system. This is the problem of inclusion. Thus, ancient Athens is typically called a democracy, but women, slaves and *metics* (resident aliens) were excluded from the rights of citizenship. The exclusion of such a large proportion of the population might lead someone, with good reason, to withhold the name of democracy for the system. Similarly, up to the time that Switzerland gave the vote to women in federal elections in 1971, we might want to say that it was not a democracy, despite its extensive participationist practices and system of proportional representation.

If we take the criterion of inclusion into account, a democracy is not simply a political system in which public choice depends upon public opinion, but also a system in which the public is defined on an inclusive basis. In this sense, the notion of inclusion can be said to be central to the definition of democracy. A democracy, on this definition, allows competition for power and influence on an inclusive basis, so that too narrow a basis of citizenship would lead us to say that though a political system rested on open competition for power, it failed to be democratic, no matter how much political participation by eligible citizens it allowed in the making of decisions.

Yet, if inclusion is so important, how are we to define principles that enable us to settle problems about exactly how inclusive or exclusive the definition of citizenship should be? After all, we cannot simply say that the public should itself decide who is a member, because this would give a licence to narrowly elite bodies of citizens to define citizenship in exclusive terms. Under apartheid in South Africa the majority of white citizens denied the political rights of citizenship to black members of society for decades. If we were simply to say that any body of citizens was entitled to define its own membership, this would produce the absurd result that apartheid South Africa was a democracy. The test of inclusion cannot therefore be the product of a decision-rule used within a political system. Rather the decision-rules that are used must pre-suppose that issues of inclusion have already been settled.

The discussion is also complicated by the fact that the term 'inclusion' has become fashionable among political theorists in recent years, so that it has collected to itself a number of quite dis-tinct and discrete problems. Robert Goodin (1996a) has pointed out, for example, that the notion of inclusion is used to discuss problems of political participation, problems of poverty and prob-lems of free movement, as well as issues connected with the definition of citizenship. In what follows, I shall seek to avoid the complications of these multiple, and not always related, issues, by focussing on a limited number of quite specific questions arising from three issues.

The first of these can be put as follows. Given that we think a people should be allowed to govern itself democratically, who should be qualified to participate in the decision-making process? This is the problem of *qualification*. We can illustrate the problem by considering the principles upon which we would give the vote to members of a society. The second issue can be expressed as follows. Even when we have defined political rights of citizenship within a community, does it follow that all qualified members of the polit-ical community should be entitled to a voice on everything? This is the problem of *partitioning* issues among sub-sets of electors, for example in terms of locality. Thirdly, there is the question of whether we should confine political representation to human inter-ests solely or whether there is a case for 'enfranchising nature'. This is the problem of *extension* beyond current human interests.

However, before looking at these three questions in detail, it will be useful to clear away another question that is sometimes raised in this context. This is the problem of *boundaries*. How do we delimit the set of persons who constitute a people entitled to govern itself? This problem would not arise if the sanguine assumptions of nineteenth-century nationalism were true (on this topic, see Kedourie, 1993).

Thus, if humanity were divided naturally into territorially discrete social groups, easily identifiable by reference to features such as language or culture, then the boundaries that defined the citizens of democracy could be drawn by reference to those characteristics or features. Some political systems do of course conform to this pattern. It could be argued that Japan is an example. It is ethnically homogenous and linguistically distinct, and the borders of its territory can be drawn largely, if not entirely, without controversy. But Japan is the exception rather than the norm. In other places different ethnic, linguistic and cultural groups are territorially intermingled. Borders exist for historical reasons but they may not correspond to any clearly identifiable pre-political features of a society.

The most acute problems arise in cases where there are three political units – let us say A, B, and C – in which a majority of A wish C to be part of A, a majority of B wish C to be part of B, and a majority of C wish C to be part of A. If the populations of A plus C form a majority of the members of all three societies and the populations of B plus C also form a majority of all three societies, then there is a serious problem of boundaries. Northern Ireland and Cyprus provide examples of political systems in which this problem arises. Simple appeal to the majority principle will not suffice to solve the problem, since the point at issue is precisely what are the boundaries within which the majority principle should operate. After all, if a majority has been artificially constructed, that would seem to disqualify it from having moral force.

With such issues, there is no answer that can be given within the terms of democratic theory itself. Instead, these questions raise issues that rest partly on historical contingency, and partly on the more general issue of the right to secession. Historical contingency simply means that what are now treated as integral political units might well have emerged in different ways. For example, Norway might never have seceded from Sweden or the plebiscites held in Schleswig after the First World War might in other circumstances have resulted in a different distribution of territory between Germany and Denmark. There is no political problem arising from this historical contingency, provided that the boundaries in question have established themselves over time as having some political legitimacy. The problem arises in cases where the boundaries do not have political legitimacy, and it is in precisely such cases that there can be no simple resort to the majority principle.

In such cases the problem of secession arises. On what basis, if at all, is one group of people entitled to separate itself from another? Clearly, that issue raises the whole question of how far we can really talk about common interests, which is a central value in the idea of democracy. There would seem to be good moral and practical arguments for allowing a right of secession under appropriate circumstances, but this is not a simple matter. Although democratic government is government that seeks to protect common interests, yet if there are no common interests, then it is difficult to see on what basis democracy can be built. Moreover, wars to prevent secession can be particularly bloody and unattractive. In the end, it seems to me that Sidgwick was right to argue that the identity of a political system was given by the willingness of the members of society to hold together independently of political authority that might be over them (Sidgwick, 1891, p. 214, compare Barry, 1989b, pp. 168–70). The boundaries of a demos are thus given by the willingness of a people to hang together politically, independently of the particular form of government under which they are living at any one time. If there is a lack of this willingness, then the conditions for a functioning political system are simply absent.

To say that a problem cannot be solved according to the principles of democratic theory is not to say that it is unimportant. It is merely to say that democratic theory is not the whole of political theory. So I shall discuss the problem of inclusion in what follows on the assumption that the boundaries of a political community are not contested, and ask on what principles we could define the political rights of citizenship and so determine the degree of inclusiveness of the political process.

The Problem of Qualification

Even if we accept, as I have suggested we must, that democracy is to be defined as a political system in which there is a high degree of inclusiveness in the rights of citizenship, it is still plausible to think that there ought to be some exclusions from political rights. One possible example is the right to vote, which is denied to children below a certain age, serving prisoners in many countries or temporary visitors from one country to another. But, unless these are to be *ad hoc* exclusions without any justification, we ought to seek for principles which would enable us to see why certain categories of those affected by political decisions ought to be excluded from influence in the making of those decisions.

In looking at this issue, I shall take the right to vote as my primary example. For some this may seem to be a purely formal right that is of little use in the absence of effective resources for broader political participation. However, whilst acknowledging the general point, it is still useful to take a particular right like that of the right to vote. In part, it is simply a way of making the analytical discussion manageable within the limits of space: the right to vote can stand as a useful place-holder for a number of other political rights. I should also want to assert, however, that focussing on the right to vote has a rationale of its own. There are, for example, a number of migrant groups in some countries of Europe who are free to organize their own political associations, but who lack the right to vote. If they were given the vote, their political power would be enhanced. The right to vote is not in itself a trivial one.

Dahl (1989, pp. 119–31) discusses two views about the rights of citizenship: citizenship as wholly contingent and citizenship as a categorical right. He shows how the first is simply inadequate, because it allows any arbitrary majority to define its own legitimacy. However, citizenship as a categorical right (everyone subject to a body of laws should have citizenship) is also inadequate, once we recognize that there are valid categories of exception. The problem is then as follows: on what principles should we define the exceptions?

One way of approaching this problem is to consider an explicit argument for exclusion on a large scale, and to see where it goes wrong. One such argument is to be found in James Mill's *Essay on Government* (Mill, 1820, p. 27), in which Mill makes the case for excluding from the right to vote all but men over forty. I take it that this reaches a conclusion that to modern intuitions is unjustifiable. Yet, Mill's argument is in strict logical terms valid, despite its reaching an unsupportable conclusion. That is to say, he does not use a pattern of argument in which false conclusions could be derived from true premises and to say that an argument is logically valid is just to say that it is one in which false conclusions cannot be derived from true premises (Salmon, 1973, pp. 1–7).

What this means is that to see why the conclusion is unsupport-able we should look at the premisses of the argument. These are that political participation is a cost and that heads of household can represent the interests of other members of the household. The costs of political participation mean that if you can advance your interests without participation, then it is to your advantage to do so. (This can be seen as a sort of participatory prisoners' dilemma.) One way in which you can protect yourself from others is to ensure that they do not participate. Hence, a rule that limited the right to vote to the minimum necessary to protect the people from government tyranny would be a sensible rule, even from the point of view of those excluded. Laid out in this way, the false premiss contained in the argument is pretty easy to spot: genera-tional and gender conflicts mean that male heads of households are not invariably good representatives for young men and women. Indeed, it may be that one of the reasons why the principle of inclu-sion is so widespread these days is that people are now (rightly) sceptical of the thought that one segment of the population can be as strongly committed to the interests of another segment of the population as they are to their own.

Be that as it may. What is interesting about James Mill's argu-ment is that it assumes that if someone can show a distinct per-sonal interest that would be protected by political inclusion then that person should be given the right to vote. This would suggest that the test of qualification should be merely that one has an interest in the outcome of a political process. But, if the original James Mill formulation seemed too narrow, the revision in terms of merely being able to demonstrate an interest seems too broad. As a short-term foreign visitor to a country, I may well have an interest in the result of the election. For example, I may be drawing my income from abroad, and know that if one party is elected to gov-ernment currency fluctuations will move in my favour, whereas if another party is elected the fluctuations will be to my disadvantage. Moreover, if I have a large income, the degree of my interest in the result might be considerable. Despite these conditions, it seems implausible to say that as a foreign visitor I should be given the vote.

Is there any other test, apart from that of possessing an interest, which can be brought in to narrow down the range of inclusion to something that seems to make more intuitive sense? At this point it is useful to compare John Stuart Mill's test, which requires both a test of interest and a test of competence, in the form of literacy and mathematical tests, to secure entitlement to the vote (Mill, 1861a, pp. 329–31). Moreover, Mill took his own test to involve the implication that there should be more votes given to those who might be thought to be more competent. For example, he favoured giving university graduates more votes than non-graduates.

We have already touched on some of these issues in discussing the principle of political equality, but it is useful to consider this implication explicitly in the present context. There are many reasons, however, why J. S. Mill's inference should be resisted. There is the doubt about the extent to which any group (including university graduates) can internalize a strong sense of competing interests. There is the historical experience of societies, for example the southern states of the USA before desegregation, where literacy tests have been misused by ruling groups to exclude challenges to political power (see the cases reported in Tribe, 1988, pp. 1092–4). And there is doubt about whether the various dimensions of intelligence actually hang together in predictable ways. We probably all know highly intelligent people that could not be trusted to buy a railway ticket, and people with lots of practical good sense who are not good at algebra. If intelligence is not homogenous, it is difficult to see how we could construct a non-contentious test of political competence.

This is not to say that competence is irrelevant, however. The sole ground for excluding children from the vote has presumably to be the fact that they are thought to lack the competence to make the relevant decisions. This is, of course, a rough and ready assumption. There are some bright ten-year-olds who could give their elders a good run for their money in any test of political knowledge. On the other hand, it would not be practicable to discriminate in favour of politically bright children as a general practice, and any injustice that might be thought done to the precocious is off-set by the fact that the disqualification is only temporary. As Rawls (1972, p. 224) puts it, such a restriction does not discriminate unfairly among persons or groups, since it falls evenly on everyone in the normal course of life. In this sense it is compatible with the requirements of political equality.

What about the case of those with learning disabilities? It might seem that any test of qualification will exclude at least some people

with severe learning difficulties. Yet people with learning difficulties
are some of the most vulnerable people is society, and therefore
count among those who have an interest to be protected. Moreover,
one of the forms of discrimination they typically suffer is an under-
estimation of their potential. For example, in the first deliberative
poll that was ever conducted (see Fishkin, 1995, pp. 161–76, for
details), a participant who characterized herself as having learning
disabilities pretty effectively routed a senior Conservative MP on
the question of legislation about the right to silence that was then
going through UK parliament and that some people feared would
put the vulnerable at a disadvantage. For these reasons, and given
that we are here talking not about a clearly identifiable group, but a
spectrum of abilities that is distributed across a population, it seems
just as easy not to try to make a categorically separate caste of one
group. This may seem anomalous if we make the comparison with
children, but it is not. Although those with significant learning disabilities can be regarded as adult children from the point of view of
competence, they are distinguished from children in the sense that
they cannot be so easily identified. In part, not excluding them formally from political rights stems from this practical circumstance.

   With these qualifications in mind, it would seem that we now
have the potential to establish a principle in terms of which we
could allocate the political rights of citizenship. If we combine the
interest test with the qualification test, does that give us a criterion
that is meaningful? Here again the case of the temporary resident
poses a difficulty. Many temporary residents will be able to pass
both a competence and an interest test. Yet, can it really be right
that, say, academic visitors spending a few months abroad should
be able to vote in elections in the country in which they are tem-
porarily living?

   Putting the question in this way might suggest that the real issue
is one of temporary versus long-term residence. However, not even
this will quite do, for it might imply that citizens ought to be
deprived of the vote once they reached a certain age. After all, it
could be argued that people above a certain age have no interest in
making present sacrifices to some future good of the sort that
might be involved in, say, reducing consumption now in order to
prevent climate change taking place over a number of decades.
Moreover, if everyone above a certain age, say eighty-five, were
deprived of the right to vote, such a restriction would pass the

Rawlsian test of fairness: it would fall evenly on everyone in the normal course of life.

Such a possibility shows that the granting of the political rights of citizenship is not simply an instrumental device to protect one's interests within a community (though it is certainly that); it also shows it to be a symbolic acknowledgement of civic dignity. To deprive the old of the right to vote would be an assault on dignity for which there is no justification. Moreover, on a more mundane level, quite apart from the fact that long-sightedness does not seem to be uniquely associated with youth, the debarring of the elderly from political citizenship would seem to indicate a defective understanding of the basis on which political rights are awarded.

In particular, what the example shows, I suggest, is that the interests underlying the granting of the right of citizenship must not only presuppose competence and be serious. They must also be tied to a commitment that the person has to the political society in question. Tribe (1988, p. 1084) puts this well in his principle that 'even though anyone in the world might have some interest in any given election's outcome, a community should be empowered to exclude from its elections persons with no real nexus to the community as such.' Such a nexus need not be a subjective one, based on attitude, but one rooted in the circumstances of the lives of individuals. Compare, for example, the temporary visitor and the indefinitely resident guestworker. After a while, the interests of the guestworker become closely bound up with those of the society in which he or she lives. It is not simply that guestworkers pay taxes – after all, so do short-term visitors – it is also that certain matters of collective concern (the state of public transport, the quality of the housing stock, policies on crime, decisions about economic management and so on) are also relevant to them. However, even this is to put the case too narrowly. Political rights may be important in enabling a group to express its own interests in relation to matters of collective concern. However, such groups typically develop their own associations and forms of political culture that enable them to make a contribution to the collective culture of the society to which they belong. In so far as debates about the balance of collective interests lead to debates about political ideals, migrant groups are in a position to make a unique contribution to that debate.

If we put the relevant criterion in terms of a nexus between the individual and the political society of which he or she is a member, we can find the rational kernel of the old property test for the right to vote. In societies in which the most important economic asset is physical property, a clear way of evidencing commitment to one's own polity is the possession of property. Hence, there is some sense in requiring the possession of property as a qualification for the franchise. It betokens a commitment to the political society in which one lives. In a modern economy the primary source of economic value is the skills and talents of workers. The commitment of human capital – one's willingness to work and participate in the collective life of the society – then becomes a way of demonstrating commitment. Once one has worked for some time, that commitment is demonstrated.

One way of stating the underlying principle of this approach is to say that the granting of political rights can be seen to be contingent on an already existing practices within a certain society, and in this sense the basis of political inclusion is a sort of consistency test. There is nothing in this theory of political rights that says that rights ought to be granted in an absolute sense. It may well be, for example, that certain societies at certain times are entitled to restrict the free movement of labour, so that outsiders cannot enter and form an economic and social nexus. The development of commitment by outsiders to a society presupposes the free movement of labour, and there is considerable disagreement as to whether there is any general human right to free movement (see Barry and Goodin, 1992). The approach I have outlined merely says that if a society does allow the free movement of labour, such that a number of guestworkers have come to live in that society, there must come a point where they are no longer denied political rights. It should also be noted that in making the test objective, I have not supposed any test of cultural compatibility. To say that guestworkers and others should culturally identify with the society in which they live seems both to overemphasize the cultural homogeneity of any reasonably large society, but also to put up an unjustifiable barrier to citizenship.

What of those who have by one means or another cut their nexus with society? There are a number of ways in which this can occur, for example crime, residence abroad or as victims of social exclusion. On the topic of crime, there are probably as many arguments against depriving prisoners of the right to vote as there are in favour. To be sure, convicted criminals have in some sense voluntarily cut their nexus with society by taking unfair advantage of the compliance of others with the law to their own benefit, and the loss of political rights, along with civil rights, might well seem an appropriate social response. On the other hand, someone could well argue that the responsibility of exercising the vote was an important part of the process of rehabilitation.

The person who emigrates from a society to live abroad seems, after a while, to fall into a different category. It seems unduly harsh to deprive someone of the vote who, say, goes to live abroad for three to four, or perhaps even five, years. On the other hand, it seems unduly generous to extend the same privilege for those who have been out of the community for up to twenty years, as was done with UK legislation passed in 1989 (Blackburn, 1995, pp. 78–80). Indeed, so generous is it that some of a cynical turn of mind might suppose that the motive was party advantage rather than a desire to be fair. Of course, there is no theoretical principle to which appeal can be made in determining the exact cut-off point, but any plausible decision would have to strike a balance between the need to ensure that people were not deprived of a voice where there was some uncertainty about their nexus with the community being restored through return and the extension of a right where there was no ground.

That leaves the category of the socially excluded, who may – say because they do not have a permanent place of residence – find themselves deprived of political rights as well as economic security. Here I am inclined to say that, although in one sense the nexus with the community has been broken, there is another sense in which such persons are even more dependent upon public choices and collective decision-making than the run of more fortunate citizens. For this reason, whatever the practical difficulties, it does not seem fair that such people should automatically be deprived of the right to vote.

The general principles of interest, qualification and commitment through a nexus to the community therefore provide a basis for the allocation of the franchise. Of course, the detailed institutional and practical recommendations that follow from these general principles are subject to particular circumstances. There is no general theory that will say that six years as a guestworker should entitle someone to the franchise whereas four years does not. Similarly, there is no way in which the age at which citizens should acquire the right to vote can be determined theoretically. However, despite these limitations, it is possible to say that the principles of political inclusion are not entirely arbitrary.

The Problem of Partitioning

If we assume that we have principles that enable us to decide who should be entitled to citizenship, we also have to consider what the scope of those citizenship entitlements should be. In particular, we should note that not all citizens in well-functioning democracies have a say in everything that passes in their society that is made a subject of political decision. For example, both local government and federalism are ways of saying that some subset of a people should have more say over particular issues than some other subset. Both presuppose that there are some issues that should be decided by local, not larger, majorities. But how can we decide the proper decision-making powers of these local majorities?

One possibility here is to say that we are confronted with a problem within a political system that is the same as the problem about how we place the boundaries around a political system. That is to say, just as I argued in the case of the boundaries problem that there was no answer within democratic theory to the problems that are raised, so one might say that the partitioning of issues among subsets of citizens was also not susceptible to theoretical resolution. There is clearly some merit in this answer and a great deal in any particular case does depend upon the details of circumstance. Thus, where local identities are very strong for cultural or other reasons, there seems to be a clear prima facie case for respecting, as much as possible, the collective preferences of those who live in the locality. However, as a general answer, this seems to me to be insufficient for a number of reasons.

Firstly, although local government may rest upon clearly identifiable and historically given identities, it need not do so, and in many areas of a modern society typically will not do so. Hence we need some principles for the case where clear identities are not given. Secondly, political cooperation among established political units may mean the transfer of powers from one level of government to another level. Clear examples of this trends at work are provided by the way in which the powers of the European Union have grown in the last twenty years. But unless we say that there

can be no principled appraisal of these transfers of powers, it seems
as though it ought to be possible at least to state a criterion in
terms of which the allocation of powers can be appraised.

John Stuart Mill offers one possible principle in his discussion
of the basis upon which powers should be assigned to local
government:

> 'after subtracting from the functions performed by most
> European governments, those which ought not to be undertaken
> by public authorities at all, there still remains so great and
> various an aggregate of duties, that, if only on the principle of
> the division of labour, it is indispensable to share them between
> central and local authorities. Not only are separate executive
> officers required for purely local duties (an amount of separa-
> tion that exists under all governments), but the popular control
> over those officers can only advantageously be exerted through a
> separate organ. Their original appointment, the function of
> watching and checking them, the duty of providing, or the dis-
> cretion of withholding, the supplies necessary for their opera-
> tions, should rest, not with the national Parliament or the
> national executive, but with the people of the locality.' (Mill,
> 1861a, pp. 411–12)

In this passage Mill locates the rationale of local government
within his broader democratic principles, and in particular within
an account of how the members of a community can best act
together to promote their common advantage. How then, on this
basis, can we approach the problem of partition?

For Mill the basic test to establish whether functions should be
carried on at a higher level than a given locality is whether citizens in other localities can be said to be *personally* indifferent or
not in how the locality treats the matter. His own examples
concern law and order, and he argues that it cannot be a matter
of personal indifference to the members of a country if one particular locality became a 'nest of robbers or a focus of demoraliza-
tion, owing to the maladministration of its police' (Mill, 1861a,
p. 420).

This test of personal indifference thus asserts that where potential causes of concern are so remote that they do not affect the personal interests of the rest of a political society, then there should be

a presumption of the devolution of political power to the locality in which there is a personal interest. It is important here that the test is that of personal interest. The test implicitly relies upon a distinction between what affects the personal interests of citizens and what affects their interests in so far as those interests are constituted by a disinterested concern for the well-being of the community at large.

An example can illustrate how this test might work. Suppose a town has to make a decision whether to build a swimming pool or a theatre. The test of personal indifference says that I am entitled to be part of that decision (and more generally the class of decisions of which this is an instance), provided that the decision is of some personal relevance to me. This need not require that I shall actually use either of the facilities in question, though it will involve changing the options that are available to me in my daily life. However, I do not get a say in the decision merely because I take an interest in such questions. Thus, neither the distant aesthete, who thinks the theatre an improving experience for people, nor the distant swimming champion, who likes the thought of a swimming pool full of people doing their lengths, is qualified by their interest to have a say in the decision.

One feature of this test of personal indifference is worth drawing attention to, namely that it does not contain the presumption that decision-making should be placed at the lowest level of government possible. Of course, within an interests account of political society, there are many arguments in favour of this assumption: the importance of individuals acquiring a sense of the public interests through their participation in public decision-making; the dangers of ignorant interference of higher authorities in the local circumstances of lower levels of government; the problems of establishing whether the harms that arise from interference outweigh the first-order benefits; and so on. Equally, however, it may be possible to show that one's personal interests require decision-making to pass to a higher level of government, as is typically the case, for example, with environmental protection.

Andrew Dobson (1996) has cited an interesting case under this last heading. Consider Scandinavians affected by the acidification of their lakes and rivers arising from emissions from British coal-fired power stations. By the test of personal indifference it would seem that they should have a vote in British energy policy. Is this a conclusion that can be sustained? The complication is that having a vote on some issues within a political system is part of participation in a wider set of issues. This is even true, it seems to me (*pace* Burnheim, 1985, pp. 107–10) in the local government case, where local rights and responsibilities are set within a broader constitutional framework. With issues like pollution that crosses national boundaries, there is lacking this broader constitutional framework. What I am inclined to say, therefore, in this sort of case is that the test of personal effect gives rise to some rights of political representation (through international negotiation, international institutions and the like) such that the offending country cannot legitimately resist being accountable for its actions. To say that a right of voting is involved, however, jumps too quickly to a particular institutional conclusion.

It is striking to observe, incidentally, how this test of personal indifference inverts the logic of some forms of democratic participation. A usual assumption is that political agents have to cast their arguments in terms of conduciveness to the public advantage if they are going to call upon the power of the state. Absence of personal interest is the test that has to be passed before one can engage in the public arguments about the general interest. More generally, we expect our political representatives to exclude themselves from participating in the vote on a certain question if they stand to gain or lose by the result. How can we square these practices with the applicability of Mill's test?

Here the relevant point would appear to be the extent to which the decision affects an interest that is purely personal. Consider, once again, the decision about the swimming pool versus the theatre. If I am an affected party, I stand to gain or lose by the decision that is taken. However, I stand to gain or lose along with others. The interest is personal in the sense that it has some effect on me personally, but it is not personal in the sense that I am the only person with a stake in the matter. Clearly we should exclude people from decision-making who have a distinctive stake in the matter at hand that may prevent their weighing the claims of others properly. But the claims of those others arise from the stake that they have.

So far, I have considered the question of partitioning in terms of territorial units. However, one question we can ask is whether the subunits have to be territorial, or whether they can be organized on some other basis. Some theorists argue for the importance of devolving power to functional, and not just territorial, groups. But if there is to be functional partitioning of decision-making responsibility, on what basis should it be assigned? The answer here is surely that the test of personal indifference is also the right one to apply. For example, if a religious group is given control of schooling, then it ought not to make any personal difference to me how they resolve any disagreements they might have within the group about what the orthodoxy is that should be taught.

However, the extent of such devolution of decision-making is not always uncontentious. For example, Young has argued that there is a case for public recognition and support for the self-organization of oppressed groups, a commitment to take into account group-generated policy proposals and a willingness to grant veto power over issues that affect them directly, for example by giving women veto power over issues to do with reproductive rights (Young, 1990, p. 184). If we ask how such a set of recommendations differs from the sort of practices that are implied by the politics of presence discussed in Chapter 6, then one important difference concerns the assumptions that need to be made about the relationship between group membership and wider citizenship. For Young, there is not a strong argument for transcending group differences in order to achieve the perspective of citizenship. Indeed, in some respects, she presents the perspective of citizenship as a totalizing category that threatens to eliminate difference.

Can we entirely repress the thought, however, that the partitioning of decisions should be located in a conception of the interests of citizens as a whole, as distinct from the interests of groups that might make up a society? It is useful here to consider the case of the consociational democracies, like the Netherlands, which Young clearly thinks offers some parallels to her own way of thinking. One of the main features of the consociational democracies like the Netherlands in the heyday of pillarization was the extent to which matters of public policy were devolved to associations representing the main social groups. Especially in areas of polity where cultural identity was important, like education, representatives of Catholics and Protestants were given power and resources to shape policy in accordance with their own sentiments.

Such a devolution of power might seem to provide a glimpse of the sort of arrangements that Young has in mind. However, the example also provides an explanation of why simple devolution needs to be embedded in wider structures of representation. Even with certain matters of policy devolved to representatives of major groups, other important matters of society-wide interest (economic and monetary policy, foreign policy and defence policy) have to be dealt with at the highest collective level. Thus, in the Netherlands, at the high point of the politics of accommodation, there were elaborate methods of inclusions, involving balanced cabinets and a balance in the staffing of the public service. But it is a plausible hypothesis that no consociational arrangement can work without some overarching sense of identity enabling members of society to think as citizens and not merely as members of specific groups. If democratic politics is about the pursuit of common interests, and not simply the mutual adjustment of otherwise contending social forces, then it will not be possible to implement a pure politics of difference.

Extension beyond Persons?

Even with these principles, we still have some troubling cases in particular: what about future generations or the rest of nature? How are such interests to be included? Should we seek to enfranchise nature or future generations in various ways? After all, we can say that both nature and future generations have interests. It would seem logical to protect these interests by finding some way of including them within the processes of political decision-making (the link between them being the assumption that short-termism in political democracy damages both).

One possibility that has been recently canvassed is that some forms of democracy are more likely to promote ecological interests than others. For example, both Goodin (1996b) and Bronwyn Hayward (1996) favour participatory, discursive forms of democracy on the grounds that these forms of democracy are more likely to be favourable to ecological concerns. Conversely there are others who have argued that this would put decision-making on too small a scale to cope with the transboundary and global nature of modern environmental problems.

Another, and more radical, possibility discussed by Dobson (1996) is that there could be proxy electorates on behalf of future generations and other species. One objection to this line of argument is to deny that having an interest alone is sufficient to constitute a ground for inclusion. This was in effect what I argued in the case of the right to vote more generally. The incapable and those without a nexus to the community could also be properly excluded. Since future generations and at least some other species will typically pass the nexus test, this leaves only the test of capacity.

Here it might seem that there was a knock-down argument against the political inclusion of nature or future generations, since it would seem that neither can communicate their interests to us. However, among proponents of enfranchising nature, this is just the assumption that has been contested. Goodin (1996b, p. 841) for example cites Stone to the effect that it is a lot easier for my lawn to communicate to me that it needs watering than it is for the 'United States' to communicate to the Attorney General that it is in its interests for Al Capone to be prosecuted. Similarly, Dryzek (1996, pp. 20–1) has argued that we should treat signals emanating from the natural world with the same respect that we accord signals emanating from human subjects.

Clearly if these claims could be made good, then nature would have satisfied all the conditions that we have determined for inclusion in the franchise. Obviously there would be practical problems about how to arrange for such representation, but these would be subsidiary to the main point of principle. Can the point of principle be carried, however, and in particular can the assumption about the communicative capacities of nature be made good? The unwatered lawn provides a good test in this context. One reason for being sceptical about the communicative competence of nature is that the signals we receive are likely to be ambiguous. My grass is brown, but the dandelions, which have deeper roots, are flourishing. Is nature telling me to water the lawn or not? Any representatives trying to decode the message are likely to disagree. Nor can we solve the situation by importing some general principle asserting the importance of species flourishing. The conservation of certain species may well involve us inhibiting the colonization by another species of a particular piece of territory.

The point is not to question the claim that we can speak about nature doing well or badly, but rather to insist that any particular judgement is likely to be contested, and that representatives who were doing their job might be expected to disagree as much as anyone else. Moreover, in some ways, talk about giving nature the vote seems to be the wrong way to think about the issues. It seems maladroit to adapt the language of rights to what is a problem of the good and its protection. A constitutional obligation to respect nature would seem to be more suitable. If this is so, then the principles of interest, competence and a nexus with the community should be sufficient to define the extension of those who should be included in the set of those entitled to political rights.

9 Democracy and Constitutionalism

Most modern democracies are the heirs of liberalism. One of the many consequences of this historical fact is that they contain an ambiguity in their institutional structure and principled rationale. On the one hand, they provide the means by which the people govern, or at least elect the representatives who are to govern. On the other hand, they usually contain constitutional devices, like the separation of powers or a system of checks and balances, that limit the scope and application of the principle of majority rule. Accordingly, constitutional democracies are typically governed according to two sets of principles: constitutionalism, which prescribes that governments should conduct their business according to rules that limit their freedom of action, and a populist principle, which prescribes that governments should implement the will of the people.

These two sets of principles can conflict with one another. Neil MacCormick puts the point with his customary clarity:

> 'Democracy says the people should be sovereign; constitutionalism denies that any sovereignty should be absolute and free of restraints or limits. Rather than plainly asserting the will of the people, it says that even the will of the people will not exercise power wisely or justly save under acknowledged limits. Constitutionalist governments are carefully respectful of the limits on state power.' (MacCormick, 1989, p. 101)

Such a distinction of principles is particularly important for the theory of democracy I have been seeking to develop, since I have sought to show that the institution of democracy can be regarded as a device for achieving certain purposes that cannot be achieved

167

within a political regime that sees government purely as a means for imposing constraints on individual interaction. Yet a significant stress upon constitutional principles would seem to undermine this rationale.

The conflict is not purely theoretical, however. In political systems where there is a clear separation of powers, constitutional courts have the power to challenge legislation on the grounds that it violates constitutionally prescribed rights. For example, the US constitution in its first amendment protects freedom of speech by imposing on the federal legislature a constraint on its freedom of legislation: 'Congress shall make no law ... abridging the freedom of speech, or of the press.' Of course, this prohibition is not self-evident in its scope. Does it protect the publication of pornography? Or the burning of the US flag as an act of protest? Or the encouragement of sedition? These are all questions that the US Supreme Court has had to decide at various times in its history. But that, of course, is precisely the point. It is up to the Court, not Congress, to determine the powers of congressional legislation. In other words, the separation of powers means that the Court takes priority in determining the limits of what the legislature can do.

In this respect, the US constitution comes closest to the ideal of constitutional government, in which a system of checks and balances and the separation of powers impose restrictions on the scope of legislation that popular majorities can adopt. For example, the first amendment to the US constitution would almost certainly mean that some forms of legislation, intended to prevent 'hate speech', would be declared unconstitutional. In the UK for instance it is a legal offence to incite racial hatred through speech or publications. Such a criminal provision would not be permissible according to the US constitution, even if there were a large majority of the population in favour of such a measure (Dworkin, 1985, p. 335).

However, it is possible to overstate the extent to which the separation of powers doctrine is unique to the US or the constitutional model of government generally. That the separation of powers has to be considered along with popular sovereignty is a view that is to be found in virtually all the models of democracy that we are considering. Within representational systems both consociational democracies and the Nordic democracies accept the need for some separation of powers, and in the case of consociational democracies there are various restrictions built into political practice that limit how governments behave. Ian Budge (1996) is also quite happy to accept, in respect to his participatory electronic democracy, that the normal constitutional protections on citizens' rights would exist. So, a commitment to constitutionalism does not vary directly with a commitment to participation. Interestingly, among indirect forms of democracy, it is Westminster systems that have been most resistant to incorporating formal constitutional devices for the separation of powers explicitly into their political arrangements. Although, at the time of writing a bill is being laid before Parliament to incorporate the European Convention on Human Rights into domestic law, the UK has long been without a documentary constitution to define the rights of its citizens and to prescribe the allocation of powers among public bodies, let alone among its constituent nations.

However, in some respects, appearances are deceptive in this regard, since we cannot infer from the absence of a formal institutional separation of powers that there is no constitutional doctrine to the effect that governments ought to limit the extent of their control over citizens. There is such a doctrine and it was stated by Dicey at the end of the nineteenth century:

'Englishmen whose labours gradually framed the complicated set of laws and institutions which we call the Constitution, fixed their minds far more intently on providing remedies for the enforcement of particular rights or (what is merely the same thing looked at from the other side) for averting definite wrongs, than upon any declaration of the Rights of Man or of Englishmen. The *Habeas Corpus* Acts declare no principle and define no rights, but they are for practical purposes worth a hundred constitutional articles guaranteeing individual liberty.' (Dicey, 1885, p. 195)

Now for present purposes it does not matter if this is an adequate constitutional doctrine (for what it is worth, my own view is that plainly it is not). What matters in the present context is that it states clearly that the idea of constitutional government is supposed to be integral to the Westminster system.

That leaves only one of our forms of democracy that does not recognize a principle of constitutionalism modifying a principle of democracy – namely the Rousseauian participatory system. In this model, of course, the assertion of the priority of the popular legislative will is explicit. What one has to say here is that Rousseau's institutional analysis presupposes his views on the importance of economic and social equality in a small-scale society. In such a society there is little need for constitutional protection, since there is little or no organized social power to tyrannize individuals. But once we see that the characterization of democracy is rooted in this particular set of social and economic circumstances, we can also readily see that the institutional analysis cannot be generalized beyond its imagined, and imaginary, setting.

Democracy and Constitutionalism

So far I argued that there is a potential conflict between constitutionalism and popular sovereignty. Dworkin (1996) has contested this assertion, however, arguing that a strong doctrine of the separation of powers is one way in which popular government can be realized. The essential premiss of this argument is that the judiciary is often in a significantly better position than elected representatives to give expression to the democratic value of equality, and in particular the principle that all citizens should be treated with equal concern and respect. The difficulty with this view, however, is that it draws too sharp a distinction between the courts as deliberative institutions, guided by an ideal of equal respect, and legislatures as aggregating institutions, responding to the weight of votes. Once we see that legislatures are necessarily deliberative institutions in their own right, the contrast fades. Once we also see that certain political rights, for example the right to petition the legislature, are ways in which social groups can participate in the shaping and interpretation of a society's morality, the contrast ceases to exist at all.

Given the uneasy relationship between constitutionalism and democracy, then, the theoretical task is to examine how deep this conflict is, and in particular to see whether the conflict is fundamental or can be accounted for in some larger theory of the democratic process. After all, there can be conflicts at the level of practice in working out a coherent complex body of principles, so that practical conflicts of this sort should not be taken to betoken a deep theoretical conflict. On the other hand, it is possible that modern constitutional democracies are the inheritors of contradictory principles among which only temporary reconciliation can be found.

Schumpeter certainly held to the latter position. Consider the way in which he expresses the conflict between democracy and the protection of individual liberties:

> 'Let us transport ourselves into a hypothetical country that, in a democratic way, practices the persecution of Christians, the burning of witches, and the slaughtering of Jews. We should certainly not approve of these practices on the ground that they have been decided on according to the rules of democratic procedure. But the crucial question is: would we approve the democratic constitution itself that produced such results in preference to a non-democratic one that would avoid them?' (Schumpeter, 1954, p. 242)

Here there is a clear identification with democracy as a method and an assertion that as a method of political decision it may issue in morally unacceptable outcomes.

Schumpeter's argument is little more than a statement of logical possibility as it stands. Much would obviously depend on the actual likelihood of democracies producing such results. However, even considered as a statement of bare logical possibility, it has problems, for we cannot simply identify democracy with the principle of majority rule. We also have to consider the underlying principle of political equality, which provides a principal part of the rationale of democratic government. Looked at from this point of view, there may well be rights that are constitutive of democratic practice (compare Ely, 1980).

If there are rights that are constitutive of democratic practice itself, they will include such rights as freedom of assembly and association, freedom to debate matters of public concern and to criticize the government of the day, freedom from arbitrary arrest and imprisonment, freedom from political obligations, like taxes and conscription, that have not been the subject of democratic decision and equality before the law, so that there are no privileged classes in terms of the scope of legal rights and duties. To say that these rights have a democratic character is not to say that any one of them, if breached, would turn a democracy into an authoritarian form of government. But it is to say that, in the absence of such

rights, temporary minorities would always have the temptation
to turn themselves into privileged groups that would be more
capable of resisting the attempt of a minority to turn itself into a
majority.

Aside from these rights, however, there will clearly also be rights
that, though they may be associated with democracy in practice, will
be logically distinct from any definition of democracy that we can
offer. Thus, a second set of principles define rights that seem essential to the idea of constitutional government, independently of the
idea of democracy. This set is formed by what may be termed civil
rights, such as freedom of religion, freedom of conscience, freedom
of non-political speech or freedom of sexual behaviour. Unlike the
first set of rights, these civil rights do not seem to be tied essentially
to the notion of democratic government. Whilst it would seem to be
inconsistent to imagine a democratic government that prohibited a
group of citizens from organizing peacefully to change public policy,
it would not be incoherent to imagine a democratic government
imposing restrictions or privileges in respect of these rights. For
example, both Sweden and Norway, which many might regard as
archetypical egalitarian democracies, have established churches and
levy taxes for their upkeep. If freedom of religion means complete
separation of church and state, which arguably it does, then there is
no reason to suppose that this separation would be respected within
functioning democracies.

The same point about the contingent relationship between
democracy and these rights to individual freedom was made by Sir
Isaiah Berlin some years ago, in his remark that 'men of imagination, originality and creative genius, and, indeed, minorities of all
kinds, were less persecuted' in the Prussia of Frederick the Great
or the Austria of Josef II than in many an earlier or later democracy (Berlin, 1969, pp. 129–30). Whether this is historically accu-
rate or not is a moot point. The conceptual point is, however, surely
correct. The degree of limitation upon the scope of the operation of
power is logically distinct from the source of that power, and if
there is a relationship it is a contingent, empirical one, rather than
a definitional one.

A third set of rights, sometimes connected by theorists to rights
to freedom but in fact logically distinct, are property rights. In one
form or another property rights are often made a matter of constitutional provision. For example, the German Basic Law secures a

right to private property for citizens, although it also prescribes (in a rather typical social Catholic way) that property has duties as well as rights. As Buchanan (1986, pp. 255–6) has noted, this is an area that tends to divide libertarians or classical liberals on the one side from social democrats on the other. Both may agree that there should be clear restrictions upon governments to interfere with the civil liberties of citizens, but they disagree on the protection that should be afforded to property rights. Whereas social democrats see property rights as institutional devices by which control of productive assets is assigned to individuals, the assignment to be judged on the consequences it produces, libertarians and classical liberals typically wish to assimilate property to the list of 'natural' rights, and to say that a person's entitlement to property depends upon their ability justly to acquire or receive property from others.

Again, the question at this stage is not whether either side in this dispute is right, but what such an example tells us about the relationship between constitutionalism and democracy. Although the social democratic account of property would not seem to present any serious problems for democratic theory (as I shall argue later), classical liberal accounts are a different matter. If the right to property is a natural right, and constitutional government aims to protect natural rights, then there could quite easily develop a conflict between the protection of property rights and democratic decision-making. The areas of policy where one would most expect this conflict to emerge would be over such matters as the state's right to take property into public ownership, the taxing of property for the purposes of redistribution or the imposition of limits upon the uses that owners made of their property rights. So, here again, we seem to have a clear case, at least under the classical liberal account of property, of the conflict between constitutional government and democratic government.

Yet another way in which the principles of constitutionalism may appear logically to clash with the principles of democracy is not in relation to a set of rights, but in respect of institutional rules and arrangements, particularly as regards economic policy. It is sometimes alleged that popular government has a tendency towards an inconsistent and self-defeating economic policy. It is prone to indulge in deficit financing, instead of facing the need to balance the public budget, and pursues inflationary monetary policies, as a way of avoiding the hard choices that are implicit in setting public spending priorities. The solution, it is then said, is to place restrictions upon the freedom of popularly elected governments to pursue such policies, and recommendations for achieving this goal have usually included constitutional limits upon governments in their budget behaviour, disallowing deficit financing, and the creation of politically independent central banks to control monetary and interest rate policy.

Here again there would seem to be a prima facie clash between the principles of democracy and the principles of constitutionalism. Democracy would seem to require that popular governments have the freedom to set their own economic priorities, and that they should not be bound by long-standing rules and institutional arrangements, whereas constitutionalism prescribes institutional arrangements that are independent of the popular policy preferences prevailing at any one time.

Taking all four examples of the potential clash between the principles of constitutionalism and populism together, it should be clear that they each raise different issues. Although they all share the feature that at any one time there may appear to be a conflict between what a constitution requires and what a popular government can do, the manner in which this conflict arises and the basis upon which it occurs differ from case to case. Moreover, it seems clear in some cases that, though there may be a clash from time to time between democratic and constitutional principles, these clashes do not reflect an underlying difference of rationale and theory but concern the practical working out of a coherent body of principle, whereas in other cases a more fundamental clash of principle is involved. Hence, if we are to understand the relation of theoretical principles involved, we need to consider each case in turn.

I have presented the conflict between constitutionalism and populist democracy as one concerned with the scope or reach of different decision procedures. Constitutional principles, in limiting the freedom of action of governments, also circumscribe the scope of the majority rule principle. However, it is also possible to characterize the conflict in terms of the source of authoritative decision-making, saying that democratic principles assign the source of authority to the people whereas constitutional principles make the source the courts, a constitutional set of documents or a set of accepted principles. On this account it would be logically possible for different arms of government to come to the same conclusions but by different routes. The only difference would then lie in the origin of the decision, rather than its scope of reach. Indeed, at various times the Supreme Court in the US seems to have played the role of legislating when there was democratic pressure to do so, but when political parties were deadlocked.

There is, incidentally in this context, an interesting question about the extent to which the US Supreme Court has functioned as a counter-majoritarian institution. Empirical analyses suggests that its decisions track with fair accuracy the movement of public opinion over time (Mishler and Sheehan, 1993; Stimson, Mackuen and Erikson, 1995). As public opinion became more liberal in the 1950s and 1960s over such issues as ethnic minority interests or abortion, so the Supreme Court became more liberal, and as public opinion began to turn more conservative, so the Supreme Court followed, so that in practice the Court may not have been such a counter-majoritarian institution as theory might suggest. The mechanism by which this tracking took place was the appointment process which allows the president the right of nomination. And, despite some spectacular 'wrong' nominations by presidents (Eisenhower is alleged to have said of Earl Warren, thought to be a safe conservative on appointment, that his nomination was 'the damndest fool thing I ever did'), it is clear that presidents seek to sense the mood of the country when making appointments.

Although it is possible to describe the conflict between the principles of constitutionalism and populist democracy in terms of the source of decision-making, I shall stick with the discussion in terms of the scope or reach of majoritarian decision-making. In part this is a matter of convenience, since it is useful to be able to discuss the conflict between populism and constitutionalism in terms of the familiar issue of majority decision-making and the protection of constitutionally guaranteed individual rights. Also this approach does not prejudge the institutional implications of the discussion, since at least one way, as we shall see, of squaring the opposition is to say that some constitutional devices can be ways of securing democratic purposes.

Democracy and Political Rights

The first case to consider is the one in which the rights at issue could themselves be regarded as constitutive of democratic practice, such as the right to freedom of assembly or freedom of political communication (Ely, 1980). In some ways we should expect these constitutional rights to be the least difficult to deal with theoretically. Even so, they are not without their problems. Moreover, we shall see that to consider constitutional rights in the context of democratic principles also carries implications for the interpretation of those rights.

I have argued that the fundamental rationale for a system of democratic decision-making is the advancement of certain common interests given the circumstances of politics. If this is so, then the chief common interest that the members of a political community will have is in the rights and powers vested in the political institutions that protect and advance those common interests. It should be clear that these interests may not be identical with the interests of the government of the day or even the popular majority on which the government of the day is based. As Holmes (1988, p. 29) points out, protection of the minority is a common good, both for the minority and for the majority. In particular, where there are sub-groups, the compromise embodied in constitutional restrictions can secure the cooperation necessary for economic prosperity and military independence. To impose no constraints on what majorities can do is to undermine the compromise between sub-groups on which any complex political order needs to be based. For example, it can be imprudent to allow majority governments to draw electoral boundaries to their own advantage as the Stormont government was allowed to do in Northern Ireland for fifty years. The build-up of resentment in the minority community can hardly be said to be in the common interest.

Moreover, the common interest in question is that of members of the political community considered as equals. As I have argued, this requirement of political equality has a number of dimensions, but a central feature is that the political system does not privilege a particular group of people within society. This requirement may be directly linked to the notion of constitutional government, since as Sidgwick (1891, p. 535) once pointed out, constitutional governments carry out their work according to certain fundamental laws. The implicit contrast here is with government by arbitrary decree; but government by arbitrary decree would be inconsistent with the demands of political equality. As Freeman (1992, pp. 12–13) puts it, a constitution organizes and qualifies ordinary government procedures 'in order to prevent the usurpation of the people's sovereignty by public or private institutions'.

So far I have argued that certain rights that may appear to have a basis in some independent idea of constitutional government can in fact be provided with a rationale in terms of democratic practice. It is sensible to establish these rights as constitutional rights, because by doing so we best achieve the underlying goal of advancing the common interest of the members of a society who regard themselves as equals. However, this coincidence between the principles of constitutionalism and democracy does not mean that the two sets of principles are entirely the same. More precisely, we may say that to provide a democratic rationale for certain constitutional principles is also to provide an interpretation of the scope and significance of those principles, and to indicate what their limits are.

Consider a right like the freedom to communicate political information. If this is treated as a free-standing constitutional right, without taking into account its democratic rationale, then it would appear to prohibit a government controlling the content and manner of political information. However, there may be good democratic reasons why there should be such control. In a world where the media of communication are owned by private individuals, unfettered freedom of political communication might result in minority points of view being driven out from public debate and the propagation of opinions favoured largely by the rich and powerful. This would be contrary both to the cause of the common interest and to the principle of political equality.

Empirical evidence suggests that these media effects exist. Cronin (1989, pp. 116–24) cites examples where the results of state referendums in the US have been affected by the amount of public broadcast time that one side of the debate has been willing and able to buy. These effects, moreover, arise despite federal regulations that require broadcasters to provide fair access to competing points of view in public debate. In fact, as Cronin (1989, p. 121) points out, no broadcaster ever lost a licence due to violations of the fairness doctrine, even when the violation occurred over a number of years. Similar worries have been raised in Italy by Berlusconi's ownership of television stations. The implication would seem to be that application of some principle of rough equality of representation in politics could require significant government control in order to uphold a central principle of democratic practice. So, rather than simply placing limits upon government, as traditional constitutional theory would do, the democratic rationale for constitutional political rights might imply vigorous government action.

Conversely, even a democratic rationale of constitutional political rights can be consistent with removing powers from elected representatives and placing those powers in independent hands. Consider, for example, the issues associated with the drawing of constituency boundaries or the financing of political parties. It would simply be unrealistic to think that these matters could be left to elected representatives, since at any one time the parties in power have too great an interest in the outcome to be able to make impartial decisions. Hence, in this sort of case, we might imagine not vigorous action by government to police the operation of constitutional rights, but the appointment of independent bodies, created to serve a longer-term public interest, by controlling the operation of the political system.

The way of reconciling democracy and constitutionalism in this case is to say that democratic practice needs to be orderly practice, if it is to serve the purposes for which it is justified, and at any one time central democratic institutions, like political parties, would be prone to distort the order on which that practice is based. The obvious analogy is also the most telling. Democratic deliberation does not consist in everyone trying to have their say at the same time, but in an orderly proceeding, with a neutral person in the chair, according to rules understood by all participants. In so far as constitutional rules and convention secure the conditions of democratic practice, there is no theoretical conflict involved, though of course there may be practical conflicts from time to time, just as there are when people from the floor challenge the ruling of the chair.

Democracy and Civil Rights

By civil rights I mean such things as the right to privacy, the right to freedom of religion, the right to freedom of sexual behaviour and the right to freedom of non-political speech (for example, speech critical of traditional social practices or of particular religions). I do not assume that these rights are always consistent with one another. Clearly, for example, the right to freedom of religion and the right to free speech can clash with one another, if for example believers in a faith hold that a particular attack amounts to 'hate speech' or an offensive practice (for one example, see Weale, 1990). However, I shall put aside these internal tensions to concentrate upon potential tensions between these civil rights and the scope of majority rule.

Consider one particular civil right, namely that of liberty of conscience. I take this as an example in part because it can be seen as a principle that lies behind a number of civil liberties, for example privacy and freedom of religion, as well as other liberties like exemption from military service. It is also a fairly strong claim, which means that if it can be made compatible with the principle of majority rule, then other, perhaps less stringent freedoms, are also likely to be compatible. Finally, there is also an argument in the history of political thought that it is a culturally distinct idea. Indeed, John Plamenatz (1963, p. 46) makes the striking claim that of the traditional freedoms it is the only one that can claim to be distinctively European. This cultural distinctiveness will turn out to be important in the development of the subsequent argument.

Suppose then that a society has a constitutional arrangement in which liberty of conscience is guaranteed, and this is an operative right in the society. By saying that it is an operative right, I mean that it is upheld against the pressures of the elected government in a significant number of cases. For example, I imagine that the courts may uphold exemptions from military service for individuals who would otherwise be conscripted into the army, or they grant charitable status to certain religious groups, giving them tax advantages, which they would otherwise be denied by public policy. How far is freedom of conscience as it operates under constitutional protection in this sort of way compatible with the principles of democracy?

Following the example of the democratic rights I shall make the test of compatibility not consistency with any majoritarian decision whatsoever, but only with those forms of majority decision-making that can be shown to be compatible with the underlying rationale of democratic institutions. In other words, the principle of liberty of conscience has to be compatible with protecting or advancing the common interests of the members of society where they wish to treat one another as political equals.

If this is the test, then there is bound to be a theoretical inconsistency between democratic practice and freedom of conscience. This is not to say that the conflict arises all the time or is invariable. But it is to say that there is no way in which the conflict can be avoided in principle. In some cases, there will be a clash. Such a conflict would not arise had John Stuart Mill been successful in *On Liberty* in showing that personal freedom had a tendency to serve the public good (Mill, 1859). But it is a commonplace of commentaries on Mill that he fails in his consequentialist justification of freedom, at least in showing that others derive a benefit – even indirectly – from the exercise of freedom by minorities. To make the argument for the protection of freedom complete, Mill has to appeal to the idea that freedom is somehow an intrinsic good for creatures who wish to transcend the 'ape-like' faculty of imitation. Such freedom can certainly be an interest of *individuals*, perhaps even their primary interest, but that does not show that there is a *public* interest in protecting and advancing such freedom. For there may be other public concerns, for example public order or protection from offence, that are harmed by the exercise of individual liberty, and a consequentialist argument will leave open how these interests balance in any particular case.

Consider the case of military conscription. Suppose that a community is fighting a just war to protect its territorial integrity. It may be simply too costly, in terms of the protection of the country, to allow the exercise of a right of freedom of conscience, since that would undermine the fighting power of the armed forces. In making this decision, there may well be concerns of course about dishonesty in the presentation of particular cases. But, abstracting from that worry, the price of freedom of conscience may well seem too high for members of the political community. Here considerations of individual freedom and the public interest appear to be in direct conflict.

It will not do at this point to invoke the principle of political equality. That principle is compatible with taking a rather hard-nosed view of the rights arising from the principle of freedom of conscience. To the argument that it is contrary to the principle of equality to override conscientiously held objections to a course of action, defenders of the action in question could well say that they would be prepared to have their rights of conscience overridden in similar circumstances. The principle of political equality requires that restrictions on freedom of conscience be even-handed; it does not require that they be generous, which is what a principle of liberty of conscience would require.

To be sure, there can be public interest reasons for favouring freedom of conscience as a principle in many cases. For example, on one account, the origins of the idea in Europe are rooted in the experience of religious wars in the sixteenth and seventeenth centuries. Toleration on this view arises because it is preferable to civil or international war (Rawls, 1993, pp. 148–9), although Skinner (1978, pp. 244–9) has noted how there were also principled arguments available at the time. As an account of the origin of the practice of toleration this has much to commend it, but the practice to which it gave rise falls significantly short of the practice that would be implied by adoption of the principle of liberty of conscience in its full sense. One way in which this can be seen is in the fact that religious toleration was typically only extended to limited groups, roughly speaking those whose dissent could kick up enough fuss to disrupt the political order, and whose interests therefore had to be accommodated within the political system. In England, for example, the eventual seventeenth-century settlement extended full religious liberty to protestant groups but not to Jews and Catholics.

The upshot of this is that, though it is possible to advance reasons of public interest for a practice that often resembles respect for liberty of conscience, the justification of toleration in the former case falls short of what would be required in the latter. There certainly is not an extensional equivalence between the principle of liberty of conscience and a public interest based rationale, in the sense that the practical implications of the two principles are distinct in a number of cases.

It would be possible to square the circle if we could provide an account of democracy in terms of autonomy. But I argued in Chapter 4 that this was not possible in any strong sense of the notion of autonomy. Democracy certainly has to be compatible with the notion that individuals are capable of reflection and choice, but that is such a minimally demanding sense of the term that it requires us merely to hold that citizens can make morally significant choices in their decision-making. It does not tell us anything about the priority to be accorded to individual liberty against other values like public order or the protection of collective interests. Moreover, as I also argued in Chapter 4, once we assert that human autonomy gives rise to some moral priority to be accorded to individual liberty, we are likely to want a libertarian political system, rather than a democratic one.

A similar point can be made if we conceive constitutional restrictions as 'gagging' clauses or ways of keeping certain contentious issues out of democratic politics. Holmes (1988) draws attention to the arguments for constitutionalizing certain issues on the grounds that making them the subject of political discussion raises the temperature too much for all the participants. Just as friends might agree among one another not to bring up certain topics in conversation, so members of a polity might benefit from having certain issues remitted to the judiciary. Holmes himself shows how both the issues of slavery in the nineteenth century and abortion in the twentieth have been kept out of politics for fear of disrupting the political relations among important groups. However, as Holmes (1988, p. 56) himself notes, such evasiveness can have serious disadvantages. It gives a premium to those willing to raise the political stakes by threatening disruption, violence and in the limit civil war.

A gap seems to open up, therefore, between the principles of democratic choice and a commitment to a strong principle of liberty of conscience. This gap of principle is institutionally represented in the political conflict that can exist between the decisions of a majoritarian political system and the constitutional protection that might be accorded to the conscientiously held practices of individuals and groups. The reason for this theoretical discrepancy is to be found in John Plamenatz's insight, I conjecture. Freedom of conscience is a culturally specific value. It is the political expression of a certain sort of individualism. A community may choose to acknowledge such a value, but that would be the result of a democratic choice.

Despite the lack of theoretical affinity between the practice of democracy and the principle of freedom of conscience, it is still possible that there is an empirical relation between them. This is, indeed, my own view. By and large, and despite Isaiah Berlin's examples to the contrary, it is democratic regimes that seem to provide the conditions within which liberty of conscience is respected rather than authoritarian ones. The reasons for this, I imagine, are that, although political equality does not require citizens to take a generous view of the conscientious claims of others, it provides the political conditions within which tolerant attitudes are promoted. Having to negotiate with the interests of others and come to some compromise is one way by which people can come to see that there are points of view other than their own, and it is in just such contexts that an attitude of toleration is likely to be developed.

Thus, in acknowledging the equal place of others to determine the common interest we necessarily recognize that we should be willing to compromise in the pursuit of our own interests. Compromise goes beyond justification, since the latter is compatible with using the procedures of the political process to your own ends, when this is possible, provided you have the power and you have explained what you are doing. Compromise, by contrast, will sometimes enjoin upon actors that they do not use their legitimate power to its full extent, even when they are able to do so, if by another course of action they can meet an opponent part of the way. Compromise, in this sense, is not an attempt to stand in a neutral position but to stand in a context-bound common position (Bellamy, 1994, pp. 436–41).

But the principle of political equality may push people at times beyond compromise to what we may call a sense of accommodation. This is stronger than compromise in the sense that it involves a willingness to take fewer advantages for oneself in the interest of getting as many people on board as possible. One of the ways in which it is manifest is in the 'politics of accommodation' as described by Lijphart (1968). The aim here then is not simply to get one's own way with some concessions to those who have competing interests, but instead to enlarge the sense of interests operative in a political situation, so as to incorporate the interests of others.

Democracy and Property Rights

Should there be constitutional limits on a democracy's right to legislate on matters of property? As I have already noted, this is an issue that divides classical liberals from social democrats, with the former wishing typically to impose only procedural limits – for example, that the treatment of property be even-handed between different groups – whilst the latter wish for stronger constitutional protection for private property in particular. A decision of this matter has considerable implications for the scope of public policy and the ability of collective mechanisms of choice to deal with the cumulative and unintended consequences of individual interaction. Stringent limits on the ability of a democracy to control and regulate the use of private property would limit measures that could be adopted in environmental policy, anti-monopoly policy, health and safety legislation, the control of pension fund investments, the relief of poverty or the adoption of measures of consumer protection.

In the US the tension between democracy and constitutionalism in this respect was manifest during the so-called 'Lochner era', after the decision in *Lochner* v. *New York*. In this case the Supreme Court ruled that minimum wage and maximum hour laws were a transfer of property from employers to employees and were as such prohibited under the constitution (Sunstein, 1988, pp. 342–3). The point about this judgement was that it went beyond simply stating that measures for worker protection had to be adopted with due process and applied according to the principle of equality before the law to a position in which the range of permissible democratic purposes was restricted. It thus conflated a constitutionalist position on the way in which the exercise of political power was to be conducted with a libertarian view of property rights.

Measures adopted by democracies to deal with the use of property will typically be forward-looking, that is to say they will seek to regulate the use of property so as to achieve a stated purpose. Libertarian accounts of property are typically backward-looking, however. That is, they ascribe ownership and entitlement in terms of the transactions that have taken place between individuals within a social order. Thus, one way in which the libertarian or classical liberal position could be made good would be in terms of a theory that showed how the existing body of property rights grew legitimately from a historically given set of transactions. But libertarian theories of property, which have normally been based on some variant of Locke's (1690, pp. 327–44) account, have proved notoriously weak in this respect. They cannot deal with the problem of how to justify initial acquisition, moving too easily to the conclusion that the existing distribution arose through a series of transactions that were either just, or should be treated as though they were just. And they presuppose what Honoré (1961) has termed 'full liberal ownership' rather than the more complex bundles of rights that in fact make up property rights in modern societies (compare Reeve, 1986, pp. 94–100).

Moreover, it seems simply a historical mistake to ignore the fact that certain forms of property have had their origin in legislative decision. The most important of these forms has been the creation of limited liability for commercial enterprises, which restricts the debt liability of owners in the event of bankruptcy, and without which the modern corporation would not exist. In Britain during the 1840s the matter was debated extensively, and it is clear that forward-looking arguments about the social benefits that might be thought to flow from the greater willingess to take risks allowed by adoption of the principle of limited liability were decisive in the passage of the legislation (Atiyah, 1979, pp. 564–7).

It does not seem, therefore, that there are strong reasons for imposing stronger constitutional restrictions upon the majority's right to legislate in matters of property than are implied by the principles of the rule of law in any case. The means employed should be proportional to the goal being sought and there should be no arbitrary discrimination in the treatment of different sorts of property owners. To entrench a right to private property in a constitution that would make it unconstitutional for a duly elected government to control and regulate property in the public good would seem to go further than is warranted by any persuasive argument.

Democracy and Independent Authority

The idea that certain sorts of issues should be removed in large measure from the legislative agenda and placed in the hands of specialist agencies or independent bodies is one that has been discussed in relation to a number of policy areas (see, for example, Majone, 1996, pp. 9–27). In some countries, like Sweden, the principle is a regular part of their public administration, whereas in other countries there are fears about the extent to which such agencies would be exempt from the normal controls of democratic accountability. One important proposal that has often been discussed in recent years in this context is the removal of certain areas of economic policy-making, most notably monetary policy and the setting of interest rates, to an independent central bank which would be free of day-to-day political control.

In any particular case the decision that is made is likely to depend upon a number of circumstances that are peculiar to the case in question and to the precise proposal that is being made. Here we shall only be able to discuss the extent to which such proposals are in principle compatible with our underlying account of democracy.

The argument that is usually advanced in favour of independent bodies controlling central aspects of economic policy is that democracies are prone by their nature to favour inflationary policies and deficit financing, for reasons that are politically acceptable in the short term but counter-productive in the long term. Hence considerations of collective prudence suggest removing instruments of monetary and interest-rate control away from political decision-makers to technical decision-makers operating according to politically agreed rules. Thus, the New Zealand central bank, which has recently acquired independence, now has a contract with the government to deliver a certain rate of inflation.

The argument against this policy is the obvious one that such an arrangement deprives a government of the flexibility that may be necessary to deal with shocks to the economy. Thus, the behaviour of governments in dealing with the price shocks associated with the fourfold increase in oil prices in the 1970s can be interpreted not as evidence that democracy is prone to inflation and deficit but simply as a complex balancing of competing policy objectives (the maintenance of high employment as well as control of inflation being the most important), and no general trends about democracy can be read into the experience, as some critics were prone to do.

By the time we are at this level of detail, however, we have gone beyond the simple point of principle and we are discussing rather complex middle-range empirical generalizations. The case for an independent central bank is certainly couched in the right sort of way, from the point of view of the principles involved, even if rests upon contestable empirical judgements. Hence, I would say that if the members of a political system were convinced of these generalizations, then there would be no objection, from the point of view of democratic principle, to their instituting independent arrangements. Of course, the empirical judgement may well turn out to be false, and in that case the members of the community would have been unwise to have instituted the reforms. All that I wish to establish here is that there can be no objection on democratic grounds to such a reform. Equally, however, the legitimating principle of the institutions would be that they had been democratically adopted.

Conclusions

No very clear or simple conclusion emerges from this review of the different ways in which constitutional devices can properly limit the scope of popular majoritarian decision-making. Instead, we need to consider the question in relation to the particular form of restriction that is being proposed. In the case of democratic rights, for example, constitutional restrictions may be regarded as ways in which the 'rules of the democratic game' are codified, and there is in principle no theoretical conflict between constitutional restrictions and democratic practice. Constitutional restrictions are necessary in order to prevent temporary holders of power from using it to their own advantage and to the disadvantage of their opponents. No doubt, in particular cases, there will be questions as to whether the constitutional umpire is entitled to make a particular decision, but those cases should not be confused with the more general theoretical issue.

Individual civil rights present a different matter, however. Here we do seem often to be faced with the choice between values that conflict, most particularly a concern with the protection of public interest and a concern for the flowering of individuality. No general theoretical reconciliation is available in this case, and the best we can hope for is that in practice the processes that foster democratic compromise will also foster a preference for individuality.

Property rights pose fewer problems. Property is a social institution that is best justified by the purposes that it serves, and its operation and terms of working can properly be modified by political decision in the general interest. Indeed, it would be absurd to suppose that an environmental problem could not be solved or the consumer's interest protected because there was a general right to use property as one pleased. Of course, changes in property rights ought to be accomplished by proper constitutional means, and principles of justice should apply (for example, that no group of property holders be discriminated against), but these are general requirements of public policy, and there is no reason to pick out issues of property as having special constitutional status.

Moving from questions of the protection of vital individual interests to matters to do with collective prudence in the management of the public budget, the conclusion was that independent bodies are at least consistent with democratic principles, if the members of society are convinced of the relevant empirical evidence and if they choose to create such institutional arrangements. However, there are no arguments of collective prudence that would indicate that it would be sensible to establish super-majoritarian institutions to ensure prudence in the management of resources. Where super-majoritarian devices have an exploitative basis, as in the ante-bellum US, then there is a strong and positive reason for wanting them abolished.

10 The Obligations of Democracy

The traditional problem of political obligation has been treated in large part as one about the obligation to obey the law or the commands of civil authority more generally. This is an important topic to which there are many possible answers (Horton, 1992). But to frame the problem of democratic obligation in this traditional way is both too wide and too narrow. It is too wide because it poses the question of obligation in relation to political authority as such, leaving aside the variety of forms that such authority can take. Even if one can show not only that there is some general obligation to obey the law under most forms of political authority but that there was some special obligation within a democracy, issues would still need to be resolved around the content and extent of these supposedly special obligations.

However, in another sense, the traditional focus is also too narrow. As Bhikhu Parekh (1993) has pointed out, the practice of democracy raises larger questions of obligation than those concerned simply with the duty to obey a democratically made law. Living in a democratic society involves duties like those of being informed about public events, being willing to play one's part in the political duties that come one's way and making sure that actions committed in one's name are in accordance with one's convictions. Of course, there is also the question of how far one is obliged to obey a democratically elected law (one's duties as a democratic subject as well as a democratic citizen, to put it in Parekh's terms), but these legal duties are only part of the full list of democratic duties that citizens owe.

It might be argued that on some conceptions of politics this sense of obligation was unnecessary. If we simply conceive politics as a process of pluralistic competition, in which self-orientated or sectional preferences for certain public goods are aggregated by

189

analogy with the way that the market aggregates preferences for private goods, then it might seem that we do not need a sense of political obligation, since generally speaking people do not need a motive of obligation to pursue their self-interest. However, if we conceive the justification of democracy to be framed in terms of political equals pursuing their common interests in conditions of fallibility, it is impossible to sustain this interpretation of democratic practice. Indeed, it is also worth noting in relation to this argument that even in its own terms it runs into paradox.

The simple reason why democratic politics cannot simply be conceived as the pluralistic pursuit of self-interest is that the logic of collective action provides political agents with an incentive to allow others sharing their interests to carry the burden of promoting those interests politically. As Olson (1965) pointed out, in large societies it will typically be rational for individuals to seek to free ride on the behaviour of those who share their interests, but this can be self-defeating from the point of view of the interest-group in question. Hence, even the pursuit of self-interest requires a sense of duty if only to one's sub-group, unless there is some hegemon to organize the collective action or special incentives are in place promoting participation.

Moreover, it would be an extremely unusual situation to suppose that any person's interests were entirely captured in their membership of some particular sectional grouping. Certainly, when things are going reasonably well, we are often not aware of how the pursuit of our particular interests depends upon the provision of major public goods like a clean environment, a well functioning system of law and administration or protection against external attack. But day-to-day lack of awareness is not the same as functional independence, and anyone with a sectional interest will also have these broader interests. We have only to think of societies where law and order have broken down to realize that for the vast bulk of the population (gun-runners and terrorists aside), the pursuit of sectional economic advantages presupposes that a large of range of public goods is already supplied.

Once we acknowledge such interdependence, then the logic of collective action gives rise to an even greater need to introduce the concept of citizen's duties. Rational choice analyses of politics that draw upon narrow and instrumentalist views of political rationality have found it impossible to account for even a simple act of political duty, like that of voting in a large electorate, without at some appealing to a notion of civic duty (Mansbridge, 1990).

If the principle of political equality is accepted, then we have a further reason for invoking the notion of citizen obligation within a democracy. Whatever else it might accomplish, there is no reason to believe that a functioning process of pluralistic competition will enable all sectional interests to be articulated in an even-handed way, since different parties will be able to bring different bargaining strengths to the negotiating table. If the value of political equality matters to the concept of democracy, then the process of bargaining will have to be nested in an account of obligations that would prevent inequalities of power from being exploited too readily.

The upshot of this discussion is that we cannot eliminate the notion of political obligation from our account of democracy. If we attempt to do so, by adopting a concept of democracy in which the notion is apparently superfluous, it will make a reappearance once we try to give an account of even the simplest political acts.

Political Obligations in a Democracy

What political obligations can we be said to have in a democracy? Bhikhu Parekh has advanced the following conception:

> 'citizens have several obligations in addition to obeying the law. These include an obligation to take an active interest and to participate in the conduct of public affairs, to keep a critical eye on the activities of government, to speak up against the injustices of their society, to stand up for those too demoralized, confused and powerless to fight for themselves, and in general to create a rich and lively community . . . citizens also have obligations to safeguard the integrity of the public realm, to do nothing to undermine the standards of public morality and debase the language of political discourse, to ensure truthfulness in public life, to pursue their interests consistently with those of the community and to conduct themselves with civility, moderation, courage and public spirit.' (Parekh, 1993, p. 243)

In commenting on this list, Parekh notes that these are moral, and not legal, obligations supported by a sense of personal responsibility rather than legal penalty, and also that they are duties owed to other citizens.

This last point is of importance in seeking to understand the underlying rationale of these obligations. To whom are the duties owed? Within the account of democracy that I have so far advanced, the duties are best conceived of as being owed to other citizens, since democracy arises out of the need to deal with the problems of collective interests. Democratic politics is thus a co-operative enterprise directed towards the solution of these common problems. Participation in this enterprise therefore brings with it obligations to play one's part on familiar grounds of fairness. These grounds have been set out, both by Hart and by Rawls, as implying a reciprocal willingness to give up one's freedom. For example, Hart renders the principle of fairness as follows:

> 'when a number of persons conduct any joint enterprise accord-ing to rules and thus restrict their liberty, those who have sub-mitted to those restrictions when required have a right to a similar submission from those who have benefited by their submission.' (Hart, 1967, p. 61)

Similarly, Rawls formulates the principle to say:

> 'that when a number of persons engage in a mutually advanta-geous cooperative venture according to rules, and thus restrict their liberty in ways necessary to yield advantages for all, those who have submitted to these restrictions have a right to a similar acquiescence on the part of those who have benefited from their submission. We are not to gain from the cooperative labours of others without doing our fair share.' (Rawls, 1972, pp. 111–12)

Thus, if we simply rely upon others to carry the burden of dealing with these collective issues, we are in effect free-riding upon their efforts.

Parekh makes the important point that these obligations do not imply that everyone needs to be active all the time, since all that successful democratic cooperation requires is that enough people play their part. In this sense, he argues, political obligation is rather like the obligation to report an accident. I have such an obligation but we need not act if someone else has done so already.

The implication that Parekh draws is that a simple failure to turn up to a public meeting should not of itself be a source of moral criticism.

It is surely right to assert that to achieve the goals of democratic practice requires only general and not universal participation. However, an obvious problem arises if we try to translate this insight into an institutional form, for in the case in which there is inadequate democratic participation, someone can always use in their defence the argument that they would have turned up if enough other people had looked like doing so as well, but in the circumstances they did not want to be one of a *minority* who turned up. In other words, in situations in which only general but not universal participation in a practice is required, we have to find a way of coordinating the actions of citizens, so that not too many and not too few are enabled to fulfil their duties.

One device for doing this is obvious, namely selection by lot. This ancient democratic device for filling public offices is attractive in the present context not only because it expresses the democratic commitment to equality but also because it can be efficiently tailored to recruit the right number of people to office. Some have gone so far as to argue that justice by lottery could be made a basic principle of political life (Goodwin, 1992). But even if we do not accept this viewpoint, it is clear that it can be successfully employed for social purposes, as its use in selecting individuals for jury service from the electoral register goes to show. Since one of the obligations of citizenship in societies that use juries is to serve when called, random selection ensures that a cross-section of one's peers will hear one's case.

It can be argued that there is an essential difference between jury service and other forms of political obligation, since serving on a jury requires participation for a limited range of tasks for a definite period of time, whereas Parekh's democratic obligations are open-ended in extent and indefinite in length. This criticism only holds, however, provided we lack sufficient imagination, for there are ways in which some of the democratic obligations can be turned into something much more like jury service, by using citizen juries or deliberative polls, which work by taking a random groups of citizens and asking them to give a view on a matter of public policy, for example the siting of hospital services. If participation involves a cost, as I argued in Chapter 5, we can fairly distribute that cost by using the principle of random selection. Clearly not all obligations could be met in this way, since some, like speaking up against the injustices of one's society or taking a stand for the powerless, cannot be organized on a principle of random selection. However, there is no reason in principle why a greater effort could not be made than is currently the case in this direction.

One question that emerges in this context is whether it is consistent with the fulfilment of one's duty to commute it to a cash payment. After all, there have been a number of societies in which people could buy exemption from military service by paying a substitute to take one's place. Less contentiously one could consider the very large number of people who pay their subscriptions to organizations like Amnesty International or Friends of the Earth without themselves participating in the political actions that they support, even if it is only writing a letter. Their reasoning presumably is that they lack to time to become fully involved in the political tasks they believe need to be carried out, but they would like to show their support by paying for someone else to take action. Paying for others to do one's citizen's duty is not like paying for someone to join the army for you, since presumably there is no risk to life and limb in doing your citizen's duty. But are the duties of citizenship sufficiently like paying your subscription to a worthwhile organization to make substitution permissible?

The obvious argument against allowing this possibility is that the purpose of citizen duties is not simply to get a particular set of jobs done but also to raise the quality of social citizenship generally. By fulfilling their duties citizens educate themselves, and this increased level of awareness then feeds into the full range of their public activities. They not only discharge their particular duty, but they become better voters, critics or members of their local government. This at least is the assumption made by authors like Mill (1861a), who see political participation as important because it promotes larger social sympathies. Of course, much here depends on the scale of selection for things like citizen juries or deliberative polls, but it would not be unreasonable so to arrange things that everyone could expect once in their life to have some serious responsibility.

So far I have only been concerned with the duties that apply to citizens generally, but it is reasonable to expect that special duties will apply to those who have particular professional responsibilities for the conduct of politics. If political decision-making is about securing the conditions for action in the public interest, then a number of duties can clearly be laid upon such professionals. Obviously, they need to use the public finances as an instrument of public purposes and not an instrument of private gain. They need to deal honestly with their opponents in public debate, taking care not to turn differences of political judgement into accusations of moral turpitude. They need to explain the basis of their decisions in government, ensuring that conditions are maintained for accountability in decision-making and maintaining data and statistics in a reliable form. And they need to avoid abuse of the political power with which they are entrusted.

The statement of these duties may seem to be apple pie. However, they are all too regularly breached. Thus, although British governments probably are entitled to their reputation for being relatively uncorrupt, there have been incidents in the postwar period when governments have delayed the implementation of boundary changes to secure electoral advantage, altered the basis on which unemployment statistics are presented, misleadingly presented public expenditure accounts and substituted unfounded slurs for rational argument in debates with their opponents. More strikingly, Italians reflecting on their post-war history might well be pleased to have had more apple pie.

Being Outvoted

No matter how well conducted the disputes of political life are, there are bound to be continuing disagreements that can only be resolved by voting. This raises what for many people will be the prime question in defining the obligations of citizenship: what are your obligations if you are outvoted and what is their basis?

In examining this question I shall assume that the political process is reasonably fair and orderly, so that the loss of the vote does not arise from corruption or bias within the system, but simply from a failure to persuade enough of one's fellow citizens to share one's point of view. I shall also assume that, though the loss of the vote sets back one's own legitimate interests or passes over one's own conscientiously held viewpoint, the setback is not so great that it can be called a severe deprivation or injustice. In other words, I shall consider the case where in being outvoted you are suffering an inevitable concomitant of democratic political life. This is obviously the most favourable case in which to ascribe an obligation to accept the result, and the logic of taking this approach is that if the obligation can be defined in such cases it will provide a reference point against which principles can be defined in more controversial cases.

In a much discussed article, Richard Wollheim (1962) once asserted that there was a paradox involved in democracy, since the practice of democracy required a commitment of citizens to accept two logically incompatible propositions. If this is so, then there can be no point in discussing any interpretation of the obligation to accept losing the vote. It cannot make sense to say that people have a duty to perform what is logically self-contradictory, just as I cannot have an obligation to paint an object green all over and red all over at the same time. Hence, if Wollheim is correct, there is either no obligation to form a judgement on alternative public policies (which is what so far we have asserted is part of the obligations of democratic citizenship) or there is no obligation to accept the result when I lose. Is it possible to resolve this problem?

There are, in fact, a number of possible solutions. One is to note an ambiguity in the way that Wollheim formulates the problem and then to see that the paradox hangs on trading on that ambiguity. The paradox that Wollheim identifies is that, in being outvoted, an individual believes that policy A ought to be enacted because it accords with his or her best judgement and a simultaneous belief that policy B ought to be enacted because it accords with the will of the majority. But there is no need ever to be forced into this dilemma. I can, for example, quite simply believe that A is the best policy (both before and after the vote) but hold that B ought to be enacted.

Wollheim misses this possibility, because he quite unconsciously glosses the belief that A is the best policy by the notion that A ought to be enacted:

'On this view when a citizen chooses a certain policy or prefers one policy to another, he is expressing not a want but an *evaluation*. He chooses A or prefers A to B, because he thinks that A is the best policy, is the policy that ought to be enacted, or, alternatively, that A is a better policy than B or ought to be enacted in preference to B' (Wollheim, 1962, pp. 77–8)

All we need at this point to do is to introduce the distinction between thinking that a policy is best and thinking that it ought to be enacted. There is no inconsistency in thinking that policy A is best but policy B ought to be enacted. It should thus be clear that there is no logical inconsistency in thinking that you have an obligation to accept a result against which you voted. That being so, we can pass on to the substantive question of why one should think that there was such an obligation.

One common answer to this question is that, in the face of disagreement, societies need a way of settling their disputes, and a refusal to accept the obligation to abide by the opinion of the majority would threaten the peaceful resolution of conflicts. The difficulty with this answer, however, is that it raises the argumentative stakes too quickly. There are certainly cases where the refusal to go along with majority opinion will lead to civil unrest and possibly civil war, thus threatening a return to the Hobbesian state of nature, but equally there are plenty of cases where disobedience will go unnoticed and undetected. For example, if there is a law forbidding me putting chemical fertilizer on my garden, this could be unenforceable and without any sense of obligation I might feel free to ignore it, particularly if I disagree with the estimate of the risks on which the policy is based. In general, with legislation intended to control the cumulative effects of individual acts that are of negligible import of themselves, only a sense of obligation will provide an individual with a reason for obeying the legislation.

If the consequences of disobeying the process of decision cannot provide a reason for obligation, then there must be something about the process itself that provides the rationale. One thought here is to appeal to the general principle of fairness, which says that one ought to play one's due part in a system of political co-operation, and to say that democratic decision-making according to the principle of majority rule is a fair scheme of decision. The reason why it is fair, as we saw in Chapter 7 in the discussion of aggregation, turns on the claim that it treats all members of the political community in a neutral or impartial way. Hence the ground of the obligation is not simply that societies need a way of settling disagreements, but that the democratic way of doing it via majority decision is a fair way of proceeding.

The relevant thought is along the following lines. In a situation of differences of judgement, where each person is voting conscientiously, each of us runs the risk that our impartial assessment of the common good will be in the minority. To be unwilling to accept the obligation to obey a rule when I am outvoted is to wish to be placed in a privileged situation compared to everyone else in registering my assessment of the common interest. Although I still think my own opinion is the correct one, I do not think I can unfairly privilege my opinion as the one on which the community ought to act.

The work here is clearly being done by a principle of fairness. Are there reasons independent of fairness, however, that are also applicable? One interesting line of argument in this context stems from the claim that the many are more likely to be right than the few. In book 3, chapter 11 of *The Politics*, Aristotle argues that 'the many, no one of whom singly is a good man, may yet taken all together be better than the few, not individually but collectively, in the same way that a feast to which all contribute is better than one given at one man's expense'. There are a number of ways of interpreting this passage (Waldron, 1995), but, taking note of his reference to judgements of art or poetry, it seems generally clear that what Aristotle has in mind is the thought that in complex matters the general public can produce a verdict that is likely to have more wisdom than the individual, because the collective sees more sides of the question than the individual.

Such a view might seem to provide a foundation for an individual obligation. After all, why would any individual think it right that partial and inaccurate views should be embodied in public policy? Aristotle's thought can be made to sound like that of Rousseau (1762, p. 250) that when in voting an opinion contrary to my own prevails, this proves that I was mistaken. However, the two approaches are subtly different. Aristotle's views relate to the processes by which public deliberation yields a better outcome than any individual could achieve singly, whereas Rousseau looks at the content of decisions that have been made.

The most important attempt to formalize the Rousseauian thought was made by Condorcet, in his other great contribution to democratic theory besides the paradox discussed in Chapter 7. Acquainted with Rousseau's work, Condorcet was able to show that, under certain conditions, a majority was more likely to be right than any individual (see McLean and Hewitt, 1994, pp. 34–40). Roughly speaking, the basic idea is that, where for a given number of voters, each voter has an equal, better than even, chance of being right, a majority of voters has a higher chance of being right than any individual (compare also Black, 1958, p. 164; Barry, 1967, pp. 119–23; and Grofman and Feld, 1988). The larger the majority, the more likely it is that the collective result is correct.

Taken in its own terms, the theorem is unassailable (it simply follows from the basic principles of probability theory). But how far does it help in the present context? Obviously, everything hangs on the assumption that everyone has a better than even chance of being right, for if they do not the probability of error rises very quickly with the size of the majority. Given that this probability is an unobservable, someone might take their minority position as evidence that this crucial assumption did not hold in any particular case. Suppose someone did make the inference from their minority position to the wrongness of the majority, would he or she be entitled to act on this assumption? The answer surely has to be no, since, by doing so, a precedent is created in which any minority could always pray in aid their status as evidence that the majority was wrong. And this would simply create a situation in which any minority was claiming a privileged situation. We are back to fairness again.

However, another source of obligation independent of fairness, some might argue, is one's participation in the political process implying consent to the outcome of the procedure. Consent may be expressed either expressly or tacitly. In express consent there is a mutually acknowledged intention to accept some offer or arrangement. For example, if I consent to my neighbour's planning application, I am saying that I will accept the proposed arrangement. In tacit consent, I act in such a way that I may validly be taken to have such intentions, or at least obligations may be ascribed to me as though I had such intentions. For example, if I do nothing to signal my disagreement with the planning application in the designated time, then I may be deemed to have consented to the plans and be held subsequently to the obligations that thereby follow.

Agreement by mutual consent is the principal means by which individuals coordinate their activities to mutual advantage. For, by expressing a positive interest in an arrangement, an individual induces other individuals to rely upon him or her to *their* advantage. My neighbours, noting my consent to their proposal, will go ahead with ordering materials, arranging builders and so on. Acts of consent, however they are conventionally expressed, are thus signals from one person to another that reliance may be placed upon the person consenting to play their part in a proposed scheme (compare Weale, 1978a).

Participation in an electoral process can be seen as one way by which persons signal to others that they are willing to abide by the result, and in receiving this signal others themselves will rely upon those so signalling. Indeed, it would not be worth the trouble voting and undertaking related acts unless one could rely upon others to play their part in the practice. Does this mean that the act of voting is an act of express or tacit consent? The answer to this question depends upon what the signal is understood to mean within a political community. If there is a general understanding that turning out to vote is a way of signalling to others that one is prepared to abide by the result, then the act of voting is equivalent to an act of express consent to the result of the election. But suppose there is not this general understanding. What then can we say? In particular, can we use the notion of tacit consent?

The notion of tacit consent, it will be recalled, is a way of ascribing meaning to an action independently of the meaning that would be ascribed to that action by the intentions of the actor. Understood in this way, I do not think that there is any clear way of ascribing meaning independently of the sort of rich institutional context that legal systems provide for interpreting actions, and I have already suggested that politics lacks such a rich institutional context. I think therefore that we have reached the limits of the notion of consent in politics once we move to the ascription of meanings that are not part of the actor's intention.

However, it is possible to recover the substance of the notion of consent by inferring an obligation from the act of participation. For if participation induces others to rely upon one, then there is a general principle of fairness which says that where one has gained from others restraining their activities to one's own advantage there is an obligation to reciprocate. Hence, the consent justification of obligation reduces to the fairness justification.

Obligations and Political Community

Obligations to play one's fair part in a practice are always obligations to play one's part in a particular practice, bounded in space and time. The question therefore arises as to what the implications of our account of democratic obligation might be for any putative duties that might exist between generations or across the boundaries of political communities. In stressing the way in which obligations arise within a political community, the present account might seem to suggest that the borders of a political community define the limits of democratic obligation. Is this so? Can there be obligations of democratic citizenship beyond borders?

Turning initially to the question of international duties, the first point to note is that a democratic state represents its citizens. Clearly if a policy is adopted by democratic vote in a direct democracy, then when the state acts in accordance with the vote it is acting in the name of its citizens. The same is also true within a representative democracy, however. A majoritarian system will presumably act according to the expressed preferences of a majority as mediated through the parliamentary representatives, and even in constitutional systems or systems of responsible government where foreign policy might be thought a paradigmatic sort of issue to be reserved to policy elites, the assumption must be that the state is acting in the national interest, and in that sense is acting in the name of citizens.

What democratic obligations do citizens have when they are members of a state that acts in their name? They are surely a special case of the obligations they have for political action more generally: to understand, scrutinize and criticize. To see how these general obligations extend the duties of citizenship beyond borders, the first necessity is to introduce some current empirical truisms of international relations, in particular that modern states are interdependent in respect of their relations and freedom of action with respect to one another (compare Beitz, 1979).

Two sorts of interdependence are particularly worth noting. The first of these is physical interdependence through the sharing of a common environment. Modern production methods have released the bounds of Prometheus, and the transformation of nature has followed in consequence. Most of the major contemporary environmental problems – acid rain, ozone depletion, global warming, the transport of hazardous waste and deforestation – are international in character, and those that are not, for example urban air pollution, arise as a consequence of the international trade in vehicles.

This international dimension means both that the action of one national actor has implications for others, and often many others, and that the solution to these problems will require international regimes of cooperation.

The second form of interdependence is economic interdependence. When price signals move around the world almost instantaneously, as happens with modern electronic stock markets, it becomes impossible for governments to insulate their economies from the effects of large monetary and capital flows, unless they practise an economic autarchy that substantially reduces their country's standard of living.

In this situation of international interdependence, the task of democratic governments is to represent faithfully the views of their citizens, and the obligations of democratic citizenship are to scrutinize, monitor and criticize where necessary the extent to which the government is faithfully representing their views. However, this conclusion does not yet get us to duties beyond borders in the strict sense of that term. It shows that citizens have democratic duties pertaining to the performance of their governments in respect of international matters, but it does not show that the opinions it is the task of the government to represent are ones that reflect a concern for international duties.

An example may help to make the problem clearer. Suppose you are a citizen of a government negotiating in your name on international agreements to tackle a serious transnational problem like global climate change. Suppose that it is the interests of your country to have an agreement that limits the emission of greenhouse gases and that the citizens of the country also think that there would be a global public benefit in an international agreement being secured. It is still consistent with these beliefs to instruct your representatives to seek an agreement that minimizes the contribution that your country makes to the costs of the agreement, rather than an agreement in which your country bears its fair share (however that is defined and assuming a fair share is higher than the minimum share that you can get away with). Is there any reason in the theory of democratic obligation why one should favour the fair share option for one's country rather than the least cost option?

This question is particularly difficult within a general theory of democracy, like the present one, which is built on the idea that democratic institutions arise from the need to solve collective action problems in societies in which members treat each other as equals. For it would appear to be an implication of that account that the function of the government in international relations was to represent the interests of citizens, and it is presumably in the interests of citizens to pay as little as they can towards the cost of an international agreement.

One possible line of argument here is to fudge the notion of interests, and to say that it is not really in a nation's interest to pay less than its fair share towards the costs of some international agreement. This attitude seems to me to be not only pious, in the pejorative sense of that term, but liable to lead us into confusion in those cases where it really would be in our interests to pay our fair share, as for example when a failure to pay our fair share would produce a reputation for being untrustworthy that would lead other countries to bargain harder on other matters. This clearly would be a case where it would be in our interests to pay our fair share, but by definition this is not the case we are considering. Instead we want to focus on the case where we could pay less without affecting our interests elsewhere.

Nor do we come any closer to a solution by saying that in attending to our common interests as members of a community we necessarily invoke certain ideals, and that the pursuit of ideals is incompatible with not paying one's fair share. Again, we may suppose that the example already encompasses that point. We are engaged in ideal reasoning when we say that it is worthwhile solving a pollution problem at a certain economic cost. In other words, we have been through the intellectual process of defining our ideals, and we are now into the process of bargaining to define exactly how they are to be implemented. There is no obvious principle of political morality that tells you that you have to pursue your ideals at greater cost to yourself than necessary.

The problem does become easier to solve once we realize that it is exactly analogous at the global level to the account of competitive pluralist democracy at the national level. In the discussion of competitive pluralism it was argued that certain elementary and essential acts to maintain the system, like voting, were incompatible with assuming that individuals were merely advancing their own sectional interests. Similarly, we might say that an international scheme of cooperation to mutual advantage is impossible if countries seek merely to pursue their own interests. Of course, in particular cases countries may be able to get away with it, but there is a sort of moral inconsistency in the stance.

The theory of democracy is a theory of how agents acquire the rightful power to act for others, and in this sense it does not say anything about the moral content of the goals that this represent-ative action involves. But in as much as it involves appeal to the idea of moral equality, it shares a principled foundation with the a theory of justice that makes moral equality its basis (compare Barry, 1989a, pp. 345–8). It is possible to participate with others in a decision process without incurring the burdens that decision-making might fairly place upon you, but at the very least it is psychologically difficult to live with the cognitive dissonance that this causes. Perhaps for this reason it is the most egalitarian democracies, as in the Nordic countries, who are also the most internationalist.

This solution to the problem of international democratic obliga-tions cannot, however, be a model for inter-generational obliga-tions. If international obligations arise as a result of participation in norm-governed regimes of international cooperation, this cannot be a model for inter-generational obligations, since we do not stand in a relationship of cooperation with future generations. In the famous words of Groucho Marx: 'Why should we do anything for posterity? What's posterity ever done for us?'

To begin to answer this question it is useful to consider the character of democratic obligations in general, and in particular the beneficiary of those obligations (compare Weale, 1991). In this context we should note that the entity to which citizens are joined by the relation of membership is a non-reducible social concept (Mellor, 1982). What I mean by this is that the duties of demo-cratic citizenship are not defined in respect of sets of individuals, strictly so called, but in respect of an entity made up of non-assignable individuals and collectively defined. To see why this is so, consider what it would be like if our account of political com-munity were based upon a strictly individualist set of obligations of the kind we find in a market economy founded on the principle of contract.

According to a strict individualist theory of obligations, persons will only be obliged when each individual is obliged. The usual method of acquiring obligations within individualist theory is by consent, though this need not be so (for example, there is nothing inconsistent with individualism in saying that parents have obligations to their children even though they are not based on contract). The essential point is that the obligations of a community will be comprised by the sum total of the obligations of its members. Take as a paradigm case the set of economic obligations and corresponding rights arising from freely negotiated contracts within a community. On the individualist account these rights and obligations will change every time that someone joins or leaves the community, since they are the rights and obligations of assignable persons. Persons will have the obligations to which they are individually liable, so that X's obligation to Y will cease when Y ceases to participate in the community. Of course, Y may have made provision for X's obligation to be transferred to Z, but this means by definition that the composition of total of rights and obligations has been altered.

The duties of citizenship do not function in this way, however. That is to say, they are not sensitive to the identity of those who are citizens at any one time. The rights and duties of citizenship can remain constant, even when the composition of the community in terms of its membership changes. The duties I owe to other citizens are not owed to other particular individuals; they are owed to the non-assignable individuals who make up the collective identity of the continuing political community. This continuing political community is the repository of our rights and duties as citizens. Without such a continuing repository we would not have a role of citizenship; all we should have would be relations between individuals that would necessarily change as the identity of those individuals changed.

On this interpretation the political community cannot be identified simply as the sum of persons living at one particular time and joined in political union. Such an arrangement would simply make citizens members of a set, not members of a continuing entity. Set membership, in the strict sense, is defined in terms of its constituent elements: change any one of the elements and the identity of the set changes. But change any one of the members of a political community and the identity of the political community does not change. The political community is not therefore reducible to its members, and cannot be identified simply with its membership at any one time.

If a political community is not reducible to its members, then the rights and obligations that repose in the political community are not as such solely in respect of current members. Moreover, since the actions of current members can affect beneficially or detrimentally the political community, including its future members, current members have duties to future generations by extension. Hence, the notion of citizenship itself implies duties to future members of one's own political community. Although this is an abstract argument, I think it has resonance in everyday moral consciousness, as when people talk about the need to do things that will benefit 'our grandchildren', even when, as with Keynes (1930), they know that they will not actually have any grandchildren. What they are referring to in this mode of speech, I suggest, are those who will be the future members of an ongoing political community of which they are currently a part.

This does not show, of course, that the obligations that citizens have to future generations are those it would be most ethically desirable for them to have. To have political duties with an indefinite forward application in time is not necessarily to have the duties that would be most beneficial for future generations. But there is unlikely to be any political community in which the duties of citizenship did not include the duty to preserve the best of the community, so that it is most likely that the duties of citizenship will include requirements to benefit the future, if not the requirement to do the best that one can do by the future.

Is There an Obligation to Bring about Democracy?

So far we have considered the obligations that are implied by the practice and presuppositions of democracy, on the implicit assumption that those who had the duties were members of a political community that is itself democratic. But is there an obligation to contribute towards bringing a democratic political community into being, and if there is how could we define its content and whose duty would it be?

In what follows I shall assume that democracies are obliged, as they are under international law, to follow the principle of non-intervention in the domestic affairs of other states. Even accepting this limitation, however, it would still be possible for democratic states to adopt policies intended to support political changes aimed at introducing those constitutional rights that define democratic practice: free association, the exchange of political views and information and the questioning of public decisions. Among these policies we might expect to find the following: making offers of international economic aid conditional upon political reform; maintaining high trade barriers until certain reforms are put in place; support for the monitoring of democratic rights in the country in question; the offering of asylum and other forms of support to dissident groups; and the avoidance of military alliances that might force a compromise in the pressure for reform.

Of course, in any particular case, there will always be grounds for argument as to whether these measures are the most appropriate to bring about democratic reform. It is always open to people to argue, for example, that increasing the volume of trade is the best way to support democratic reform in a country. What matters in the present case, however, is not the effectiveness of particular measures in any one case, but the idea that there are measures that could be taken, which represent a break from normal diplomatic relations and which are intended to foster democracy.

Those defending the freedom of countries not to adopt democratic institutions are likely to do so on one or more of three grounds. Firstly, that it is implausible under all circumstances to apply the principle of political equality, since there may be stages of economic development at which we cannot reasonably assume that no member of the community is better qualified to judge the public good than any other. Secondly, that the introduction of democratic institutions is likely to disrupt an existing cultural consensus and foster competitive and ultimately destructive political practices. Thirdly, that the morality underlying the rights of democracy is alien to the society in question. Let us consider each of these three points in turn.

The view that it is not always plausible to accept the assumption of political equality may be reasonably held under certain circumstances. For example, in peasant-dominated societies in which only few are educated and many are uneducated, it may be unreasonable to suppose that all are equally qualified to make decisions. Even though a society like India manages to maintain a form of democracy with a high proportion of poorly educated peasants, there is no reason to suppose that there is an underlying linear pattern of political development through which countries can pass on their way to stable democracy (compare Randall, 1997). Hence, it would not be unreasonable for an educated elite to claim in good faith that it would not be conducive to the underlying collective interests of their society to rule without popular methods of ratification. Yet, even under these circumstances, the acceptance of the situation may be qualified, and there may be a whole series of obligations to improve the situation over time.

One way in which this could be done is to distinguish between the arguments for democracy at national level and the arguments for democracy at local level. Whilst there may be in principle arguments for elite rule at national level, particularly in the early stages of economic development, there are seldom arguments for not encouraging and nurturing democracy at local level. National urban elites may be much better than the mass of their fellow citizens at questions of international finance, foreign policy and development strategies, but by definition they are likely to be poor at local issues, since they lack the contextual knowledge. Allowing democracy at the local level may be a short-term burden, since effective local governments may veto certain projects that are thought to be in the national interest, for example by preventing land take to improve water supplies. But there is enough experience of the long-term disasters of centrally planned development to suggest that local opposition may often more informed than many national, or even international, experts.

A second condition that needs to be applied before one can easily accept the suspension of the political equality assumption is that the relevant elites accept seriously a duty to ensure that education is provided as quickly as possible, to create the conditions in which democracy is possible. If lack of education is the only argument against the introduction of democratic practices, then those arguing the case have a duty to ensure that they are not simply adopting a strategy of convenience, by making mass public education a priority of public policy. This duty to promote democracy may well extend to the inhabitants of existing democracies in relation to the educational needs of poorer countries. If aid and other forms of economic cooperation and development can legitimately be made conditional, this implies that the sums involved should be large enough seriously to tackle the problems on which the conditionality hangs.

What then of the second defence, that the introduction of conventional democratic practices is likely to disrupt a social consensus and create damaging competitive processes into a society? Here again, there does not appear to be an *a priori* argument that would render this argument invalid taken by itself, and there may well be available empirical evidence to support the proposition. For example, in post-independence Tanzania in the 1960s the leading party, TANU, secured over 90 per cent of the vote in elections, and there was a good argument for seeking to contain such political differences as there were within this broad consensus to prevent destructive ethnic conflict. However, it cannot be evidence for a consensus simply to note that there is ineffective political opposition to a ruling group, since the lack of opposition may simply be a consequence of the imposition of authoritarian rule. Without some opportunity for competition, it is impossible to know whether a consensus is real or manufactured. Moreover, as the development of Tanzania itself suggests, the lack of institutionalized contestation of public policies, as happened in the 1970s with the policy of villageization, brings its own disadvantages (see Mwansasu and Pratt, 1979).

I have also tried to stress in the discussion of the models of democracy that making competition the essence of democracy is only one way of looking at the possibilities. Certainly competition for office by means of elections is the best institution we have for testing claims to a popular mandate, but that does not imply that the winners are entitled to use their political power for their own advantage or the advantage of their sectional supporters. The implication of the consensus argument may simply be not that competitive elections as such should be rejected but that the institutional arrangements associated with protective and pluritarian models of democracy should be rejected.

The third set of arguments concerned cultural particularity. Here I shall be brief, since I do not see how this can be an argument having any independent force from the two arguments that I have just cited. If there are forces in a society pushing for the introduction of democracy, it is no argument to say to them that this would be an innovation. Of course, it can be argued (see Parekh, 1993, p. 169) that there is the possibility of non-liberal democratic societies, in which the political practice is democratic but the content of the public policies non-liberal, in the sense that there is no commitment to values like freedom of conscience, freedom of religion or freedom of sexual behaviour. Since I have already argued that these are values that are not conceptually tied to the principles of democracy, I am bound to agree. But this point then simply amounts to the claim that where societies that maintain traditional values adopt democratic practices we should expect their policies to be intolerant of individual freedoms. This cannot be an argument for preventing the citizens of those societies debating and contesting how much of their traditions they wish to maintain. In conclusion, then, there are obligations to bring about democracy, but acting on the obligation is conditional upon the circumstances for the effective introduction of democracy holding.

11 An Ideal of Democracy?

Having now set out a series of arguments about the most important dimensions of democracy, are we in a position to evaluate the five institutional conceptions of democracy that I distinguished in Chapter 2? I considered towards the end of that chapter the argument that no such impartial evaluation was possible, since democracy was an essentially contested concept and that any comparative evaluation of its various forms would have to draw on ideological presuppositions that were unarguable in intellectual terms. Yet, each model makes, either implicitly or explicitly, various assumptions about the value of democracy, the role of participation, the place of representation and inclusion and the aggregation of preferences. Moreover, different conceptions of democracy are also associated with views on the role of constitutional constraints and the obligations that citizens have in a democracy. Although comparing one model with another is bound up with complex sets of beliefs about the character of democratic political life, it is still possible to isolate those beliefs and subject them to critical analysis. Simply because political values or rather intangible empirical assumptions are involved, is there reason to think that we cannot have, in John Stuart Mill's felicitous phrase (Mill, 1861b, p. 135), considerations 'capable of determining the intellect' in such matters?

Summarizing the argument as I have tried to present it, we can outline its logic as follows. If we ask what the justification is of a system of government in which the content of laws and public policies is formally, if only indirectly and intermittently, related to the state of public opinion, then the principal answer is that such a system of government enables citizens to attend to their common interests, and recognize themselves as both fallible and the political equals of all other members of the society.

211

By contrast, it is not possible to base a justificatory argument for democracy on a strong notion of individual autonomy. Had it been possible, such an account of democracy would have clearly underwritten the conclusion that the only justifiable form of democratic political organization would be that of direct democracy. In the absence of such a justification, however, a representative system of government is not only justified but could also be said to have certain advantages compared to direct democracy, not least that it enables all citizens to take advantage of the political division of labour to live their lives according to competing conceptions of the good. This is not to say that participation, and the virtues it stimulates, are unimportant; it is to say that direct democracy does not set a standard against which representative government somehow falls short.

Turning to the ways in which we might evaluate representative systems, we can see that there are good arguments for a politics of presence, in which political representatives themselves reflect not only a broad range of political opinions but also a wide span of social characteristics. The diversity of opinion to which this gives rise can be dealt with in a system of aggregation based upon the majority principle, interpreted so that it incorporates the Condorcet criterion. There is no argument from the paradox of voting and its extensions in Arrow's theorem for a liberal constitutionalist conception of democracy.

A defensible system of representative government will not only be inclusive, in the sense that it will seek to be fair to all those who have a nexus to the political community, it will also ensure constitutional protection for democratic rights of participation and political contestation. There is, however, no conceptual connection between the principles of democracy and the principles of liberalism that would lead to the constitutional protection, in all democracies, of strong rights of individual conscience. However, to the extent to which democratic citizenship requires a distinct account of civic virtues, it is possible to give these determinate content.

The ideal to which these arguments lead is what I have termed a representational system of government, in which there is inclusiveness of citizenship, broad representation of interests and opinions and acceptance of majoritarian devices to break deadlocks of disagreement. At a local level and through non-governmental organizations, active citizens in such a system would not only play their fair part in a scheme of political cooperation that was necessary to maintain the

system in being, they would themselves hold civic office and contribute to the common life. At a national level they would also scrutinize the acts and decisions of their representatives with a critical
rationality to ensure that what was being done in their name was justifiable in the court of public opinion, both in their own country and
abroad. I think this not so very far from the conception of democracy
advanced by John Stuart Mill, but without the fancy franchise and the
metaphysics about national character. If we couch this conclusion in
terms of the comparative political science analysis that I have taken
as the closest real-world embodiment to these normative principles,
then the practices of some of the smaller European democracies
approximate most closely to this conception of political life.

If we identify such an ideal, does it also follow that we could read
off from that ideal a political programme? After all, to say that the
choice of model is subject to considerations capable of determining
the intellect might suggest that we can move from evaluation to political prescriptions. Is this so? I suggest not for a number of reasons.

In the first place, the models that I have laid out are static and
deliberately oversimplified, even if we allow that some approximation to their principles is exemplified in some of the working
democracies. But the models are presented to clarify thought
rather than inform a political programme. Although in distinguishing between representational government and Westminster
systems I sought to draw upon a literature in comparative politics
that has identified two powerfully discriminating variables – electoral laws and executive dominance on legislative committees –
dividing countries into statistical clusters, the classification
involved was nevertheless one which left many important features
of political institutions out.

Secondly, to lay out an ideal, even one that is more fully described
than the models that I have presented here, is not to furnish a guide
to its implementation. Social and political systems are enormously
complex with inter-relations that are often difficult to fathom and
replete with possibilities for unintended effects from human action.
The history of the twentieth century is littered with intellectual projects whose implementation has caused countless misery to millions
of people. Suitable modesty about our lack of understanding of the
laws of the evolution of society, if there are any, should incline us to
Popper's 'piecemeal social engineering' rather than any more ambi-
tious forms of politics. Even Rousseau saw that political ideals did

not translate simply and directly into political prescriptions. His constitution for Poland is a representative scheme that has none of the elemental simplicity of the social contract.

When we discuss issues of the redesign or reform of political institutions, in the light of general principles, issues of scale, social conditions and historical experience are likely to be important. If we try to move from ideal to prescription, or even evaluation, without bearing these dimensions of institutional performance in mind, then difficulties will arise.

Scale is important because it affects the way in which we think about issues of participation and preference aggregation. I have argued, for example, that Rousseauian assumptions about preference homogeneity are typically rather over-optimistic in the degree to which they assume that social consensus is possible. However, on a small scale, in local communities where there is a high degree of civic involvement, a Rousseauian conception may be most appropriate. Where people interact frequently with one another and know that they have to conduct a common life together, it may well be that they can run their affairs with little political division of labour, with a high degree of agreement and without the need for elaborate checks and balances. Yet, carried even to rather modest higher level of scale, Rousseauian political practices are likely to break down.

Social conditions, and in particular the way in which attitudes interact with social position, are also likely to be important. The clearest example here is provided by the contrast between the Westminster system and systems of representational government. I argued in the chapter on aggregation that an important assumption built into the operation of Westminster systems was that political issues took a binary form, and that when this assumption broke down reliance on the plurality rule rather than a rule embodying the Condorcet-winner violated the requirements of political equality. It follows from this that a political system that may well have been suitable for a country at one stage of its political development, when issues took a binary form, may be unsuited at later stage when there is a higher degree of political pluralism and issues do not fall simply into a left–right spectrum.

The difficulties of mapping a Westminster system onto plural social conditions are reinforced when we consider its lack of suitability to societies that are socially plural by virtue of deep religious, ethnic, linguistic or cultural cleavages. Where one important set of political conflicts is likely to be overlaid with another set, the way in which the Westminster system herds different issues together is prone to cause problems. Conversely, however, where the problem is seen to be 'over-representation', as was the case with the Fourth French Republic, the opposite may be true. The creation of institutional pressures to reduce the representation of the political system may be what is called for.

Historical pressures may also work to limit or direct change in ways that are at odds with the conclusions of an ideal analysis. In part, of course, this is simply a matter of political agents holding on to the power they have been bestowed by chance or fortune. Political parties in power advantaged by a certain pattern of electoral laws are not going to want to change those laws unless special circumstances obtain. Similarly, political systems with elaborate arrangements for institutional checks and balances will not find change easy.

Bringing scale, social conditions and historical experience together poses severe problems in moving from abstract argument to concrete recommendation. The problems are made more difficult by the fact that the reform of democratic institutions has to take place in a world in which economic and social change is driving a great deal of political change. Robert Dahl (1989, pp. 317–21) speaks about a third democratic transformation. Just as democracy had to learn how to move out of the city-state and live in the nation-state, so now the political system needs to be adapted to a world in which the boundaries of political decision are smaller than the economic, physical and security environment within which those decisions are taken. David Held (1995) raises the issues of how a political system can move from the modern state to internationalized governance.

It is, I think, a merit of the view of democracy presented here that it does not link democratic values to a strong, pre-political notion of identity. To speak of common interests is not to assume that there is one, and only one, way of politically segmenting humanity. Democratic institutions are primarily means with which we deal with our common problems. As the scale and character of those problems changes, so we should expect out conception of democracy to adjust. We cannot simply transpose our understanding of democracy from one level of political association to another. Even if the best form of democratic polity at the level of the nation-state is the system of representational government, it does not follow that a democratic system of internationalized governance should simply seek to replicate the institutions of the nation-state. Our major common interests with others may now be more highly segmented among the different layers of the complex system of multi-level governance in which many now live.

We can illustrate these points with the example of the European Union (EU). At present there is considerable concern over the 'democratic deficit' within the EU. Yet, it is difficult to see how we could even think about reform without considering the issues of scale, social conditions and historical context as they affect the Union.

Consider first the problem of scale. Suppose we were convinced that the representational system of government had much to recommend it. Suppose, that is to say, we thought it right that all the member states of the EU should have representational systems. Since most of them are, or come close to it, this would really involve change only in France and the UK. Would it follow that the EU itself should be modelled on the pattern of a representational system? By no means. Even leaving aside the variety of institutional arrangements within the set of representational democracies, it would still be possible to argue that moving the level of political decision-making to a higher level of aggregation had implications for the design of satisfactory institutions.

One reason for this concerns the role of political parties. Within representational systems the political party is an important institution, both practically and normatively. It organizes debate, structures competition and recruits representatives. Normative proposals for reform have often therefore focussed on political parties – for example, in the form of quotas for selecting more women candidates. However, within the EU, political parties operate at the level of the member states. There simply is no functioning European party system in terms of electoral competition. Hence, simply to assert that the EU should become a representational system, on the model of its member states, would be to ignore the vital role that political parties play in the process of representation.

The argument can also be reversed, however. It does not follow from the fact that the design of political institutions for the EU has to satisfy certain conditions that the political institutions of the member states had to follow the same pattern. For example, someone might argue that a liberal constitutional arrangement, with checks and balances and a clear separation of powers, was called for at the European level, without implying that such a system was the right one for the member states. Here again, scale alone can make a difference.

A similar point can be made with respect to social conditions. Social and economic conditions within the EU are highly variable. Countries and regions stand at different levels of economic development. There are the obvious linguistic differences, and geographical spread imposes its own limits on the degree to which there is an homogeneity of outlook or interest among the populations of Europe. This heterogeneity of social conditions is likely to have implications for the type of political design that one can reasonably recommend. For example, it is unlikely, given this heterogeneity, that the device of the referendum would work well at the European level. Indeed, it is striking that even in the US, where participatory devices like the initiative and the referendum have been developed in recent years at state level, there is little movement to use the referendum as a policy-making device at the federal level, presumably a reflection of the fact that the US does not contain a sufficiently homogeneous public to make common popular voting on a particular issue desirable.

Finally, historical circumstance affects questions of institutional design as much in the EU as elsewhere. One of the features of the EU is the role played by the Commission in the making of policy. This is a product of the Monnet method by which technocratic collaboration replaced grand political design as the device to secure integration (Hayward, J., 1996). It cannot be assumed that the role of the Commission is somehow merely an historical accident, however. European integration may have got to the point that it has precisely because no other method, other than Monnet's, would have worked. Hence, moving from the technocratic assumptions of the present set-up to a more democratic one may be more difficult than is sometimes supposed. Simply transferring the powers of policy initiative from the Commission to the Parliament, for example, may have important structural implications.

The example of the EU is just one possible one, of course, but it does illustrate how difficult it is to move from an ideal of theory to a prescription of practice. Speaking personally I find it difficult to see an alternative to liberal constitutionalism at the level of the EU itself, but I should be more reconciled to this view if I also saw greater inclusiveness and representation at the national level and active forms of civic involvement at the local levels. Such a judgement is necessarily personal, since there are obviously many detailed considerations that need to be taken into account when coming to any particular conclusion.

For this reason, there is a great deal of merit in the view that the models of democracy that I have set out, with the associated discussion about the merits of their different normative and empirical assumptions, should be regarded as thought-experiments, intended to clarify the discussion of standards of evaluation, rather than as blueprints to which we would expect any political system to correspond. Even if it turned out, as I believe, that systems of representational government had merits that other forms of government lacked, there would still be a great deal of work involved in showing what the implications were for the construction of any particular political system.

However, there is a danger in being too complacent about the limited power of analysis. If we treat competing conceptions of democracy simply as thought-experiments, designed to clarify thinking, but with no prescriptive or practical implications, then we lose the critical potential provided by the discussion of normative political principles. Political systems are certainly held together by more than simply the power of argument. But the critical analysis of political institutions cannot escape the practical implications of its conclusions. If a particular institutional arrangement has faults from the normative point of view, and there appears to be an alternative that is superior on the relevant counts, then the system should be reformed.

In this context it is easy to overlook the fact that there is intellectual discussion in all societies about the merits of their democratic arrangements. In the UK, for example, critics of the first-past-the-post system of elections have existed since the early nineteenth century and as various times their campaigns have looked as though they might be successful (Hart, 1992). Great concern over democratic performance is present in many European countries arising from the changes that the single European market has brought about. And democratization in many parts of the world, whilst it has brought problems, has also brought the liberation to think independently about those problems. Least of all in democratic theory can we separate our principles from our practice.

Guide to Further Reading

As well as a global resurgence in democracy, there appears to be a global resurgence in writing about democracy. Consequently, what follows is suggestive rather than definitive.

Probably the most comprehensive introduction is provided by Dahl (1989). In many ways this summarizes and synthesizes a lifetime's thinking about democracy. It is written by someone of enormous scholarship, who is both conceptually acute and empirically well informed. For my taste the dialogues that pepper the book are a distraction, but non-scientific surveys among my students suggest that mine is a minority viewpoint.

Broad introductions to the topic are provided by Held (1996) and Lakoff (1996). Held's book is more sociological, whereas Lakoff has more historical detail. Both give great weight to the idea of autonomy in connection with democracy, and therefore contrast with the treatment that I have tried to offer here. There are also useful historical essays in Dunn (1992), and much of the material in Duncan (1983) remains relevant, as does the minor classic of Plamenatz (1973). Harrison (1993) covers both the historical and the conceptual issues, but with a sharper eye to philosophical questions.

All the above volumes will discuss various aspects of the history of democratic theory, but there is, of course, no substitute for reading the originals. I have been struck, going over this book for publication, how much I have returned to five works: Rousseau (1762), *The Federalist Papers* (1787), James Mill (1823), John Stuart Mill (1861a) and Schumpeter (1954). In many ways, taken together, they cover the broad span of theoretical possibilities, and all become richer the more they are reread – which to my mind is the crucial test. Bryce (1888) and Sidgwick (1891), who were friends, had many of the prejudices of their day, but were also first-rate intellects, and will repay persistence. Popper (1945) gains more force as the belief in human reason wanes.

All democrats should have, once in their lifetimes at least, the chastening experience of reading Thucydides's *The Peloponnesian War*, which, with its historical detail, is more telling to my mind than Plato's metaphysics in *The Republic*.

For those with an interest in the philosophical, rather than historical, issues Hyland (1995) offers a reflective and thoughtful text, and in a similar vein Lively (1975) is still worth reading. Graham (1986) too is philosophically sophisticated. Birch (1993) is in many ways a remarkable *tour de force*, made more remarkable by the fact that the learning is worn lightly. It covers a wide variety of topics, including those in the methodology of the social sciences, and it is always shrewd. It should have been longer. Holden (1988) is sound on all that it discusses. Arblaster (1987) is too brief on too many topics, which is a shame, since what is said is often interesting.

There are useful collections of essays written in the light of the current process of democratization and changing patterns of citizenship and political organization. Held (1993) offers a wide selection, and the pieces in Mouffe (1992) are both intelligent and thoughtful. Beetham (1994) offers a collection of essays on measuring democracy that are worth looking at. Lehning and Weale (1997) collect essays on democracy and citizenship in the European Union.

Burnheim (1985) offers a radical prospectus, though I am tempted to say that it is done with more verve than persuasiveness. I feel the same about Green (1985) and, to a lesser extent, Barber (1984), though this probably says more about me than the works themselves.

No approach to democratic theory seems complete without offering its own typology. I have relied upon the article by Bingham Powell (1989), but there is an influential discussion in comparative politics by Lijphart (1984). Lijphart also deserves credit for having discovered one of the few really original concepts in post-war political science, namely that of consociational democracy (see Lijphart, 1968 and 1977). Macpherson (1966 and 1977) offers alternative ways of classifying democracy. Deliberative democracy is sometimes picked out by contrast with pluralism, and a good collection to look at is Bohman and Rehg (1997). Pluralism should, however, be looked at through its own writings: Dahl (1961) is exemplary; Truman (1951) much under-rated. Schattschneider (1960), a critic of pluralism, is about as insightfully wrong, to my mind, as it is possible to be.

Central to the justification of democracy is the value of equality. Dahl (1989) is often at his best when writing on this topic. Vlastos (1962) produced an essay on the principle of equality many years ago that it still worth reading. Barry (1995) offers an egalitarian theory of justice, which ought to issue, sometime, in an interesting theory of democracy. Beitz (1989) is both insightful and sensitive on the topic. In all his writings Dworkin (1977, 1985, and 1996) seeks to reinterpret US democracy in the light of the principle of equal concern and respect. As I have tried to suggest in this book, it is not easy to reconcile constitutional and democratic norms, but, if anyone can, it is Dworkin.

Participation is a complex issue. Pateman (1970) deserves credit for starting so much of the discussion off, and for drawing attention to the role of participation in the history of democratic thought. Mansbridge (1980) is a sensitive study for participation in practice. Parry, Moyser and Day (1992) look at the empirical evidence on participation in the UK and Verba, Schlozman and Brady (1995) present a rich vein of evidence for the US. Putnam (1993) opened up the discussion on social capital and democracy.

On the subject of representation Birch (1972) is a good introduction. Pitkin (1972) is still worth reading, particularly in the light of Anne Phillips's (1995) attempt to reconstruct the idea of demographic representation. Manin (1997) is a brilliant history of the idea of representation and the way in which the principle of election came to replace that of selection by lot. Young (1989, 1990) produces challenging work on the extent to which there is a common interest to be represented.

The application of social choice theory to the understanding of politics has raised the issue of aggregation to the fore. Riker (1982 and 1986) offers particularly incisive analyses, the latter volume being a series of short stories to illustrate the general theme of the manipulability of voting schemes. I have tried to offer an appraisal in Weale (1984 and 1995). McLean (1987) still remains a useful introduction to rational choice approaches to politics. Hargreaves Heap *et al.* (1992) provide a general introduction to theories of rationality and social choice.

Constitutionalism is well treated in Bellamy and Castiglione (1997) and by Bellamy (1996) as well as the issue of *Political Studies* in which it appears. Elster and Slagstad (1988) is a useful collection of essays and Rawls (1993) can be read as the apotheosis of a certain form of constitutional democracy. In the text I have drawn attention to the interesting speculation in Plamenatz (1963) on the cultural distinctiveness of the idea of freedom of conscience.

On political obligation in general, Horton (1992) is a good guide. To my mind the article by Parekh (1993) is a splendid refocussing of the notion in democratic terms. Brennan and Lomasky (1993) offer an expressive theory of voting, which if it could be made to work would undermine the appeal to the duty of fairness in the present text.

This is a book about normative democratic theory rather than democratization, but for those who like their theory to have some reference to the great global transformation, Diamond and Plattner (1996), Linz and Stepan (1996) and Potter *et al.* (1997) are obvious places to start.

Bibliography

Ackerman, B. A. (1980) *Social Justice in the Liberal State* (New Haven and London: Yale University Press).

Amy, D. (1987) *The Politics of Environmental Mediation* (New York: Columbia University Press).

Arblaster, A. (1987) *Democracy* (Milton Keynes: Open University Press).

Arendt, H. (1958) *The Human Condition* (Chicago: University of Chicago Press).

Aristotle (1962) *The Politics*, translated with an introduction by T. A. Sinclair (Harmondsworth: Penguin).

Arrow, K. J. (1963) *Social Choice and Individual Values*, second edition (New Haven: Yale University Press).

Atiyah, P. S. (1979) *The Rise and Fall of Freedom of Contract* (Oxford: Clarendon Press).

Bagehot, W. (1867) *The English Constitution*, edited with an introduction by R. H. S. Crossman (London: Fontana/Collins, 1963).

Bambrough, R. (1956) 'Plato's Political Analogies', in P. Laslett (ed.), *Philosophy, Politics and Society* (Oxford: Basil Blackwell), pp. 98–115.

Barber, B. R. (1984) *Strong Democracy* (Berkeley: University of California Press).

Barry, B. (1965) *Political Argument* (London: Routledge & Kegan Paul).

Barry, B. (1967) 'The Public Interest', in A. Quinton (ed.), *Political Philosophy* (Oxford: Oxford University Press), pp. 112–26.

Barry, B. (1989a) *Theories of Justice* (London: Harvester-Wheatsheaf).

Barry, B. (1989b) *Democracy, Power and Justice* (Oxford: Clarendon Press).

Barry, B. (1995) *Justice as Impartiality* (Oxford: Clarendon Press).

Barry, B. and Goodin, R. E. (eds) (1992) *Free Movement: Ethical Issues in the Transnational Migration of People and Money* (New York and London: Harvester Wheatsheaf).

Beetham, D. (1991) *The Legitimation of Power* (London: Macmillan).

Beetham, D. (1993) 'Liberal Democracy and the Limits of Democratization', in D. Held (ed.), *Prospects for Democracy* (Cambridge: Polity Press), pp. 55–73.

Beetham, D. (ed.) (1994) *Defining and Measuring Democracy* (London: Sage).

Beitz, C. R. (1979) *Political Theory and International Relations* (Princeton: Princeton University Press).

Beitz, C. R. (1989) *Political Equality* (Princeton: Princeton University Press).

Bellamy, R. (1994) '"Dethroning Politics": Liberalism, Constitutionalism and Democracy in the Thought of F. A. Hayek', *British Journal of Political Science*, 24:4, pp. 419–41.

Bellamy, R. (1996) 'The Political Form of the Constitution: The Separation of Powers, Rights and Representative Democracy', *Political Studies*, 44:3, pp. 435–56.

Bellamy, R. and Castiglione, D. (1997) 'Constitutionalism and Democracy – Political Theory and the American Constitution', *British Journal of Political Science*, 27:4, pp. 595–618.

Bentham, J. (1780) *An Introduction to the Principles of Morals and Legislation*, edited by J. H. Burns and H. L. A. Hart (London: Athlone Press, 1970).

Berelson, B., Lazarsfeld, P. F. and McPhee, W. N. (1954) *Voting* (Chicago: University of Chicago Press).

Berlin, I. (1969) *Four Essays on Liberty* (Oxford: Oxford University Press).

Berry, J. M., Portney, K. E. and Thomson, K. (1993) *The Rebirth of Urban Democracy* (Washington, DC: The Brookings Institution).

Birch, A. H. (1972) *Representation* (London: Macmillan).

Birch, A. H. (1993) *The Concepts and Theories of Modern Democracy* (London and New York: Routledge).

Black, D. (1958) *The Theory of Committees and Elections* (Cambridge: Cambridge University Press).

Blackburn, R. (1995) *The Electoral System in Britain* (London: Macmillan).

Bohman, J. and Rehg, W. (eds) (1997) *Deliberative Democracy* (Cambridge, Mass.: MIT Press).

Brennan G. and Buchanan, J. M. (1985) *The Reason of Rules* (Cambridge: Cambridge University Press).

Brennan, G. and Lomasky, L. (1993) *Democracy and Decision* (Cambridge: Cambridge University Press).

Bryce, J. (1888) *The American Commonwealth*, volume 3 (London: Macmillan).

Buchanan, A. (1991) *Secession: The Morality of Political Divorce from Fort Sumter to Lithuania and Quebec* (Boulder: Westview Press).

Buchanan, J. M. (1986) *Liberty, Market and State: Political Economy in the 1980s* (Brighton: Wheatsheaf Books).

Buchanan, J. M. and Tullock, G. (1962) *The Calculus of Consent* (Ann Arbor: University of Michigan Press).

Budge, I. (1996) *The New Challenge of Direct Democracy* (Cambridge: Polity Press).

Bullock, A. (1962) *Hitler: A Study in Tyranny* (Harmondsworth: Penguin).

Burnheim, J. (1985) *Is Democracy Possible?* (Cambridge: Polity Press).

Calhoun, J. C. (1853) *A Disquisition on Government*, ed. C. Gordon Past (Indianapolis: Bobbs-Merrill, 1953).

Castoriadis, C. (1987) *The Imaginary Institution of Society* (Cambridge: Polity Press).

Castoriadis, C. (1993) *Political and Social Writings* (Minneapolis: University of Minnesota Press).

Chan, J. and Miller, D. (1991) 'Elster on Self-Realization in Politics: A Critical Note', *Ethics*, 102:1, pp. 96–102.

Cohen, J. (1986) 'An Epistemic Conception of Democracy', *Ethics*, 97:1, pp. 26–38.

Coleman, J. and Ferejohn, J. (1986) 'Democracy and Social Choice', *Ethics*, 97:1, pp. 6–25.

Converse, P. E. (1964) 'The Nature of Belief Systems in Mass Publics',
    in D. E. Apter (ed.), *Ideology and Discontent* (New York: Free Press),
    pp. 206–61.
Coote, A. and Lenaghan, J. (1997) *Citizens' Juries: Theory into Practice*
    (London: Institute of Public Policy Research).
Cronin, T. E. (1989) *Direct Democracy: The Politics of Initiative, Referendum and
    Recall* (Cambridge, Mass.: Harvard University Press).
Dahl, R. A. (1956) *A Preface to Democratic Theory* (Chicago: University of
    Chicago Press).
Dahl, R. A. (1961) *Who Governs?* (New Haven: Yale University Press).
Dahl, R. A. (1970) *After the Revolution?* (New Haven: Yale University Press).
Dahl, R. A. (1989) *Democracy and Its Critics* (New Haven and London: Yale
    University Press).
Davie, G. (1961) *The Democratic Intellect* (Edinburgh: Edinburgh University
    Press).
Dews, P. (1986) 'Editor's Introduction', in J. Habermas, *Autonomy and
    Solidarity: Interviews* (London: Verso).
Diamond, L. and Plattner, M. F. (eds) (1996) *The Global Resurgence of
    Democracy*, second edition (Baltimore and London: The Johns Hopkins
    University Press).
Dicey, A. V. (1885) *Introduction to the Study of the Law of the Constitution*,
    eighth edition 1915 (London: Macmillan).
Dobson, A. (1996) 'Representative Democracy and the Environment', in
    W. M. Lafferty and J. Meadowcroft (eds) *Democracy and the Environment:
    Problems and Prospects* (Cheltenham: Edward Elgar), pp. 124–39.
Downs, A. (1957) *An Economic Theory of Democracy* (New York: Harper &
    Row).
Dryzek, J. (1996) 'Political and Ecological Communication', in F. Mathews
    (ed.), *Ecology and Democracy* (London: Frank Cass), pp. 13–30.
Duncan, G. (ed.) (1983) *Democratic Theory and Practice* (Cambridge:
    Cambridge University Press).
Duncan, G. and Lukes, S. (1963) 'The New Democracy', *Political Studies*,
    11:2, pp. 156–77, repr. in S. Lukes, *Essays in Social Theory* (London:
    Macmillan, 1977), pp. 30–51.
Dunn, J. (ed.) (1992) *Democracy: The Unfinished Journey* (Oxford: Oxford
    University Press).
Duverger, M. (1964) *Political Parties*, fourth edition, translated by B. and
    R. North (London: Methuen).
Dworkin, R. (1977) *Taking Rights Seriously* (London: Duckworth).
Dworkin, R. (1985) *A Matter of Principle* (Oxford: Clarendon Press).
Dworkin, R. (1996) *Freedom's Law* (Cambridge, Mass.: Harvard University
    Press).
Elster, J. (1983) *Sour Grapes: Studies in the Subversion of Rationality*
    (Cambridge: Cambridge University Press).
Elster, J. (1997) 'The Market and the Forum: Three Varieties of Political
    Theory', in J. Bohman and W. Rehg (eds), *Deliberative Democracy*
    (Cambridge, Mass.: MIT Press), pp. 3–33.

Elster, J. and Slagstad, R. (eds) (1988) *Constitutionalism and Democracy* (Cambridge: Cambridge University Press).

Ely, J. H. (1980) *Democracy and Distrust* (Cambridge, Mass.: Harvard University Press).

Featherstone, K. (1994) 'Jean Monnet and the "Democratic Deficit" in the European Union', *Journal of Common Market Studies*, 32:2, pp. 149–70.

The Federalist Papers (1787), edited C. Rossiter (New York: New American Library, 1961).

Feinberg, J. (1970) 'The Nature and Value of Rights', *The Journal of Value Enquiry*, 4, pp. 243–57, repr. in J. Feinberg, *Rights, Justice and the Bounds of Liberty* (Princeton: Princeton University Press, 1980), pp. 143–55.

Feinberg, J. (1973) *Social Philosophy* (Englewood Cliffs, New Jersey: Prentice-Hall, Inc.).

Finer, S. (1970) *Comparative Government* (Harmondsworth: Penguin).

Fishkin, J. S. (1995) *The Voice of the People: Public Opinion and Democracy* (New Haven and London: Yale University Press).

Freeman, M. (1996) 'Human Rights, Democracy and "Asian Values"', *The Pacific Review*, 9:3, pp. 352–66.

Freeman, S. (1992) 'Original Meaning, Democratic Interpretation, and the Constitution', *Philosophy and Public Affairs*, 21:1, pp. 3–42.

Fukuyama, F. (1989) 'The End of History?', *The National Interest*, 16, pp. 3–18.

Gallie, W. B. (1955–66) 'Essentially Contested Concepts', *Proceedings of the Aristotelian Society*, 56, pp. 167–98.

Gamble, A. (1990) 'Theories of British Politics', *Political Studies*, 38:3, pp. 404–20.

Goodin, R. E. (1996a) 'Inclusion and Exclusion', *Archives Européennes de Sociologie*, 37:2, pp. 343–71.

Goodin, R. E. (1996b) 'Enfranchising the Earth and Its Alternatives', *Political Studies*, 44:5, pp. 835–49.

Goodwin, B. (1992) *Justice by Lottery* (Hemel Hempstead: Harvester Wheatsheaf).

Graham, K. (1986) *The Battle of Democracy* (Brighton: Wheatsheaf Books).

Green, P. (1985) *Retrieving Democracy* (London: Methuen).

Grofman, B. and Lijphart, A. (eds) (1986) *Electoral Laws and Their Political Consequences* (New York: Agathon).

Grofman, B. and Feld, S. (1988) 'Rousseau's General Will: A Condorcetian Perspective', *American Political Science Review*, 82:2, pp. 567–76.

Habermas, J. (1979) *Communication and the Evolution of Society*, translated with an introduction by T. McCarthy (London: Heinemann).

Habermas, J. (1985) *The Philosophical Discourse of Modernity*, translated by Frederick Lawrence (Cambridge: Polity Press).

Hargreaves Heap, S. *et al.* (1992) *The Theory of Choice: A Critical Guide* (Oxford: Blackwell).

Harrison, R. (1993) *Democracy* (London and New York: Routledge).

Hart, H. L. A. (1961) *The Concept of Law* (Oxford: Clarendon).

Hart, H. L. A. (1967) 'Are There Any Natural Rights?', in A. Quinton (ed.), *Political Philosophy* (Oxford: Oxford University Press), pp. 53–66.

Hart, J. (1992) *Proportional Representation: Critics of the British Electoral System 1820–1945* (Oxford: Clarendon Press).

Hayek, F. A. (1973) *Law, Legislation and Liberty, volume 1: Rules and Order* (London: Routledge).

Hayward, B. M. (1996) 'The Greening of Participatory Democracy', in F. Mathews (ed.), *Ecology and Democracy* (London: Frank Cass), pp. 215–36.

Hayward, J. (1996) 'Has European Unification by Stealth a Future?' in J. Hayward (ed.), *Élitism, Populism, and European Politics* (Oxford: Clarendon Press), pp. 252–7.

Hegel, G. W. F. (1956) *The Philosophy of History* (New York: Dover Publications).

Held, D. (ed.) (1993) *Prospects for Democracy* (Cambridge: Polity Press).

Held, D. (1995) *Democracy and the Global Order* (Cambridge: Polity Press).

Held, D. (1996) *Models of Democracy*, second edition (Cambridge: Polity Press).

Hirsch F. (1977) *The Social Limits to Growth* (London and Henley: Routledge & Kegan Paul).

Hobbes, T. (1651) *Leviathan*, edited with an introduction by M. Oakeshott (Oxford: Basil Blackwell, n.d.).

Hofferbert, R. I. and Budge, I. (1992) 'The Party Mandate and the Westminster Model: Election Programmes and Government Spending in Britain, 1948–85', *British Journal of Political Science*, 22:2, pp. 151–82.

Holden, B. (1988) *Understanding Liberal Democracy* (Oxford: Philip Allan).

Holmes, S. (1988) 'Gag Rules or the Politics of Omission', in J. Elster and R. Slagstad (eds), *Constitutionalism and Democracy* (Cambridge: Cambridge University Press).

Honoré, A. M. (1961) 'Ownership', in A. G. Guest (ed.), *Oxford Essays in Jurisprudence* (Oxford: Oxford University Press), pp. 107–47.

Horton, J. (1992) *Political Obligation* (London: Macmillan).

Hume, D. (1742) *Essays, Moral, Political, and Literary*, edited by T. H. Green and T. H. Grose (London: Longmans, Green & Co., 1889).

Hyland, J. L. (1995) *Democratic Theory: The Philosophical Foundations* (Manchester: Manchester University Press).

Janis, I. L. (1982) *Groupthink* (Boston: Houghton Mifflin).

Jones, P. (1988) 'Intense Preferences, Strong Beliefs and Democratic Decision-Making', *Political Studies*, 36:1, pp. 7–29.

Kedourie, E. (1993) *Nationalism*, fourth edition (Oxford: Blackwell).

Keynes, J. M. (1930) 'Economic Possibilities for Our Grandchildren', in *The Collected Writings of J. M. Keynes: volume IX, Essays in Persuasion* (London: Macmillan, 1972), pp. 321–32.

Khilnani, S. (1992) 'India's Democratic Career', in J. Dunn (ed.), *Democracy: The Unfinished Journey* (Oxford: Oxford University Press), pp. 189–205.

King, A. (1997) *Running Scared* (New York: The Free Press).

Kitschelt, H. (1986) 'Political Opportunity Structures and Political Protest: Anti-Nuclear Movements in Four Democracies', *British Journal of Political Science*, 14:1, pp. 57–85.

Knei-Paz, B. (1978) *The Social and Political Thought of Leon Trotsky* (Oxford: Clarendon Press).

La Rochefoucauld (1678) *Maxims*, translated with an introduction by
 L. Tancock (Harmondsworth: Penguin, 1959).
Lakoff, S. (1996) *Democracy: History, Theory, Practice* (Boulder: Westview Press).
Larmore C. E. (1987) *Patterns of Moral Complexity* (Cambridge: Cambridge
 University Press).
Lau, S.-K. (1982) *Society and Politics in Hong Kong* (Hong Kong: The Chinese
 University Press).
Leftwich, A. (1983) *Redefining Politics* (London and New York: Methuen).
Lehning, P. and Weale, A. (eds) (1997) *Citizenship, Democracy and Justice in
 the New Europe* (London and New York: Routledge).
Lijphart, A. (1968) *The Politics of Accommodation – Pluralism and Democracy in the
 Netherlands* (Berkeley and Los Angeles: University of California Press).
Lijphart, A. (1977) *Democracy in Plural Societies* (New Haven and London:
 Yale University Press).
Lijphart, A. (1984) *Democracies* (New Haven and London: Yale University
 Press).
Lijphart, A. (1994) *Electoral Systems and Party Systems* (Oxford: Oxford
 University Press).
Lijphart, A. and Waisman, C. H. (eds) (1996) *Institutional Design in New
 Democracies* (Boulder: Westview Press).
Linz, J. J. and Stepan, A. (1996) *Problems of Democratic Transition and
 Consolidation* (Baltimore and London: The Johns Hopkins University
 Press).
Lively, J. (1975) *Democracy* (Oxford: Basil Blackwell).
Locke, J. (1690) *Two Treatises of Government*, edited P. Laslett (New York:
 Mentor, 1965).
Lucas, J. (1966) *The Principles of Politics* (Oxford: Clarendon Press).
Macaulay, T. B. (1829) 'Mill on Government', in *Speeches on Politics and
 Literature by Lord Macaulay* (London: J. M. Dent).
Macaulay, T. B. (1906) *The History of England from the Accession of James II*
 (London: J. M. Dent).
MacCormick, N. (1989) 'Unrepentant Gradualism', in O. W. Edwards
 (ed.), *A Claim of Right for Scotland* (Edinburgh: Polygon), pp. 99–109.
McLean, I. (1982) *Dealing in Votes* (Oxford: Martin Robertson).
McLean, I. (1987) *Public Choice* (Oxford: Basil Blackwell).
McLean, I. and Hewitt, F. (1994) *Condorcet: Foundations of Social Choice and
 Political Theory* (Aldershot: Edward Elgar).
Macpherson, C. B. (1966) *The Real World of Democracy* (Oxford: Clarendon
 Press).
Macpherson, C. B. (1977) *The Life and Times of Liberal Democracy* (Oxford:
 Oxford University Press).
Maier, C. S. (1992) 'Democracy since the French Revolution', in J. Dunn
 (ed.), *Democracy: The Unfinished Journey* (Oxford: Oxford University Press),
 pp. 125–53.
Majone, G. (1996) *Regulating Europe* (London and New York: Routledge).
Manin, B. (1997) *The Principles of Representative Government* (Cambridge:
 Cambridge University Press).
Mansbridge, J. J. (1980) *Beyond Adversary Democracy* (New York: Basic Books).

Mansbridge, J. (1990) 'Self-Interst in Political Life', *Political Theory*, 18:1, pp. 132–53.

Mapel, D. R. (1990) 'Civil Association and the Idea of Contingency', *Political Theory*, 18:3, pp. 392–410.

May, K. O. (1952) 'A Set of Independent, Necessary and Sufficient Conditions for Simple Majority Decision', *Econometrica*, 20, pp. 680–4.

Mellor, D. H. (1982) 'The Reduction of Society', *Philosophy*, 57, pp. 51–75.

Mill, J. (1820) *Government*, reprinted 1823 in T. Ball (ed.), *James Mill: Political Writings* (Cambridge: Cambridge University Press).

Mill, J. S. (1859) *On Liberty*, repr. in J. Gray (ed.), *John Stuart Mill: On Liberty and Other Essays* (Oxford: Oxford University Press, 1991).

Mill, J. S. (1861a) *Considerations on Representative Government*, repr. in J. Gray (ed.), *John Stuart Mill: On Liberty and Other Essays* (Oxford: Oxford University Press, 1991).

Mill, J. S. (1861b) *Utilitarianism*, reprinted in J. Gray (ed.), *John Stuart Mill: On Liberty and Other Essays* (Oxford: Oxford University Press, 1991).

Miller, D. (1983) 'The Competitive Model of Democracy', in G. Duncan (ed.), *Democratic Theory and Practice* (Cambridge: Cambridge University Press), pp. 133–55.

Miller, D. (1993) 'Deliberative Democracy and Social Choice', in D. Held (ed.), *Prospects for Democracy* (Cambridge: Polity Press), pp. 74–92.

Miller, D. (1995) *On Nationality* (Oxford: Clarendon Press).

Mishler, W. and Sheehan, R.S. (1993) 'The Supreme Court as a Counter-majoritarian Institution? The Impact of Public Opinion on Supreme Court Decisions', *American Political Science Review*, 87:1, pp. 87–101.

Mouffe, C. (ed.) (1992) *Dimensions of Radical Democracy* (London and New York: Verso).

Mulhall, S. and Swift, A. (1992) *Liberals and Communitarians* (Oxford: Blackwell).

Mwansasu, B. U. and Pratt, C. (eds) (1979) *Towards Socialism in Tanzania* (Dar es Salaam: Tanzania Publishing House).

Nagel, J. (1993) 'Populism, Heresthetics and Political Stability: Richard Seddon and the Art of Majority Rule', *British Journal of Political Science*, 23:2, pp. 139–74.

Nagel, J. (1998) 'Social Choice in a Pluritarian Democracy: The Politics of Market Liberalization in New Zealand', *British Journal of Political Science*, 28:2, pp. 223–67.

Norris, P. and Lovenduski, J. (1993) '"If Only More Candidates Came Forward": Supply-Side Explanations of Candidate Selection in Britain', *British Journal of Political Science*, 23:3, pp. 373–408.

North, D. (1990) *Institutions, Institutional Change and Economic Performance* (Cambridge: Cambridge University Press).

Nozick, R. (1974) *Anarchy, the State and Utopia* (Oxford: Basil Blackwell).

Nozick, R. (1989) *The Examined Life: Philosophical Meditations* (New York: Simon & Schuster).

Nursey-Bray, P. (1983) 'Consensus and Community: The Theory of African One-Party Democracy', in G. Duncan (ed.), *Democratic Theory and Practice* (Cambridge: Cambridge University Press), pp. 96–111.

Oakeshott, M. (1975) *On Human Conduct* (Oxford: Clarendon Press).
Olson, M. (1965) *The Logic of Collective Action* (Cambridge, Mass.: Harvard University Press).
Ordeshook, P. C. (1986) *Game Theory and Political Theory* (Cambridge: Cambridge University Press).
Parekh, B. (1993) 'A Misconceived Discourse on Political Obligation', *Political Studies*, 41:2, pp. 236–51.
Parry, G., Moyser, G. and Day, N. (1992) *Political Participation and Democracy in Britain* (Cambridge: Cambridge University Press).
Pateman, C. (1970) *Participation and Democratic Theory* (Cambridge: Cambridge University Press).
Paterson, W. E. (1989) 'Environmental Politics', in G. Smith, W. E. Paterson and P. H. Merkl (eds), *Developments in West German Politics* (London: Macmillan), pp. 267–88.
Pennock, J. R. (1979) *Democratic Political Theory* (Princeton: Princeton University Press).
Phillips, A. (1993) *Democracy and Difference* (Cambridge: Polity Press).
Phillips, A. (1995) *The Politics of Presence* (Oxford: Clarendon Press).
Pitkin, H. F. (1972) *The Concept of Representation* (Berkeley: University of California Press).
Plamenatz, J. (1963) *Man and Society*, volume 1 (London: Longman).
Plamenatz, J. P. (1968) *Consent, Freedom and Political Obligation*, second edition (London: Oxford University Press).
Plamenatz, J. (1973) *Democracy and Illusion* (London: Longman).
Plato, *The Republic* translated F. M. Cornford (Oxford: Clarendon Press).
Popper, K. R. (1945) *The Open Society and Its Enemies*, volume 2 (London: Routledge & Kegan Paul).
Potter, D., Goldblatt, D., Kiloh, M. and Lewis, P. (eds) (1997) *Democratization* (Cambridge: Polity Press).
Powell Jr., G. Bingham (1989) 'Constitutional Design and Electoral Control', *Journal of Theoretical Politics*, 1:2, pp. 107–30.
Putnam, R. D. (1993) *Making Democracy Work: Civic Traditions in Modern Italy* (Princeton: Princeton University Press).
Rae, D. W. (1975) 'The Limits of Consensual Decision', *American Political Science Review*, 69, pp. 1270–94.
Randall, V. (1997) 'Why Have the Political Trajectories of India and China Been Different?', in D. Potter *et al.*, *Democratization* (Cambridge: Polity Press), pp. 195–218.
Rawls, J. (1972) *A Theory of Justice* (Oxford: Oxford University Press).
Rawls, J. (1993) *Political Liberalism* (New York: Columbia University Press).
Raz, J. (1986) *The Morality of Freedom* (Oxford: Clarendon Press).
Reeve, A. (1986) *Property* (London: Macmillan).
Riker, W. H. (1982) *Liberalism against Populism* (San Francisco: Freeman & Co.).
Riker, W. H. (1986) *The Art of Political Manipulation* (New Haven and London: Yale University Press).
Roberts, L. and Weale, A. (1991) *Innovation and Environmental Risk* (London and New York: Belhaven Press).

Rogowski, R. (1981) 'Representation in Political Theory and Law', *Ethics*, 91:3, pp. 395–430.

Rousseau, J.-J. (1762) *The Social Contract* translated by G. D. H. Cole (London: J. M. Dent & Sons, 1973).

Rueschemeyer, D., Stephens, E. H. and Stephens, J. D. (1992) *Capitalist Development and Democracy* (Cambridge: Polity Press).

Runciman, W. G. (1969) *Social Science and Political Theory* (Cambridge: Cambridge University Press).

Salmon, W. C. (1973) *Logic* (Englewood Cliffs, New Jersey: Prentice-Hall).

Scanlon, T. M. (1982) 'Contractualism and Utilitarianism', in A. Sen and B. Williams (eds), *Utilitarianism and Beyond* (Cambridge: Cambridge University Press), pp. 103–28.

Scharpf, F. W. (1988) 'The Joint-Decision Trap: Lessons from German Federalism and European Union', *Public Administration*, 66:3, pp. 229–78.

Scharpf, F. W. (1989) 'Decision Rules, Decision Styles, and Policy Choices', *Journal of Theoretical Politics*, 1, pp. 149–76.

Schattschneider, E. E. (1960) *The Semi-Sovereign People: A Realistic View of Democracy in America* (New York: Holt, Rinehart & Winston).

Schumpeter, J. A. (1954) *Capitalism, Socialism and Democracy* (London: Allen & Unwin, first edition, 1943).

Sidgwick H. (1891) *The Elements of Politics* (London: Macmillan).

Sidgwick, H. (1901) *The Methods of Ethics*, sixth edition (London: Macmillan).

Simon, H. (1983) *Reason in Human Affairs* (Oxford: Basil Blackwell).

Skinner, Q. (1978) *The Foundations of Modern Political Thought: The Age of Reformation* (Cambridge: Cambridge University Press).

Skinner, Q. (1992) 'On Justice, the Common Good and the Priority of Liberty', in C. Mouffe (ed.), *Dimensions of Radical Democracy* (London and New York: Verso), pp. 211–24.

Smith, A. (1776) *An Inquiry into the Nature and Causes of The Wealth of Nations*, two volumes (Indianapolis: Liberty Classics).

Steiner, J. (1971) 'The Principles of Majority and Proportionality', *British Journal of Political Science*, 1:1, pp. 63–70.

Stimson, J. A., MacKuen, M. B. and Erikson, R. S. (1995) 'Dynamic Representation', *American Political Science Review*, 89:3, pp. 543–65.

Sunstein, C. R. (1988) 'Constitutions and Democracy: An Epilogue', in J. Elster and R. Slagstad (eds), *Constitutionalism and Democracy* (Cambridge: Cambridge University Press), pp. 327–56.

Sunstein, C. R. (1991) 'Preferences and Politics', *Philosophy and Public Affairs*, 20:1, pp. 3–34.

Taylor, M. (1976) *Anarchy and Cooperation* (London: John Wiley & Sons).

Thompson, D. F. (1970) *The Democratic Citizen* (Cambridge: Cambridge University Press).

Thucydides, *History of the Peloponnesian War*, translated by R. Warner with an introduction by M. I. Finley (Harmondsworth: Penguin, 1954).

Tocqueville, A. de (1835) *Democracy in America, volume 1*, edited by Phillips Bradley (New York: Vintage Books, 1945).

Tribe, L. (1988) *American Constitutional Law*, second edition (Mineola, NY: Foundation Press).

Truman, D. B. (1951) *The Governmental Process* (New York: Alfred A. Knopf).

Verba, S., Schlozman, K. H. and Brady, H. E. (1995) *Voice and Equality: Civic Voluntarism in American Politics* (Cambridge, Mass.: Harvard University Press).

Vlastos, G. (1962) 'Justice and Equality', in R. B. Brandt (ed.), *Social Justice* (Engelwood Cliffs, NJ: Prentice-Hall), pp. 31–72, partially reprinted in J. Feinberg (ed.), *Moral Concepts* (Oxford: Oxford University Press, 1969), pp. 141–52.

Waldron, J. (1995) 'The Wisdom of the Multitude: Some Reflections on Book 3, Chapter 11 of Aristotle's *Politics*', *Political Theory*, 23:4, pp. 563–84.

Warren, M. (1996) 'What Should We Expect From More Democracy: Radically Democratic Responses to Politics', *Political Theory*, 24:2, pp. 241–70.

Weale, A. (1978a) *Equality and Social Policy* (London: Routledge & Kegan Paul).

Weale, A. (1978b) 'Consent', *Political Studies*, 26:1, pp. 65–77.

Weale, A. (1984) 'Social Choice Versus Populism? An Interpretation of Riker's Political Theory', *British Journal of Political Science*, 14:3, pp. 369–85

Weale, A. (1990) 'Freedom of Speech versus Freedom of Religion?', in Commission for Racial Equality, *Free Speech*, Discussion Papers 2, pp. 49–58.

Weale, A. (1991) 'Citizenship Beyond Borders', in M. Moran and U. Vogel (eds), *Frontiers of Citizenship* (Houndmills: Macmillan), pp. 155–65.

Weale, A. (1995) 'William Riker and the Theory of Democracy', *Democratization*, 2:3, pp. 377–95.

Weale, A. (1998) 'From Contracts to Pluralism?', in P. Kelly (ed.), *Impartiality, Neutrality and Justice* (Edinburgh: Edinburgh University Press), pp. 9–34.

Weber, M. (1947) *The Theory of Social and Economic Organization*, translated by A. M. Henderson and T. Parsons (New York: Oxford University Press).

Wolff, R. P. (1970) *In Defense of Anarchism* (New York: Harper Colophon Books).

Wollheim, R. (1962) 'A Paradox in the Theory of Democracy', in P. Laslett and W. G. Runciman (eds), *Philosophy, Politics and Society* (Oxford: Basil Blackwell), pp. 71–87.

Young, I. M. (1989) 'Polity and Group Difference: A Critique of the Ideal of Universal Citizenship', *Ethics*, 99:2, pp. 250–74.

Young, I. M. (1990) *Justice and the Politics of Difference* (Princeton: Princeton University Press).

Young, O. (1989) *International Cooperation: Building Regimes for Natural Resources and the Environment* (Ithaca, NY: Cornell University Press).

Index